Delitefully
HEALTHMARK

... cooking for the health of it!

D1314957

By Susan Stevens, M.A., R.D.
HealthMark Centers, Inc.

HealthMark Centers, Inc.
Englewood, Colorado

Delitefully HealthMark

Acknowledgments

Many thanks to the following people without whom this book would have not been possible: Kathy Mohn for her marketing and business expertise; Sally Daniel for her invaluable technical and marketing advice; John Cruise for creative typesetting; Pattee Speck for her lively graphics ...

... and to my family for their adventuresome tastebuds and unfailing patience;

... and to Rob Gleser for his vision and inspiration.

Additional copies of this book may be obtained by sending a check for $16.95* plus $2.50 shipping and handling to:

HealthMark Centers, Inc.
5889 Greenwood Plaza Boulevard, Suite 200
Englewood, Colorado 80111
303/694-5060

*Colorado residents add $1.13 tax

Order blanks are included in the back of the book

Published by HealthMark Centers, Inc., Englewood, Colorado
Fifth printing, October, 1992

ISBN # 0-9624784-0-7

Printed on recycled paper

Dedication

This book is dedicated to my grandmother,
Josephine Middleton, who taught me at an early
age that good food is essential for a happy, healthy life —
and who, at 95 years of age, is living proof
that she is right.

Delitefully HealthMark

Table of Contents

Dedication iii

Table of Contents v

Foreword vi

Introduction vii

Nutrition Analysis Information viii

Recipe Modification Guidelines ix

Cook's Notes xv

Appetizers 1

Soups 23

Sandwiches 41

Salads 49

Breads 69

Breakfast 93

Pasta and Grains 111

Beans 131

Poultry 145

Fish and Seafood 177

Meat 203

Vegetables 215

Desserts and Cookies 237

Sauces and Dressings 277

Cookbook Order Form 297

Index 299

HealthMark Philosophy 321

Delitefully HealthMark

Foreword

Hot on the heels of her best seller *Cooking for a Healthier Ever After*, comes *Delitefully HealthMark* written by Susan Stevens, M.A., R.D., the Director of Nutrition at HealthMark Centers, Inc.

Ms. Stevens has been instrumental in the success of the HealthMark programs in Denver. She has developed the most successful supermarket and restaurant programs in the country. Over 170 restaurants provide HealthMark approved entrees and 200 supermarkets shelf-label more than 2000 HealthMark-approved items. These programs help make Denver one of the healthiest places to live and a city where adapting to a new health-conscious lifestyle becomes very easy.

Lifestyle change is never easy, especially eating habits. At HealthMark our goal is to teach that eating healthfully is tasty, pleasurable and fun. The old adage that health food looks brown and tastes bad has been utterly dispelled by the efforts of Ms. Stevens. The cookbooks she has created are testimony to the fact that good-for-you food can look and taste great.

There is no doubt that our basic lifestyle — bad eating habits, lack of exercise, smoking, excess alcohol and caffeine consumption and stress — are at the root of many of the leading causes of death in this country. Heart disease, strokes, high blood pressure, adult onset diabetes, lung, colon, breast and prostate cancer, obesity and osteoporosis are related to our unhealthy lifestyle.

Fortunately, many of these diseases are preventable, controllable or — in some cases — even reversible (e.g. heart disease) by making positive changes in our lifestyle. We should be smart enough to realize that what happens to us is directly a result of what we do to ourselves.

As we move into the 1990's we are finding that the cost of treating the end stage of these illnesses is far too great for the medical system to bear, as evidenced by the rising cost of medical care. It is much easier and less costly to teach someone to prevent heart disease by eating correctly, exercising regularly and stopping smoking. The cost of prevention is far less than a $30,000 coronary bypass operation.

Evidence is now accumulating that by controlling cholesterol levels in our blood we can prevent cholesterol build-up in the arterial wall and even reverse this build-up in some people. Our bad eating habits are obviously one of the cornerstones of our lifestyle that need to be changed.

This cookbook will provide you with the necessary ammunition to win the food fight and achieve a healthier and happier life.

Eat healthfully, it's no yolk.

Rob Gleser, M.D.
Founder and Director
HealthMark Centers, Inc.

Introduction

HealthMark: the name conjures up images of a healthy lifestyle — regular exercise and good-for-you food that tastes great. Shelf-tags on grocery shelves, logos on dozens of menus and thousands of HealthMark graduates all testify to the success of this concept.

What is HealthMark? Founded in 1985 by Dr. Robert A. Gleser, HealthMark's preventive medicine approach took Denver by storm. To date, over 6,000 people have graduated from HealthMark Programs, over 170 restaurants offer HealthMark approved menu items and 200 grocery stores identify HealthMark-approved foods on their shelves. In addition, the *HealthMark Program for Life* by Dr. Gleser and the first HealthMark cookbook, *Cooking for a Healthier Ever After* have become best sellers.

And so comes the second HealthMark cookbook in response to a demand for more quick, easy recipes and preparation techniques for low-fat, low-cholesterol, low-sodium foods. This book, in conjunction with *Cooking for a Healthier Ever After,* shows you the wide variety of ways in which healthy ingredients can be combined to create delicious food that promotes good health.

In addition, this book shows you HOW to do it, that is how to trim the fat, cholesterol and sodium from your own collection of family favorites so that eating "HealthMark style" can become the norm rather than the exception in your household.

The introductory chapter on recipe modification will teach you the tricks and techniques for creating healthy recipes that will become family favorites as well as elegant fare for guests and special occasions. Making ingredient substitutions and modifications to recipes will soon become second nature. Meals will be as appealing and tasty as ever — but much healthier.

Trial and error is the best way to perfect your new skills in light cuisine. Your occasional mistake — usually edible — will show what works and what doesn't for a particular recipe. Some recipes, such as layer cakes, custards and certain sauces — don't tolerate ingredient substitutions. But you will find that many recipes can be adjusted successfully to reduce fat, cholesterol, sodium and calories without sacrificing taste or appearance.

The adage — "The way to a man's heart is through his stomach" — takes on new meaning in light of the grim statistic that heart disease is the number one killer in the United States. Other diseases, such as strokes, diabetes, certain cancers and obesity, also stem from our over-abundant and under-exercised lifestyle. By learning new, creative ways of preparing foods as kind to your palate as to your heart and waistline, we can make these diseases rare instead of routine.

Bon Appetit

S.S.

Delitefully HealthMark

Nutrition Analysis Information

Recipes have been analyzed for calories, fat, cholesterol, dietary fiber and sodium. Nutrition information is given for a single serving, based on the largest number of servings given for the recipe. Serving sizes have been specified for appetizers, sauces and dressings.

Recipes have been developed to be as low in fat, cholesterol, sodium and calories as possible while retaining optimal flavor and appearance. Use the nutrition information to help you select recipes to fit within the HealthMark Daily Dietary Guidelines:

- 150 milligrams of dietary cholesterol
- 20 to 25 percent of calories from fat; not more than 45 grams of fat per day
- 2300 milligrams of sodium
- 25 to 35 grams of dietary fiber

Recipe Modification Guidelines

As we become more aware of the relationship between lifestyle choices and diseases such as heart disease, stroke, diabetes, certain cancers and obesity, eating habits are changing. The health-conscious cook reads recipes with an eye toward reducing or eliminating some of the ingredients that play havoc with our health. With a bit of modification most recipes can be "lightened" without sacrificing taste or visual appeal.

Read every recipe with an eye toward eliminating as much fat, cholesterol, sodium and sugar as possible without sacrificing flavor or quality. Don't hesitate to experiment with recipes to find out what works best. Fat, salt and sugar can usually be reduced without significantly altering flavor or texture.

Use the following tips and techniques to guide you as you modify favorite recipes and develop new dishes destined to become family — and company — favorites.

Reducing Cholesterol

1. Reduce the amount of meat, fish or poultry in a recipe — 3 to 4 ounces per serving is ample.

2. Avoid organ meats, which are very high in cholesterol. Also, use seafoods such as shrimp, crab, lobster and calamari (squid) sparingly (two to three ounces per serving) as they are high in cholesterol.

3. Use fewer egg yolks and whole eggs. In baking, substitute 1–2 egg whites for each whole egg. As the number of eggs in a recipe increases, decrease the whites. For example, in place of 2 eggs use 4 whites, but in place of 4 eggs, use 1 whole egg plus 6 whites.

4. Use eggless pasta in place of pasta made with egg yolks (most, by the way, is eggless unless specified on the label).

5. Use non-fat or 1% dairy products to reduce cholesterol, fat and calories.Replace whole milk cheese with cheeses made from skim or part-skim milk, such as part-skim mozzarella.

Reducing Fat

1. Use lean cuts of meat and trim all visible fat before cooking.

2. Serve poultry, fish, whole grains, dried beans, peas and entils more often. All are excellent sources of low fat protein.

3. Cook poultry without the skin; reduce cooking time slightly to keep it moist. To roast whole birds, wrap in foil and baste often or use a cooking bag.

4. Substitute skinless chicken and turkey for red meats. Turkey works well in recipes using pork or veal.

5. Use cooking methods and utensils that minimize or eliminate cooking fat. Broil, bake, roast, poach or stir-fry instead of pan frying or deep-fat frying. Be sure to use non-stick cookware; coat lightly with cooking spray or brush lightly with oil, if necessary, to keep food from sticking (e.g. egg white omelettes).

6. Saute in non-stick cookware using a minimum of oil, one to two teaspoons, or saute with broth, wine or water (cover the pan if necessary to prevent liquid from evaporating). Chefs call this "sweating". Also, microwave mushrooms, onions, zucchini, etc. in a covered container in place of sauteeing

7. Make stock, soups, sauces and stews ahead of time; chill, then remove all hardened fat. If there is no time to do this, skim off as much fat as possible, then add several ice cubes. Fat will congeal and cling to the ice cubes, which can then be discarded.

8. Reduce the amount of fat in baked goods by one-third to one-half. Use vegetable oil (canola oil is the least saturated) or soft margarine whenever possible. Quick breads, muffins, pancakes and waffles are just as good made with oil rather than a more saturated fat such as butter, shortening or stick margarine.

   To add moisture to baked goods (such as muffins) when reducing oil add any of the following: applesauce, mashed bananas, crushed pineapple, cranberries, pumpkin, grated zucchini, grated carrots.

   Substitute soft margarine for butter or stick margarine when a recipe calls for creaming butter and sugar together. This will give better results than using oil. Experiment with recipes to see what works best; soft (tub) margarines contain more air and water than stick margarine and will not work in all circumstances.

   Certain recipes, such as cakes, are too difficult to adjust; enjoy these as a special treat occasionally.

9. Use non-fat or 1% dairy products (milk, yogurt or cottage cheese). Use evaporated non-fat milk in soups, sauces and baking.

10. Buy low-fat or part-skim cheese (no more than 5 grams of fat per ounce) and use less than the recipe calls for, as even low-fat cheese is high in fat. Look for skim milk ricotta cheese.

11. To make rich sauces without cream, blend 1/4 to 1/3 cup non-fat dry milk into one cup of liquid non-fat milk. Stir well before using to dissolve powdered milk. Use this "HealthMark cream" in place of the cream or whole milk called for in a recipe.

    Use this same technique to create creamy sauces with a chicken or beef flavor. Substitute salt-free, defatted chicken or beef stock for liquid non-fat milk. Add a touch of dry white or red wine or sherry for an elegant flavor.

12. Replace sour cream with either non-fat yogurt or HealthMark Sour Cream (page 287), depending on the consistency and flavor desired in the recipe. Non-fat yogurt is tart and thinner than HealthMark Sour Cream (pureed cottage cheese). Use yogurt for dips and salad dressings. To use in cooking, blend one to two tablespoons flour or one table-spoon cornstarch into the yogurt before adding it to the recipe. Heat gently to prevent curdling.

For a thicker consistency, drain yogurt overnight in the refrigerator. Place yogurt in a strainer lined with cheesecloth or several coffee filters. Cover and suspend over a bowl to catch the liquid that will drain off. This is called yogurt cheese and may be eaten plain or with herbs added. It is good for dips and salad dressings.

Use HealthMark Sour Cream for dips and thicker salad dressings. Also may be used to replace sour cream in baked goods (e.g. sour cream cakes), but does not work well in cooked dishes (e.g. stroganoff) as it will separate.

13. Use light, cholesterol-free mayonnaise mixed with equal parts of non-fat yogurt. Good for salad dressings as well as a sandwich spread.

14. Substitute 3 tablespoons unsweetened cocoa powder and 1 tablespoon oil for 1 ounce baking chocolate.

15. Eliminate nuts from a recipe or use only one-fourth to one-third cup.

Reducing Salt and Sodium

1. Your taste for salt will diminish as you gradually reduce the amount you use. If salt is necessary in a recipe, use sparingly. Try Lite Salt™ to reduce sodium but not flavor.

2. Even though nothing else tastes exactly like salt, other seasonings will enhance the flavor of foods and compensate for the salt you have eliminated. Use the following season-ings to add zest to foods: fresh lemon or lime juice; lemon or lime zest; flavored vine-gars (e.g. tarragon, raspberry, wine); dried onion flakes; onion or garlic powder; pepper; hot pepper sauce; mustard.

3. Condiments such as Worcestershire sauce, hot pepper sauce, mustard and so on are rel-atively high in sodium, but if used sparingly can enliven foods without overdoing the sodium.

4. Eliminate or reduce salt in all recipes except yeast breads where salt is necessary to con-trol growth of the yeast. Even in yeast breads salt can usually be reduced.

5. Use onion and garlic powders instead of salts.

6. Replace salt with salt-free herb mixtures (available in grocery stores or make your own).

7. Crush dried herbs before using to release more flavor.

8. Buy salt-free canned vegetables, soups and tuna. Use salt-free tomato sauce and tomato paste

9. Use light (reduced sodium) soy sauce - sparingly. For added flavor mix with orange juice, pineapple juice or sherry.

10. Use wines and liqueurs — sparingly — to flavor foods. If cooked at or above boiling temperature, the alcohol evaporates, eliminating most of the calories while the flavor remains.

11. Use salt-free canned beef and chicken broth. For more flavor, boil until reduced by half. Be sure to defat canned broth by chilling until fat hardens, then skim. Keeping a can in the refrigerator will make this easier.

12. Rinse canned seafood (such as tuna, salmon, shrimp, crab, clams), vegetables, and beans to reduce salt content.

13. Eliminate salt when cooking pasta, rice and other grains. Flavor with salt-free herb mixtures.

Reducing Sugar

1. In most recipes, sugar can reduced by one-third to one-half. In cookies, bars and cakes, replace the sugar you have eliminated with non-fat dry milk.

2. Brown sugar or honey may be substituted for white sugar; both are slightly sweeter than white sugar, therefore less can be used (as above). Nutritionally, they are all similar; there is no nutritional advantage to brown sugar or honey.

3. When sugar is decreased, enhance flavor with spices (cinnamon, nutmeg or cloves) and extracts (vanilla, almond, orange or lemon). Doubling the amount of vanilla called for increases the sweetness without adding calories.

   The amount of spice may also be increased to boost flavor when sugar is decreased, but be careful of strong spices, such as cloves and ginger, as they can easily overpower the recipe. Safest spices to increase are cinnamon, nutmeg and allspice.

4. When reducing sugar in quick breads, cakes and cookies, use fruits which add sweetness naturally such as raisins, dried apricots, dates or bananas.

5. For added sweetness, soak raisins and other dried fruit in hot water (or a liqueur) for 10 to 15 minutes then add to the batter along with the soaking liquid.

6. Use juice- or water-packed fruits.

Adding Fiber

1. Use whole wheat flour whenever possible. It is heavier than white flour, so use less: 7/8 cup whole wheat flour to 1 cup white flour. Experiment to find out what works best in a recipe. Some recipes will turn out well with all whole wheat flour, others are better when half whole wheat and half white (unbleached) flour is used.

    Also, try whole wheat pastry flour. It can be substituted for all of the white flour in a recipe as it is lighter than whole wheat flour.

2. Add wheat bran, oat bran or oatmeal to baked goods, cereals, casseroles, soups and pancakes. Start with one or two tablespoons and increase gradually.

    Substitute up to 1/2 cup oatmeal or oat bran for part of the flour in baked goods.

3. Use potatoes unpeeled ("country style") whenever possible in soups, stews or for oven fries.

4. Use more vegetables, whole grains (bulgur, brown rice, corn, barley and oatmeal), dried beans, split peas and lentils.

HealthMark Recipe Modifications

The following examples show you how to create lighter recipes:

Chicken in Orange Sauce

(Original)	(Modified — page 159)
3 to 4 lb. roasting chicken, cut up	6 skinless, boneless chicken breasts
2 tsp. salt	
1/2 cup butter	2 Tbsp. liquid margarine
4 Tbsp. flour	4 Tbsp. unbleached flour
1/4 tsp. cinnamon	1/2 tsp. cinnamon
1/8 tsp. cloves	1/8 tsp. cloves
3 cups orange juice	2 cups fresh orange juice
1 cup sliced almonds	1/4 cup sliced almonds
1 cup raisins	1/2 cup golden raisins
2 cups orange sections	1 1/2 cups orange sections
Cooked egg noodles	Cooked brown rice or eggless pasta

Oriental Dip

(Original)

1 cup mayonnaise
2 Tbsp. soy sauce
1 Tbsp. oriental sesame oil
2 tsp. Dijon mustard
Dash Worcestershire sauce

(Modified — page 9)

1 cup non-fat yogurt
2 Tbsp. cholesterol-free light mayonnaise
2 to 3 tsp. Dijon mustard
1 Tbsp. low-sodium soy sauce

Pineapple Oatmeal Cake

(Original)

1 1/4 cups sugar
1 cup butter
1/2 cup sour cream
2 eggs
1/2 tsp. vanilla
2 cups flour
1 tsp. baking soda
1 tsp. baking powder
1 tsp. salt
1/2 tsp. cinnamon
1/4 tsp. nutmeg
1/4 tsp. ginger
1 1/2 cups rolled oats
1 cup crushed pineapple, undrained

(Modified — page 261)

3/4 cup brown sugar
1/2 cup liquid margarine
1/2 cup plain non-fat yogurt
4 egg whites
1 tsp. vanilla
1 cup *each* whole wheat and unbleached flour
1 tsp. baking soda
1 tsp. baking powder
1 tsp. orange zest
1 tsp. cinnamon
1/2 tsp. nutmeg
1/2 tsp. ginger
1 1/2 cups rolled oats
1 cup crushed pineapple (juice-pack),
    undrained

Cook's Notes

- Add flavor to baked goods, sauces and other dishes by adding zest, the thin outer layer of an orange, lemon or other citrus peel. Use a zester (a tool available in cookware stores) or a grater to remove the zest.

- Fresh herbs have the best flavor, but if not available, substitute 1/2 to 1 tsp. dried herb per tablespoon of fresh herb. Give dried herbs a fresh taste by mixing with an equal amount of chopped fresh parsley, then let stand 10 to 15 minutes before using.

- Olive, canola and safflower are best choices for cooking oils. Use olive oil for sauteeing and salad dressings; choose canola or safflower for baking.

- Bake in non-stick pans coated with cooking spray or brush pan lightly with oil.

- Line muffin pans with paper liners to minimize clean-up.

- A 1/4 cup measure is just the right size for scooping muffin batter into a muffin cup.

- Muffins and other baked goods can easily be prepared in the food processor: measure dry ingredients into work bowl first and pulse until just blended; add nuts and/or dried fruit and pulse until chopped. Add liquid ingredients and pulse until batter is just blended.

- Microwave lemons and limes for 30 to 60 seconds before juicing.

- Honey is easier to measure when warmed.

- To substitute honey for sugar, decrease liquid in the recipe by 1/4 cup. If recipe has no liquid added, add 4 tablespoons flour. Decrease baking temperature by 25° to prevent over-browning.

- Measure oil first, then honey will slide easily out of the cup.

- If unsalted nuts are not available, rinse salted nuts then toast briefly before using.

- Eggs are easiest to separate when cold; the whites beat up to greatest volume at room temperature.

- If fresh orange juice is not available, substituted frozen orange juice concentrate - one tablespoon equals about 1/4 cup fresh juice.

- For best results, preheat oven before baking.

- Prick meat all over with a fork to allow marinade to penetrate thoroughly.

- To prevent skinless chicken from drying out, reduce cooking time by a few minutes.

- Wash poultry with warm water before using to decrease bacteria and minimize chance of illness. Be sure to wash hands, utensils, cutting board, sink and anything else that comes in contact with raw poultry.

**Trim the excess fat, cholesterol
and calories from appetizers by replacing
cream cheese and sour cream with low-fat (1%)
cottage cheese whirled smooth in the blender.
All the taste and much healthier!**

Delitefully HealthMark

Chips

Bagel Chips 11
Pita Chips 11
Tortilla Crisps 12

Dips

Avocado Cilantro Dip 7
Avocado Sesame Dip 7
Green Chile-Cilantro Dip 8
Creamy Garlic Dip 3
English Tavern Dip 9
Green Onion Dip 6
Mary's Guacamole 6
Mexican Salsa 10
Oriental Dip 9
Red Pepper Dip 5
Roquefort Dip 5
Salsa Dip 7
Salsa Verde 10

Spreads

Chutney Cheese Spread 8
Confetti Spread 3
Herbed Cheese Spread 4
Pesto Cheese Spread 4
Tangy Onion Spread 4

Hot

Chicken Rumaki 18
Golden Chicken Nuggets 18
Herbed Tomato Bread 14
Mandarin Chicken Bites 17
Marinated Flank Strips 20
 Horseradish Mustard 20
Mexican Pizza 12
Oriental Meatballs 16
Pizza Potato Skins 14
Turkey Montmorency 16

Cold

Ceviche 13
Chicken Pate 19
Citrus Marinated Seafood 19
Crisp Garbanzo Nuts 21
Hot and Sour Nuts 21
Salsafied Seafood 15
Spicy Cucumber Bites 15

Creamy Garlic Dip

1 cup 1% cottage cheese
2 tsp. fresh lemon juice
2 tsp. Dijon mustard

1 clove garlic
1 Tbsp. chopped fresh basil *or* tarragon *or*
  1 tsp. dried

Combine all ingredients in a food processor or blender and process until smooth. Serve as a dip or as a salad dressing, adding milk or vinegar as needed to thin.

Yield: 1 cup
Serving size: 2 Tbsp.

Per serving:	Calories	Fat (g)	Cholesterol (mg)	Fiber (g)	Sodium (mg)
	23	0	1	0	131

Confetti Spread

2 cups 1% cottage cheese
1 Tbsp. horseradish
1 tsp. Worcestershire Sauce
1/2 tsp. celery salt

1 1/2 cups finely chopped radishes
4 green onions, thinly sliced
Thin rye crackers
Raw vegetables

Process cottage cheese, horseradish, Worcestershire and celery salt in a food processor or blender until smooth. Transfer to a bowl and stir in radishes and green onion. Cover and chill.

Serve with rye crackers and raw vegetables.

Yield: about 2 1/2 cups
Serving size: 2 Tbsp.

Per serving:	Calories	Fat (g)	Cholesterol (mg)	Fiber (g)	Sodium (mg)
	14	0	1	0	52

Herbed Cheese Spread

1 cup 1% cottage cheese
1/4 cup plain non-fat yogurt
1 Tbsp. chives

1/4 tsp. tarragon
1/4 tsp. dried minced onion

Place ingredients in blender or food processor and puree until very smooth. Serve with low-fat crackers or use as a topping for baked potatoes. Also good as a base for creamy salad dressings.

Variation: Pesto Cheese Spread — Eliminate chives, tarragon and dried onion. Add 2 to 3 Tbsp. Pesto (page 293) to pureed cheese. Chill before serving. (Increases fat to 1/2 gram per serving)

Yield: about 1 cup
Serving size: 2 Tbsp.

Per serving:	Calories	Fat (g)	Cholesterol (mg)	Fiber (g)	Sodium (mg)
	20	0	2	0	8

Tangy Onion Spread

3 onions, thinly sliced
1 Tbsp. olive oil
1 cup plain non-fat yogurt

1 to 2 Tbsp. rice *or* cider vinegar
Thinly sliced green onions

In a large skillet, saute onions in oil over medium heat for 10 to 15 minutes or until onions are limp. Reduce heat to low and continue cooking, stirring often, until onions are golden brown and have developed a sweet flavor, 15 to 30 minutes. Let cool.

Before serving, combine onions with yogurt and vinegar. Garnish with thinly sliced green onions.

Serve with low-fat rye crackers and/or crudites.

Yield: about 2 cups
Serving size: 2 Tbsp.

Per serving:	Calories	Fat (g)	Cholesterol (mg)	Fiber (g)	Sodium (mg)
	29	1	1	0	13

Red Pepper Dip

1 red bell pepper, grilled (see page 226)
3/4 cup 1% cottage cheese
1 Tbsp. fresh lemon juice

1 clove garlic
1/8 tsp. white pepper

Combine all ingredients in blender or food processor; blend until very smooth.

To serve, spoon dip into a hollowed out green or red bell pepper. Serve with low fat crackers and raw vegetables.

Yield: about 1 cup
Serving size: 2 Tbsp.

Per serving:	Calories	Fat (g)	Cholesterol (mg)	Fiber (g)	Sodium (mg)
	23	1	1	0	87

Roquefort Dip

2 cups 1% cottage cheese
1/4 cup plain non-fat yogurt

1/4 cup (2 oz.) crumbled blue cheese
Dash hot pepper sauce

Puree cottage cheese and yogurt in blender or food processor until very smooth. Stir in crumbled blue cheese and hot pepper sauce to taste. Chill before serving.

Serve with crudites (raw vegetables); celery is especially good.

Yield: 2 1/2 cups
Serving size: 2 Tbsp.

Per serving:	Calories	Fat (g)	Cholesterol (mg)	Fiber (g)	Sodium (mg)
	28	1	3	0	131

Green Onion Dip

1 cup plain non-fat yogurt
$^1/_4$ cup low-fat sour cream
$^1/_2$ cup thinly sliced green onions

$^1/_4$ cup minced fresh cilantro
1 Tbsp. lime juice
1 tsp. lime zest

In a small bowl, combine all ingredients. Cover and chill before serving.

Serve with raw vegetables, including small romaine lettuce leaves.

Yield: about 1$^3/_4$ cups
Serving size: 2 Tbsp.

Per serving:	Calories	Fat (g)	Cholesterol (mg)	Fiber (g)	Sodium (mg)
	18	1	2	0	18

Mary's Guacamole

Although high in fat, avocados contain primarily monounsaturated fat — the type
that helps lower cholesterol. Enjoy, but in moderation.

3 avocados, peeled and pitted
$^1/_4$ tsp. cumin
Lemon pepper to taste
Mrs. Dash to taste

1 tomato, cored and diced
4 to 6 scallions, thinly sliced
$^1/_2$ cup Mexican Salsa (page 10)
2 cloves garlic, minced

In a medium bowl, mash avocados. Stir in cumin, lemon pepper and Mrs. Dash. Fold in
remaining ingredients. Spoon into a serving bowl. If made ahead, place one avocado pit in
center of guacamole to prevent browning.

Serve with Tortilla Crisps (page 12) or raw vegetables — jicama is especially good.

Yield: about 2 cups
Serving size: 2 Tbsp.

Per serving:	Calories	Fat (g)	Cholesterol (mg)	Fiber (g)	Sodium (mg)
	86	7	0	2	0

Salsa Dip

1 cup 1% cottage cheese
1 tsp. lemon *or* lime juice

1 cup Mexican Salsa (page 10)

In a food processor, puree cottage cheese with lemon juice until very smooth. Add remaining ingredients and pulse 4 or 5 times until well mixed.

Serve as a dip for Tortilla Crisps (page 12) or as a salad dressing (especially good with Fiesta Salad (page 205).

Yield: about 2 cups
Serving size: 2 Tbsp.

Per serving:	Calories	Fat (g)	Cholesterol (mg)	Fiber (g)	Sodium (mg)
	38	1	1	1	119

Avocado-Sesame Dip

1 ripe avocado, peeled and pitted
2 tsp. fresh lemon *or* lime juice
1/4 cup Tahini (sesame seed paste)
1 clove garlic, minced

1 cup plain non-fat yogurt
2 green onions, minced
Freshly ground black pepper
1 Tbsp. toasted sesame seeds

Mash avocado with lemon or lime juice. Beat in tahini, garlic and yogurt. Stir in minced green onions and black pepper to taste. Spoon into a serving bowl and sprinkle with toasted sesame seeds and additional chopped green onion, if desired.

Serve with toasted pita bread wedges.

Tip: can also be made in a food processor

Variation: Avocado-Cilantro Dip — Eliminate tahini and sesame seeds. Add 1/4 cup chopped fresh cilantro, 1 jalapeño pepper, seeded and minced and 1 tomato, cored and diced.

Yield: about 1 1/2 cups
Serving size: 2 Tbsp.

Per serving:	Calories	Fat (g)	Cholesterol (mg)	Fiber (g)	Sodium (mg)
	85	7	1	1	1

Green Chile-Cilantro Dip

This tasty dip can be spiced up or down to suit your tastebuds

1¹/₂ cups 1% cottage cheese
2 Anaheim chiles, diced *or*
 1 Anaheim chile and 1 jalapeño chile, diced
¹/₄ cup chopped green chile

¹/₂ cup chopped red onion
¹/₂ tsp. cumin
¹/₄ cup chopped fresh cilantro

Puree cottage cheese in food processor or blender until smooth. Add remaining ingredients and process until well mixed. Chill before serving.

Serve with Tortilla Crisps (see page 12) or raw vegetables; jicama is especially good.

Variation: Add crushed red chile peppers or cayenne pepper to taste for a spicier dip.

Yield: about 2 cups
Serving size: 2 Tbsp.

Per serving:	Calories	Fat (g)	Cholesterol (mg)	Fiber (g)	Sodium (mg)
	22	0	1	0	95

Chutney Cheese Spread

Creamy cottage cheese blends well with the spicy tang of chutney

1¹/₂ cups 1% cottage cheese
2 Tbsp. dry sherry
1 8-oz. jar chutney

3 green onions, thinly sliced
¹/₂ tsp. curry powder
¹/₂ tsp. dry mustard

Place cottage cheese in food processor or blender and puree until smooth. Add remaining ingredients and process until well combined.

Chill before serving with low-fat crackers or toasted pita bread wedges

Yield: about 2 cups
Serving size: 2 Tbsp.

Per serving:	Calories	Fat (g)	Cholesterol (mg)	Fiber (g)	Sodium (mg)
	29	0	1	0	86

Oriental Dip

1 cup non-fat yogurt
2 Tbsp. fat free or cholesterol-free
   light mayonnaise
2 to 3 tsp. Dijon mustard (to taste)

1 Tbsp. low-sodium soy sauce
2 tsp. oriental sesame oil
Dash Worcestershire sauce

In a small bowl, whisk together all ingredients until well blended. Chill before using.

Use as a dip for fresh vegetables (lightly steamed asparagus is especially good), a salad dressing, a sauce for grilled fish or chicken, or as a dip for artichokes.

Yield: about 1 cup
Serving size: 2 Tbsp.

Per serving:	Calories	Fat (g)	Cholesterol (mg)	Fiber (g)	Sodium (mg)
	52	1-4	1	0	161

English Tavern Dip

Wasabi adds a nice bite to this hearty dip

1½ cups 1% cottage cheese
⅓ cup non-fat yogurt
½ cup ground smoked turkey (skinless)

1 tsp. to 1 Tbsp. wasabi powder* *or*
2 tsp. dry mustard

Puree cottage cheese in food processor or blender until very smooth. Add remaining ingredients and blend 10 seconds. Spoon into a serving bowl, cover and refrigerate overnight before serving.

* Wasabi powder, or Japanese horseradish, is available in the specialty section of most grocery stores

Yield: about 2 cups
Serving size: 2 Tbsp.

Per serving:	Calories	Fat (g)	Cholesterol (mg)	Fiber (g)	Sodium (mg)
	24	1	1	0	124

Mexican Salsa

Select chiles to suit your tastebuds: Anaheims are mild, jalapeños
are hot and the tiny serrenos are hotter!

2 to 3 green onions, cut in 2" pieces
1/4 red onion, cut into pieces
1 to 2 cloves garlic
1 Anaheim chile *or*
  1 to 2 jalapeño chiles, seeded and chopped

3 tomatoes, cored and diced
1/4 to 1/2 cup chopped fresh cilantro (to taste)
1 tsp. dried oregano
1/4 tsp. cumin
1 Tbsp. fresh lime juice *or* red wine vinegar

Combine all ingredients in a food processor and pulse 6 to 8 times or until coarsely chopped.

Serve as a dip with Tortilla Crisps (page 12), a topping for grilled fish or chicken or as a omelette filling

Yield: about 1 1/2 cups
Serving size: 2 Tbsp.

Per serving:	Calories	Fat (g)	Cholesterol (mg)	Fiber (g)	Sodium (mg)
	16	0	0	0	3

Salsa Verde

1 12-oz can tomatillos, drained
2 to 3 Anaheim *or* jalapeño chiles, seeded
2 cloves garlic
4 green onions, cut into 2" pieces

1/4 cup fresh cilantro
1 tsp. olive oil
Pinch salt

Combine all ingredients in a food processor and puree until chunky. Serve with Tortilla Crisps (page 12) or raw vegetables.

Yield: about 2 cups
Serving size: 2 Tbsp.

Per serving:	Calories	Fat (g)	Cholesterol (mg)	Fiber (g)	Sodium (mg)
	12	0	0	1	30

Bagel Chips

2 bagels (eggless)
Olive oil cooking spray
1 tsp. oregano, crushed

With a sharp serrated knife, slice bagel into very thin slices. Arrange on a non-stick baking sheet. Spray with cooking spray. Sprinkle with oregano. Bake at 350° for 10 to 12 minutes or until lightly browned. Cool, then store in an airtight container.

Variation: Use other dried herbs such as dill, basil or tarragon; or try chili powder or cinnamon.

Yield: 24 rounds
Serving size: 4 rounds

Per serving:	Calories	Fat (g)	Cholesterol (mg)	Fiber (g)	Sodium (mg)
	74	0	0	0	87

Pita Chips

Whole wheat pita bread, split in half
Canola *or* safflower *or* olive oil
Poppy *or* sesame seeds

Brush pita bread lightly with oil. Sprinkle with seeds and cut into eight wedges. Arrange on a baking sheet; bake at 350° for until crisp, 5 to 10 minutes.

Variation: Sprinkle lightly with Parmesan cheese.

Serving size: one-half pita

Per serving:	Calories	Fat (g)	Cholesterol (mg)	Fiber (g)	Sodium (mg)
	65	2	1	2	9

Tortilla Crisps

1 pkg. corn tortillas
Water *or* cooking spray

Lite Salt™
Chili powder (optional)

Brush each tortilla lightly with water (use a pastry brush) or coat with cooking spray. Sprinkle lightly with Lite Salt and chili powder (if desired). Cut into six to eight wedges. Bake at 350° for 10 to 12 minutes or until crisp. Be careful not to burn.

Variations:

• Substitute flour tortillas (made with soy oil).

• Sprinkle chips with the following seasoning mix: 1/2 tsp each garlic powder, onion powder, chili powder, celery salt, crushed oregano, paprika and 1/4 tsp. cumin.

Yield: about 6 dozen
Serving size: one tortilla (six to eight pieces)

Per serving:	Calories	Fat (g)	Cholesterol (mg)	Fiber (g)	Sodium (mg)
	189	2	0	1	180

Mexican Pizza

1 12" flour tortilla (made with soy oil)
1/3 cup vegetarian refried beans
1/4 cup Mexican Salsa (page 10)
1/2 cup grated part-skim Mozzarella cheese
2 Tbsp. sliced black olives
  (rinse and drain before slicing)

2 green onions, thinly sliced *or*
  1/4 cup chopped red onion
1–2 Tbsp. chopped fresh cilantro

Brush tortilla lightly with oil. Place on a baking sheet and bake at 400° for 3 to 5 minutes or until slightly crisp. Spread with refried beans then top with remaining ingredients. Broil until cheese bubbles. Cut into 8 wedges.

Serves 2 to 4
Serving size: one-fourth pizza

Per serving:	Calories	Fat (g)	Cholesterol (mg)	Fiber (g)	Sodium (mg)
	120	6	8	2	225

Ceviche

This delicious ceviche, served at the Fresh Fish Company, is the best I have ever eaten!

1/2 lb. bay scallops *or* large scallops, quartered
1/2 lb. snapper, bass, grouper *or* other firm white fish, diced
1 cup fresh lime juice
3/4 cup lemon juice
1/4 cup white vinegar

Sauce:
4 tomatoes, cored and diced
2 Tbsp. diced green pepper
2 Tbsp. diced red bell pepper
1/4 cup diced red onion
1 small jalapeño pepper, seeded and diced
2 Tbsp. chopped fresh cilantro
3/4 cup tomato juice

1/8 cup fresh orange juice
1/8 cup fresh lemon juice
1 Tbsp. tequila (optional)
1 Tbsp. olive oil
2 tsp. white vinegar
2 Tbsp. sugar
1/2 tsp. freshly ground black pepper

In a medium bowl, combine scallops, diced fish, lime juice, lemon juice and vinegar. Cover and marinate in refrigerator for 24 hours or until scallops and fish are white all the way through. Drain and rinse with cold water.

Sauce: Combine all ingredients in a large bowl and mix well. Add well drained fish mixture and mix thoroughly. May be served at room temperature or chilled.

Serve in small bowls or on plates lined with romaine or red leaf lettuce and garnished with lime wedges and cilantro.

Serves 6 to 8
Serving size: 3/4 cup

Per serving:	Calories	Fat (g)	Cholesterol (mg)	Fiber (g)	Sodium (mg)
	127	3	3	1	167

Herbed Tomato Bread

2 Tbsp. olive oil
1 clove garlic, crushed
1 16-oz. loaf unsliced Italian bread
3 ripe tomatoes, thinly sliced
2 Tbsp. chopped fresh basil *or*
  1 tsp. dried basil

1 Tbsp. chopped fresh oregano *or*
  1 tsp. dried oregano
2 Tbsp. chopped fresh parsley
3/4 cup grated part-skim mozzarella cheese

Combine olive oil and garlic in a tightly covered container and let stand overnight.

Slice bread in half crosswise, then lengthwise. Broil until lightly browned. Brush with garlic oil. Arrange tomato slices evenly over bread. Sprinkle with herbs and cheese. Broil until cheese melts. Slice and serve.

Serves 16
Serving size: one piece

Per serving:	Calories	Fat (g)	Cholesterol (mg)	Fiber (g)	Sodium (mg)
	104	3	4	2	171

Pizza Potato Skins

4 baked potatoes
2 Tbsp. olive oil
1 tsp. dried oregano, crushed
1 tsp. dried basil, crushed
1 clove garlic, minced

Topping:
1 cup grated part-skim mozzarella cheese
1/3 cup diced green (*or* red) pepper
2 green onions, thinly sliced
1/4 cup sliced black olives (rinse
  and drain before slicing)

Cut potatoes in half, then cut each half into thirds. Scoop out pulp leaving a 1/4" shell (reserve pulp for another use). Combine olive oil, oregano, basil and garlic. Brush on inside of skins. Place on a non-stick cookie sheet and bake at 400° for about 10 minutes or until crisp.

Combine topping ingredients and sprinkle evenly over potato skins. Return to oven and bake 5 to 10 minutes longer or until cheese melts.

Yield: 24 appetizers
Serving size: one piece

Per serving:	Calories	Fat (g)	Cholesterol (mg)	Fiber (g)	Sodium (mg)
	53	3	5	1	58

Salsafied Seafood

This is also good as a salad on a hot summer day

1¹/2 cups Mexican Salsa (page 10)
¹/4 lb. cooked small shrimp
¹/4 lb. cooked bay scallops

1 avocado, peeled and diced
1 head romaine lettuce

Combine Salsa with shrimp, scallops and avocado. Cover and chill 1 to 2 hours.

Remove small lettuce leaves and fill with 1 to 2 Tbsp. seafood mixture. Arrange on a serving platter.

Variation: Also good served on cucumber slices or stuffed into large cherry tomatoes. May also be served as a first course on a bed of lettuce.

Serves 10
Serving size: one-fourth cup

Per serving:	Calories	Fat (g)	Cholesterol (mg)	Fiber (g)	Sodium (mg)
	60	4	1	1	9

Spicy Cucumber Bites

2 English cucumbers, seeded
¹/4 tsp. paprika
¹/8 tsp. cayenne pepper (*or* to taste)

¹/8 tsp. turmeric
4 Tbsp. orange juice

Cut cucumbers into bite-size chunks. Blend spices into orange juice, then mix in cucumber pieces. Cover and chill 1 hour. Drain well. Serve on toothpicks for an appetizer or serve as a salad.

Serves 4 to 6
Serving size: four to five pieces

Per serving:	Calories	Fat (g)	Cholesterol (mg)	Fiber (g)	Sodium (mg)
	16	0	0	0	3

Oriental Meatballs

Replacing ground beef with ground turkey reduces
the fat — but not the flavor — in these delicious meatballs

1 lb. ground turkey
1 8-oz. can water chestnuts, chopped
4 green onions, thinly sliced
3 Tbsp. low-sodium soy sauce
1/4 cup chopped fresh cilantro

2 Tbsp. minced fresh ginger
2 cloves garlic, minced
2 tsp. oriental sesame oil
Freshly ground black pepper
Cilantro *or* parsley sprigs

In a large bowl, combine all ingredients and mix well. Form into 1" balls. Arrange on a broiler pan coated with cooking spray and broil about 6 to 8 minutes or until tops of meatballs brown.

To serve: arrange meatballs on a platter garnished with cilantro or parsley sprigs.

Tip: To prepare in food processor, mince water chestnuts and onions, then add remaining ingredients. Do not overprocess.

Yield: about 24
Serving size: four meatballs

Per serving:	Calories	Fat (g)	Cholesterol (mg)	Fiber (g)	Sodium (mg)
	150	4	49	1	363

Turkey Montmorency

1 cup currant jelly
1 cup Dijon mustard
1 1/2 lbs. cooked turkey (white meat), cubed

In a skillet, combine jelly and mustard. Heat, stirring, until blended. Add turkey to sauce and simmer 15 to 20 minutes. Serve in a chafing dish with toothpicks.

Variation: Slice turkey, heat in sauce and serve as an entree.

Serves 8 to 10
Serving size: 2 1/2 ounces

Per serving:	Calories	Fat (g)	Cholesterol (mg)	Fiber (g)	Sodium (mg)
	227	4	51	0	371

Mandarin Chicken Bites

This lovely appetizer, adapted from the *Creme de Colorado*
cookbook, is colorful as well as delicious

2 cups low-sodium chicken broth
1/4 cup low-sodium soy sauce
2 tsp. Worcestershire sauce
4 skinless, boneless chicken breasts
1 lb. fresh spinach leaves, rinsed and stemmed
8 cups boiling water
2 16-oz. cans mandarin oranges,
   rinsed and drained

Curry Dip:
1 cup plain non-fat yogurt
2 Tbsp. fat free or light, cholesterol-free
   mayonnaise
1/4 cup chutney, chopped
1 Tbsp. minced fresh ginger
1 to 2 tsp. curry powder
1 tsp. orange zest

In a large skillet, boil chicken broth until reduced to about 1 1/2 cups. Add soy and Worcestershire sauce. Reduce heat to simmer and add chicken breasts. Cover and cook until tender, about 10 to 15 minutes or until chicken is no longer pink in the center. Remove chicken from broth and cool slightly. Cut into strips about 1/2" wide.

Place spinach leaves in a colander and pour boiling water over to wilt. Drain and set aside to cool.

Place a piece of chicken at stem end of a spinach leaf and roll leaf around chicken leaving some chicken showing on the ends. Secure leaf with a toothpick then place a mandarin orange on the end of the toothpick. Arrange on a serving platter, cover and refrigerate one hour.

Prepare dip: combine yogurt, mayonnaise, chutney, ginger, curry powder and orange zest; mix well. Spoon into a serving bowl. Refrigerate one hour to blend flavors. To serve, set dip in center of serving platter surrounded by chicken.

Yield: about 5 dozen
Serving size: 4 pieces

Per serving:	Calories	Fat (g)	Cholesterol (mg)	Fiber (g)	Sodium (mg)
	108	3	28	1	160

Chicken Rumaki

A low-fat, low-cholesterol, low-sodium version of a classic appetizer

4 skinless, boneless chicken breasts
24 water chestnuts
24 pineapple chunks (juice-pack), drained
1/4 cup low-sodium soy sauce

1/4 cup reserved pineapple juice
2 Tbsp. dry sherry
1 Tbsp. minced fresh ginger
1 clove garlic, minced

Freeze chicken slightly, then thinly slice across the grain into 24 slices. Cut each water chestnut and pineapple chunk in half. Wrap a chicken strip around each water chestnut and pineapple half. Secure with a toothpick.

Combine remaining ingredients in a plastic zip-top bag and mix well. Add chicken to bag. Seal and marinate, refrigerated, overnight; turn occasionally.

Coat a broiler pan with cooking spray. Arrange chicken pieces on broiler rack, then broil 3 to 4 minutes, turning once. Baste with marinade while cooking.

Yield: 24
Serving size: four pieces

Per serving:	Calories	Fat (g)	Cholesterol (mg)	Fiber (g)	Sodium (mg)
	227	4	67	0	472

Golden Chicken Nuggets

1/3 cup honey
1/2 cup dry sherry *or* white wine
3 Tbsp. fresh lime juice
1 Tbsp. minced fresh ginger

2 tsp. cinnamon
1 tsp. lime zest
1 clove garlic, minced
8 skinless, boneless chicken breasts, cubed

Combine honey, sherry, lime juice, ginger, cinnamon, zest and garlic in a zip-top plastic bag. Add chicken cubes, seal and marinate overnight in the refrigerator. Turn occasionally.

Drain chicken pieces. Arrange on a broiler pan coated with cooking spray. Broil for 5 to 6 minutes, basting with marinade. Serve with toothpicks.

Yield: about 60 pieces
Serving size: four pieces

Per serving:	Calories	Fat (g)	Cholesterol (mg)	Fiber (g)	Sodium (mg)
	130	3	54	0	53

Chicken Paté

An elegant substitute for liver paté, which is high in cholesterol and fat

¹/₂ cup chopped carrot
2 thin slices fresh ginger, peeled
1 shallot
1 clove garlic
1 cup cubed cooked chicken
  (cooked without skin)

¹/₄ cup fat free or light, cholesterol-free
  mayonnaise
2 Tbsp. plain non-fat yogurt
1 tsp. rice *or* white wine vinegar
2 tsp. low-sodium soy sauce
3 green onions, thinly sliced
Pita bread *or* rye crackers

Place carrot, ginger, shallot and garlic in a food processor and process until chopped. Add chicken and process 5 seconds or until chicken is minced. Add mayonnaise, yogurt, vinegar and soy sauce; pulse 3 to 4 times or until well blended. In a small bowl, combine chicken mixture with green onions; cover and chill 8 hours or overnight.

Serve on pita wedges or rye crackers

Yield: about 16 appetizers
Serving size: two appetizers

Per serving:	Calories	Fat (g)	Cholesterol (mg)	Fiber (g)	Sodium (mg)
	68	3	16	0	123

Citrus Marinated Seafood

Using a mixture of shrimp and scallops helps to reduce
the cholesterol in this tangy appetizer

1 Tbsp. olive oil
2 tsp. Worcestershire sauce
2 tsp. fresh lime *or* lemon juice

1 tsp. lime *or* lemon zest
4 large shrimp, shelled and deveined
6 large scallops

Combine olive oil, Worcestershire, lime juice and zest. Add shrimp and scallops; marinate for 1 to 2 hours. Drain and broil until shrimp is pink and seafood is opaque.

Serve garnished with parsley and a lime wedge.

Serves 2

Per serving:	Calories	Fat (g)	Cholesterol (mg)	Fiber (g)	Sodium (mg)
	172	8	63	0	307

Marinated Flank Strips

4 Tbsp. red wine vinegar	1 tsp. freshly ground black pepper
2 cloves garlic, minced	1/2 cup olive oil
2 tsp. dry mustard	2 lbs. flank steak, trimmed of all fat
1/4 cup low-sodium soy sauce	
2 tsp. Worcestershire sauce	Cocktail rye bread, toasted
1 tsp. hot pepper sauce	Horseradish Mustard (recipe follows)

Whisk together vinegar, garlic and dry mustard in a medium bowl. Mix in soy sauce, Worcestershire, hot pepper sauce and pepper. Gradually whisk in olive oil in a slow, steady stream.

Place steak in a shallow glass pan. Pour marinade over; prick all over with a fork and turn steak over. Cover and refrigerate at least 8 hours or overnight.

Broil or grill steak 3 to 4 minutes per side or until medium rare. Slice diagonally across the grain into paper-thin strips. Arrange on toasted rye bread. Serve with Horseradish Mustard Sauce.

Serves: 16
Serving size: 2 ounces

Per serving:	Calories	Fat (g)	Cholesterol (mg)	Fiber (g)	Sodium (mg)
	185	11	38	0	187

Horseradish Mustard

1/2 cup coarse-grained mustard
1/4 cup horseradish (freshly grated, if available)

Mix mustard and horseradish together in a small bowl. May be prepared up to 3 days ahead and refrigerated.

Yield: about 3/4 cup
Serving size: 1 Tbsp.

Per serving:	Calories	Fat (g)	Cholesterol (mg)	Fiber (g)	Sodium (mg)
	12	0	0	0	240

Hot and Sour Nuts

1/4 tsp. garlic powder
2 tsp. hot chili oil *or*
  1/4 tsp. tabasco
3 Tbsp. brown sugar

3 Tbsp. reduced-sodium soy sauce
3 Tbsp. cider vinegar
2 cups assorted raw nuts
  (e.g. almonds, cashews, pecans)

In a medium bowl, mix together garlic powder, chili oil, brown sugar, soy sauce, and vinegar. Add nuts and mix to coat thoroughly. Spread mixture onto a non-stick baking sheet.

Bake at 300° until liquid has evaporated, about 15 to 20 minutes. Stir twice during cooking. Nuts burn easily so watch carefully. Cool, then break apart if necessary. Store in airtight container.

Tip: After cooking, nuts may be mixed with dry cereal (e.g. Chex, bite-size Shredded Wheat, Crispex) to reduce fat content of this recipe.

Yield: about 2 cups
Serving size: 1/4 cup

Per serving:	Calories	Fat (g)	Cholesterol (mg)	Fiber (g)	Sodium (mg)
	355	28	0	6	231

Crisp Garbanzo Nuts

3 Tbsp. low-sodium soy sauce
2 Tbsp. dry white wine *or* water
1 tsp. onion powder
1/2 tsp. garlic powder

1/2 tsp. curry powder
1/4 tsp. paprika
4 cups canned garbanzo beans, rinsed
  and drained

Mix together soy sauce, wine and seasonings. In a large bowl, combine beans with soy mixture. Marinate one hour, stirring frequently.

Place beans on a non-stick baking sheet. Bake at 325° for 60 minutes or until browned and crisp. Stir occasionally.

Yield: about 2 cups
Serving size: 1/4 cup

Per serving:	Calories	Fat (g)	Cholesterol (mg)	Fiber (g)	Sodium (mg)
	144	2	0	2	232

Soups

Whether light and refreshing or hearty and filling, soups add variety to meals. Homemade soups are far lower in sodium than those off the shelf.

Cold

Avocado Bisque 25
Chilled Beet 25
Citrus Melon 26
Cold Spinach 27
Cool Mango 26
Ruby Fruit 27
Summmer Tomato 28
Sweet Potato Vichyssoise 28
Zucchini Pesto 40

Hot

Asparagus 29
Bean 'n' Greens 29
Blackeye Pea 31
Broccoli 29
Calico Bean 30
Corn Chowder 36
Cream Soup Mix 29
Creamy Cheesy Broccoli 33
Curried Broccoli 34
Four Onion 37
Gingered Carrot 33
Golden Pepper 34
Green and Gold 35
Mushroom 29
Quick Tomato Barley 38
Pinto Bean 31
Sherried Cream of Mushroom 38
Shredded Cabbage 35
Spanish Rice 37
Spinach and Black Bean 32
Summer Tomato 28
Sweet Potato Vichyssoise 28
Turkey 39

Avocado Bisque

1 ripe avocado, pitted and peeled
3 Tbsp. fresh lemon juice
2 Tbsp. chopped fresh dill
2 cups non-fat buttermilk
2 cups salt-free chicken broth, defatted
1/4 tsp. Lite Salt™
1/4 tsp. white pepper
1/8 lb. small shrimp, cooked and peeled
Fresh dill sprigs

In a blender or food processor puree avocado, lemon juice, dill, buttermilk, broth, Lite Salt and pepper until very smooth. Pour into a bowl, cover and chill before serving.

Serve garnished with shrimp and dill sprigs.

Serves 4 to 6

Per serving:	Calories	Fat (g)	Cholesterol (mg)	Fiber (g)	Sodium (mg)
	114	6	15	1	179

Chilled Beet Soup

1 15-oz. can diced beets
1/2 cup plain non-fat yogurt
1/4 cup low-fat sour cream
1/4 cup white vinegar (*or* to taste)
2 Tbsp. chopped fresh dill

6 to 8 green onions, thinly sliced
1 cup sliced English cucumber
Ice cubes
Freshly ground black pepper

Drain beet liquid into a medium bowl. Whisk in yogurt, sour cream and vinegar, mixing well. Stir in beets, dill, green onion and cucumber. Add 4 to 6 ice cubes. Cover and chill 2 to 4 hours before serving. Season to taste with pepper.

Serves 4

Per serving:	Calories	Fat (g)	Cholesterol (mg)	Fiber (g)	Sodium (mg)
	90	2	4	1	302

Cool Mango Soup

1 orange
3 ripe mangos, peeled, pitted and cubed
Zest of 1 orange
1¹/₂ cups fresh orange juice

1 to 3 tsp. honey
1¹/₂ cups non-fat buttermilk
1 to 2 teaspoons fresh lemon juice (optional)
Mint leaves

Peel and slice orange; reserve slices for garnish.

Puree mango with orange zest, orange juice and honey. Blend in buttermilk. Pour into a bowl and refrigerate, covered, until well chilled. Taste and add lemon juice (or more honey) if necessary.

To serve, ladle into chilled bowls and garnish with orange slices and mint leaves.

Yield: 6 servings

Per serving:	Calories	Fat (g)	Cholesterol (mg)	Fiber (g)	Sodium (mg)
	130	1	1	1	85

Citrus-Melon Soup

1 cantaloupe (*or* other melon
  of your choice)
1 6-oz. can frozen tangerine *or* orange
  juice concentrate, partially thawed

1 tsp. lime zest
1/2 tsp. grated fresh ginger
Orange *or* lime slices
Mint sprigs

Cut melon in half, discard seeds and scoop out flesh. Cut into large cubes. Place in blender or food processor with juice concentrate and process until smoothly pureed. Stir in zest and ginger.

May be served immediately or transfer to a large bowl and chill up to 24 hours before serving. Serve garnished with orange or lime slices and mint sprigs.

Variation: Add 1 to 2 Tbsp. orange-flavored liqueur.

Serves 4

Per serving:	Calories	Fat (g)	Cholesterol (mg)	Fiber (g)	Sodium (mg)
	114	1	0	2	22

Ruby Fruit Soup

5 cups raspberry *or* cran-raspberry juice
1/2 cup red wine *or* 1/2 cup sherry
1/2 cup tapioca
1/4 cup honey
1 tsp. almond extract

1 Tbsp. lemon *or* orange zest
2 cups fresh raspberries *or*
  2 12-oz. bags frozen raspberries
1 cup sliced strawberries
Vanilla non-fat yogurt

In a medium saucepan, combine juice, wine, tapioca, honey, almond extract and zest. Let stand five minutes. Bring to a boil over medium heat, stirring constantly. Add berries. Cool to room temperature, stirring occasionally.

Cover and chill. Serve topped with a dollop of vanilla yogurt. Garnish with orange zest and toasted sliced almonds, if desired.

Serves 10 to 12

Per serving:	Calories	Fat (g)	Cholesterol (mg)	Fiber (g)	Sodium (mg)
	124	0	0	1	2

Cold Spinach Soup

1 lb. fresh spinach, washed and stemmed
4 green onions, thinly sliced
1 shallot, minced
1 tsp. curry powder

2 cups non-fat buttermilk
1/8 tsp. pepper
1 tsp. fresh lemon juice
1/8 tsp. nutmeg

Steam spinach for 3 to 4 minutes or until wilted. Place in food processor and puree. Add remaining ingredients and process until smooth. Spoon into a large bowl and chill 30 to 60 minutes before serving.

Serves 2 to 4

Per serving:	Calories	Fat (g)	Cholesterol (mg)	Fiber (g)	Sodium (mg)
	80	1	3	4	239

Sweet Potato Vichyssoise

6 cups salt-free chicken broth, defatted
1 1/2 cups dry white wine
4 leeks (white part only), sliced
3 sweet potatoes, peeled and diced
1/4 tsp. Lite Salt™

1 tsp. lime zest
3 Tbsp. lime juice
2 cups evaporated non-fat milk
Lime wedges

In a large saucepan, combine chicken broth, wine, leeks, potatoes and salt. Simmer until potatoes are tender, about 15 minutes. Add lime zest, juice and milk. Puree soup in batches in food processor or blender until very smooth.

Soup may be served hot or cold. Garnish with lime wedges

Serves 6

Per serving:	Calories	Fat (g)	Cholesterol (mg)	Fiber (g)	Sodium (mg)
	215	1	3	2	156

Summer Tomato Soup

Tomatoes from your garden make this soup a summer favorite

1 Tbsp. olive oil
2 cups chopped onion
1 cup chopped carrot
1 clove garlic, minced
1/4 tsp. Lite Salt™

1/4 tsp. cayenne pepper
4 cups salt-free chicken broth, defatted
4 lb. tomatoes, cored, seeded and diced
1/2 cup Avocado-Cilantro Dip (page 7)
   (optional)

Heat oil in a large saucepan; saute onion, carrot and garlic until onion is lightly browned. Add Lite Salt, pepper and broth. Simmer for 30 to 40 minutes. Add tomatoes and cook over medium heat until softened, 10 to 15 minutes. Cool slightly. Puree in food processor or blender. May be served warm or chilled.

Garnish with a dollop of Avocado-Cilantro Dip (page 7) if desired.

Serves 4 to 6

Per serving:	Calories	Fat (g)	Cholesterol (mg)	Fiber (g)	Sodium (mg)
	74	3	0	1	59

Cream Soup Mix

Use as a substitute for canned cream soup.

2 cups non-fat dry milk
3/4 cup cornstarch
2 Tbsp. chicken bouillon granules
2 Tbsp. dried onion flakes
1 1/2 tsp. dried basil

1 tsp. dried savory
1/2 tsp. dried marjoram
1/2 tsp. dried thyme
1/2 tsp. white pepper

Combine all ingredients and store in an airtight container. To replace one 10 1/2-oz. can of cream soup, combine 1/3 cup of dry mix with 1 1/4 cups low-sodium chicken broth. Bring to a boil over medium heat, then cook and stir until thickened.

Variations:

• Mushroom soup: add 1/2 cup finely diced mushrooms before bringing to a boil.

• Asparagus or broccoli soup: add 3/4 cup steamed, chopped vegetable to the cooked mixture.

Yield: 3 cups mix

Per serving:	Calories	Fat (g)	Cholesterol (mg)	Fiber (g)	Sodium (mg)
	160	1	5	0	784

Bean 'n' Greens Soup

1 tsp. olive oil
1/2 cup chopped onion
2 cloves garlic, minced
2 15-oz. cans garbanzo beans
5 cups salt-free chicken broth, defatted

1 pkg. frozen chopped spinach, mustard
   greens *or* swiss chard, thawed and drained
1 cup cooked small pasta shells
   or 1/2 cup cooked brown rice
1 tsp. Lite Salt™

Heat olive oil in a skillet; saute onion and garlic until soft. Set aside.

Puree one can of beans. Combine with remaining ingredients including onion and garlic. Simmer 30 minutes.

Serves 6 to 8

Per serving:	Calories	Fat (g)	Cholesterol (mg)	Fiber (g)	Sodium (mg)
	119	2	6	2	151

Calico Bean Soup

1/2 cup each: great northern, small lima, garbanzo, kidney, and black beans; lentils; and barley
8 cups low-sodium beef broth, defatted
2 bay leaves
1 tsp. olive oil
1 onion, chopped
2 cloves garlic, minced
2 Tbsp. dry sherry
1 green *or* red bell pepper, cored, seeded and chopped

1 carrot, diced
2 stalks celery, sliced
1/2 tsp. cumin
1 tsp. coarsely ground coriander *or* fennel seeds
1 tsp. orange zest
Freshly ground black pepper
1/4 tsp. dried red pepper flakes
Hot brown rice
Plain non-fat yogurt
Chopped fresh parsley

Rinse and sort beans. Place in a large pot; add cold water to cover by 2 to 3 inches. Let stand overnight. Drain and return to pot. Add beef broth and bay leaves. Bring to a boil then simmer, covered, for 1 1/2 to 2 hours or until beans are tender.

Meanwhile, heat oil in a large skillet. Saute onion and garlic until soft, 10 to 15 minutes. Add sherry, remaining vegetables, cumin, coriander seeds, orange zest, black pepper to taste and red pepper flakes. Cover and simmer until vegetables are tender, about 15 minutes, stirring occasionally. Add vegetables to beans; simmer 10 to 15 minutes longer.

Place a scoop of rice in a soup bowl and ladle soup over top. Garnish with a dollop of yogurt and chopped parsley.

Serves 6

Per serving:	Calories	Fat (g)	Cholesterol (mg)	Fiber (g)	Sodium (mg)
	350	2	0	7	37

Blackeye Pea Soup

1 lb. dry blackeye peas
8 cups water
1/2 lb. smoked turkey, skinned and cubed
1 onion, chopped
1 stalk celery (including leaves), chopped
2 cloves garlic, minced

1 jalapeño pepper, diced (optional)
1 16-oz. can salt-free tomato sauce
1 Tbsp. beef bouillon granules
1/2 tsp. dried savory
1/4 tsp. dried thyme
1/8 tsp. pepper

Wash and sort peas. Combine with remaining ingredients in a large pot. Simmer over medium heat, covered, for about 3 hours or until peas are very soft. Stir occasionally. Add water as necessary.
Serves 6

Per serving:	Calories	Fat (g)	Cholesterol (mg)	Fiber (g)	Sodium (mg)
	351	3	0	5	752

Pinto Bean Soup

1 cup dried pinto beans
1 onion, quartered
2 to 3 cloves garlic, minced
1 bay leaf
1/2 tsp. dried thyme

1/2 tsp. Lite Salt™
1/2 tsp. white pepper
1 12-oz. can evaporated skim milk
Thinly sliced green onion *or* cilantro

Soak beans overnight in water to cover. Drain and rinse well. In a large saucepan, combine beans with 3 quarts fresh water and bring to a boil. Add onion, garlic, bay leaf, thyme, Lite Salt and pepper. Reduce heat and simmer, covered, until beans are tender, about to 4 hours. Add more water as needed.

Remove bay leaf. Let beans cool to room temperature then puree in food processor or blender. Return to pan over medium heat. Add milk and heat gently. Serve garnished with green onion or cilantro.

Serves 4 to 6

Per serving:	Calories	Fat (g)	Cholesterol (mg)	Fiber (g)	Sodium (mg)
	173	1	3	2	161

Spinach and Black Bean Soup

1 lb. dry black beans, rinsed and sorted	1 small onion, studded with 2 cloves
1 tsp. olive oil	1/4 tsp. dried oregano
1 onion, chopped	1/8 tsp. cayenne pepper *or* dash hot sauce
2 cloves garlic, minced	2 tsp. red wine vinegar
12 cups salt-free beef *or*	2 Tbsp. dry sherry (optional)
chicken broth, defatted	1 pkg. frozen chopped spinach, thawed *or*
1-2 Tbsp. liquid smoke	4 cups fresh chopped spinach
2 bay leaves	Fresh cilantro

Soak beans overnight or use quick soak method: Cover beans with three times as much water. Bring to a boil, cook for 1 to 2 minutes then remove from heat and let stand for an hour. Drain beans.

Heat oil in a large pot. Saute onion and garlic until onion is soft, about 5 minutes. Add beans, broth, liquid smoke, bay leaves, onion and oregano. Bring to a boil, then reduce heat and simmer for 1 1/2 to 2 hours or until beans are tender. Add water as necessary. When beans are done, remove about half and puree then return to soup.

Add cayenne, vinegar, sherry and spinach. Simmer until soup thickens, about 30 minutes. Garnish with cilantro and serve.

Serves 6 to 8

Per serving:	Calories	Fat (g)	Cholesterol (mg)	Fiber (g)	Sodium (mg)
	255	3	0	4	47

Creamy Cheesy Broccoli Soup

1 cup non-fat dry milk
2 cups non-fat milk
1 tsp. olive oil
1/2 cup chopped onion
2 cups salt-free chicken broth, defatted
2 cups chopped broccoli

1/4 cup water
1/4 cup unbleached flour
1 cup grated low-fat cheddar cheese
1 to 2 Tbsp. dry sherry
1/4 tsp. white pepper

Blend dry milk into liquid non-fat milk; stir well and set aside.

Heat olive oil in a large saucepan. Saute onions until soft, 2 to 3 minutes. Add chicken broth and broccoli. Simmer 10 to 15 minutes or until broccoli is tender.

Blend water into flour and add to soup along with milk mixture, cheese, sherry and pepper. Bring to a boil, stirring constantly; reduce heat and simmer until thickened.

Variation: Puree cooked broccoli before adding remaining ingredients.

Serves 4 to 6

Per serving:	Calories	Fat (g)	Cholesterol (mg)	Fiber (g)	Sodium (mg)
	188	3	9	1	570

Gingered Carrot Soup

1 tsp. olive oil
1 onion, chopped
3 to 4 Tbsp. minced fresh ginger
2 to 3 cloves garlic, minced
8 cups salt-free chicken broth, defatted
1 cup dry white wine

1 1/2 lbs. carrots, sliced
2 Tbsp. fresh lemon *or* lime juice
1 tsp. lemon *or* orange zest
1/8 tsp. curry powder
Freshly ground pepper
Snipped fresh chives *or* chopped fresh parsley

Heat oil in a large pot and saute onion, ginger and garlic until onion is soft, 5 to 10 minutes. Add broth, wine and carrots. Simmer, uncovered, until carrots are very soft, about 45 minutes.

Puree soup in a food processor or blender. Return to pot and add lemon juice, lemon zest, curry powder and pepper to taste. Serve garnished with chives or parsley.

Serves 6

Per serving:	Calories	Fat (g)	Cholesterol (mg)	Fiber (g)	Sodium (mg)
	129	3	0	2	64

Curried Broccoli Soup

Serve this hearty soup as a main dish with whole wheat rolls

1¹/₂ lbs. broccoli
1 tsp. olive oil *or* liquid margarine
2 tsp. curry powder
¹/₄ tsp. cumin
1 onion, chopped
1 leek, sliced

6 cups salt-free chicken broth, defatted
2 new potatoes, cubed
4 carrots, sliced
1 cup evaporated skim milk
1 cup grated low-fat cheddar cheese

Chop broccoli into bite-size pieces and set aside. Heat oil in a large pot; add curry powder, cumin, onion and leek. Saute until onion is soft, about 5 minutes. Add broth, potatoes and carrots; cover and simmer until vegetables are soft and potatoes mash easily, about 30 minutes. Puree, half at a time, in a food processor or blender. Return to pot and bring to a boil. Add broccoli and evaporated milk. Simmer, uncovered, until broccoli is just tender. Add cheese gradually, stirring until melted.

Serves 6 to 8

Per serving:	Calories	Fat (g)	Cholesterol (mg)	Fiber (g)	Sodium (mg)
	148	3	4	4	469

Golden Pepper Soup

1 tsp. olive oil
1 onion, chopped
2 cloves garlic, minced
¹/₈ tsp. crushed red pepper flakes

4 yellow bell peppers, cored, seeded
  and chopped into large pieces
2 cups salt-free chicken *or* beef broth, defatted

In a large pot, heat olive oil; saute onion, garlic and red pepper flakes about 5 minutes. Add bell peppers. Cover and cook over low heat for 10 to 15 minutes, stirring frequently. Add broth. Simmer until peppers are tender, about 30 minutes.

Puree in batches in a food processor or blender. Return to pan and heat gently before serving.

Serves 4 to 6

Per serving:	Calories	Fat (g)	Cholesterol (mg)	Fiber (g)	Sodium (mg)
	47	2	0	1	12

Shredded Cabbage Soup

Serve with crisp bread sticks for a light first course

6 cups salt-free chicken *or* beef broth, defatted
1 potato (unpeeled), diced
4 tomatoes, cored and diced
1/2 cup grated carrots
1/2 cup diced celery
1/2 cup chopped onion
1/4 cup chopped fresh parsley

2 bay leaves
4 to 6 peppercorns
1/2 tsp. Lite Salt™
1/4 tsp. thyme
2 cups shredded green cabbage
2 cups shredded red cabbage
1/4 cup fresh lemon juice
1 Tbsp. brown sugar

In a large pot, combine broth, potato, tomatoes, carrots, celery, onion, parsley, bay leaves, peppercorns (place in bouquet garni), salt and thyme. Cover and simmer for 1 hour, stirring occasionally. Add cabbages and simmer an additional 10 minutes. Add lemon juice and sugar. Remove bay leaves and bouquet garni before serving.

Variation: Add 1 cup cooked brown rice or 1 15-oz. can white (Great Northern) beans.

Serves 6 to 8

Per serving:	Calories	Fat (g)	Cholesterol (mg)	Fiber (g)	Sodium (mg)
	68	1	0	3	94

Green and Gold Soup

2 tsp. olive oil
1 onion, thinly sliced
1 leek, thinly sliced
2 cloves garlic, minced
1/4 cup unbleached flour
2 zucchini, sliced
2 crookneck squash, sliced

3 cups salt-free chicken broth, defatted
1 12-oz. can evaporated non-fat milk
1 Tbsp. minced fresh basil *or* 1 tsp. dried
2 tsp. minced fresh oregano *or* 1/2 tsp. dried
1/4 tsp. Lite Salt™
Freshly ground pepper

Saute onion, leek and garlic in olive oil until onion is soft, about 5 minutes. Add flour and cook, stirring, 3 minutes. Add squash and cook until softened, about 5 minutes. Stir in chicken stock, evaporated milk, basil, oregano and Lite Salt. Season to taste with pepper. Reduce heat and simmer for 20 minutes.

Serves 6 to 8

Per serving:	Calories	Fat (g)	Cholesterol (mg)	Fiber (g)	Sodium (mg)
	106	2	2	1	92

Corn Chowder

Serve with Sesame Spinach Salad (page 52) and
crusty whole wheat rolls for a simple summer meal

1 tsp. olive oil *or* liquid margarine
1/4 cup diced celery
1/4 cup diced onion
1/4 cup chopped green *or* red bell pepper
2 cups fresh corn kernels *or*
  1 10-oz. pkg. frozen corn
1 cup diced potatoes (unpeeled)
2 Tbsp. chopped fresh parsley

1 cup salt-free chicken broth
1/2 tsp. Lite Salt™
1/4 tsp. paprika
1/8 tsp. white pepper
2 Tbsp. unbleached flour
2 cups non-fat milk *or*
  1 cup non-fat milk and
  1 cup non-fat evaporated milk

Heat oil in a large saucepan. Saute celery, onion and green pepper until soft. Add corn, potatoes, parsley, broth, salt, paprika and pepper. Bring to a boil, then simmer for 10 to 15 minutes or until potatoes are tender.

In a jar with a tightly fitting lid, combine flour and 1/2 cup of milk. Shake to blend thoroughly. Add to chowder along with remaining milk. Cook and stir, over medium heat, until mixture thickens.

Variation: Add 1 cup cubed smoked turkey.

Serves 4 to 5

Per serving:	Calories	Fat (g)	Cholesterol (mg)	Fiber (g)	Sodium (mg)
	158	3	2	4	159

Four Onion Soup

1 Tbsp. olive oil	1 Tbsp. unbleached flour
3 onions, sliced	8 cups salt-free chicken broth, defatted
3 leeks, sliced	1 cup dry white wine (optional)
8 green onions, thinly sliced	2 tsp. chicken bouillon granules
1/4 cup minced shallots	2 Tbsp. brandy (optional)
2 tsp. minced fresh ginger	1 tsp. fresh lemon juice
2 garlic cloves, crushed	Freshly ground pepper

Heat olive oil in a large saucepan. Add onions, leeks, green onions, shallots, ginger and garlic. Saute over low heat until soft, about 20 minutes; stir occasionally.

Add flour and stir. Add broth, wine and bouillon granules.

Simmer 20 minutes. Blend in brandy, lemon juice and pepper. Simmer 15 minutes more. Serve hot.

Yield: 8 servings

Per serving:	Calories	Fat (g)	Cholesterol (mg)	Fiber (g)	Sodium (mg)
	112	3	0	1	256

Spanish Rice Soup

1 tsp. olive oil	1 cup dry white wine
1 red onion, chopped	(*or* chicken broth)
1 clove garlic, minced	1 4-oz. can chopped green chiles
3/4 cup brown rice	2 Tbsp. paprika
3 cups salt-free chicken broth, defatted	1 tsp. dried oregano
2 cups chopped celery	1 tsp. cumin
2 carrots, thinly sliced	1 tsp. to 1 Tbsp. chili powder (to taste)
3 15-oz. cans salt-free tomatoes, pureed	

Heat oil in a large saucepan and saute onion, garlic and rice until onion is soft. Add broth, celery and carrots. Bring to a boil, then simmer, covered, for 30 to 40 minutes. Add remaining ingredients and simmer 15 to 20 minutes or until rice is done.

Serves 6 to 8

Per serving:	Calories	Fat (g)	Cholesterol (mg)	Fiber (g)	Sodium (mg)
	172	2	0	6	83

Sherried Cream of Mushroom Soup

This creamy soup has a fraction of the fat of its canned counterpart

1 tsp. liquid *or* soft margarine
1/2 lb. mushrooms, sliced
1/2 cup chopped onion
1/2 cup non-fat dry milk

2 Tbsp. unbleached flour
1 cup salt-free chicken broth, defatted
1 12-oz. can evaporated skim milk
2 to 3 Tbsp. dry sherry (optional)

Melt margarine in a medium saucepan and stir in mushrooms and onion. Cover and saute over low heat until mushrooms are soft and liquid has accumulated in the pan. Cool slightly. Pour mushrooms and juice into a food processor. Add dry milk, broth and flour; process until mushrooms are finely chopped.

Return mushroom mixture to saucepan. Blend in milk and sherry. Heat gently.

Variation: Reserve half of sauteed mushroom mixture; puree remaining half in food processor with flour and dry milk. Proceed as above.

Serves 4

Per serving:	Calories	Fat (g)	Cholesterol (mg)	Fiber (g)	Sodium (mg)
	193	2	7	3	239

Quick Tomato Barley Soup

1 28-oz can Italian tomatoes
2 10-oz. cans salt-free chicken broth,
  defatted
1/2 cup pearl barley

1 Tbsp. chopped fresh basil *or* 1/2 tsp. dried
1/8 tsp. celery seed, ground
Dash allspice

Puree tomatoes in a food processor. Pour into a saucepan and add remaining ingredients. Bring to a boil. Reduce heat and simmer, stirring occasionally, for about 30 minutes or until barley is soft.

Serves 4 to 6

Per serving:	Calories	Fat (g)	Cholesterol (mg)	Fiber (g)	Sodium (mg)
	47	1	0	4	175

Turkey Soup

The only meal better than a turkey dinner is the soup that follows

1 turkey carcass	**2 bay leaves**
1 onion, chopped	**1 tsp. Lite Salt™**
2 carrots, peeled and sliced	**1 cup barley, wild *or* brown rice**
3-4 stalks celery (including leaves), sliced	**(*or* a combination)**
1 leek, sliced	

Break carcass into pieces. Place in a large soup pot; add remaining ingredients, except barley. Cover with water (2 to 3 quarts). Bring to a boil over medium heat. Skim foam if necessary. Partially cover and simmer for 2 to 3 hours skimming foam as necessary.

Add barley; continue cooking an additional hour or until barley is done. Remove carcass pieces and cool. Remove meat and return to soup.

Variations:

• Add sliced fresh mushrooms.

• Add sliced fresh green beans during last 30 minutes of cooking.

• Add peas: place thawed frozen peas in soup bowl, then pour hot soup over. Stir and serve.

Serves 6 to 8

Per serving:	Calories	Fat (g)	Cholesterol (mg)	Fiber (g)	Sodium (mg)
	86	2	22	2	164

Zucchini Pesto Soup

3 zucchini, trimmed and sliced
3 cups salt-free chicken broth, defatted

2 Tbsp. Pesto (page 293)
Fresh basil leaves

Combine zucchini and chicken broth in a 2 to 3 quart pot. Bring to a boil; reduce heat and simmer until zucchini is tender, 10 to 15 minutes. Let cool to room temperature.

Strain zucchini, reserving broth, and place in food processor or blender. Add pesto and puree until very smooth, adding ¼ to ½ cup broth as necessary to make a smooth puree. Blend puree with remaining broth and stir well. Heat gently and serve, or cover and chill before serving. Garnish with thin slices of zucchini and top with a fresh basil leaf.

Serves 4 to 6

Per serving:	Calories	Fat (g)	Cholesterol (mg)	Fiber (g)	Sodium (mg)
	59	4	0	1	5

Skip the high-fat processed lunch meats and make lunch out of the ordinary with low-fat sandwich fillings stuffed in a pita pocket or layered between whole grain bread.

Delitefully HealthMark

California Avocado 43
Chicken Club 45
Chicken Fajita 44
Grilled Eggplant 44
Salad 43
Hummus in Pita Bread 45
Lentils in Pita Pockets 43
Salmon in Pita Bread 46
Seafood Avocado Salad in Pita 46
Skinny Chicken Salad 47
Tuna Pita 48
Zucchini Pockets 49
Quick Pizzas 49

California Avocado Sandwich

2 slices whole wheat *or* sourdough bread   **1 slice red onion**
2 tsp. HealthMark Mayonnaise (page 287)   **2 slices tomato**
1/8 avocado, sliced   **Alfalfa sprouts**

Spread bread with mayonnaise. Arrange avocado, onion, tomato and sprouts on one slice of bread; top with second slice.

Serves 1

Per serving:	Calories	Fat (g)	Cholesterol (mg)	Fiber (g)	Sodium (mg)
	204	7	3	7	306

Salad Sandwich

Salad (lettuce, tomatoes, cucumbers, etc.)
    tossed lightly with dressing
Kidney *or* garbanzo beans —
    1/4 cup per serving
Whole wheat pita bread

Toss salad and beans together. Cut pita pockets in half and stuff with salad mixture.

Per serving:	Calories	Fat (g)	Cholesterol (mg)	Fiber (g)	Sodium (mg)
	148	1	1	9	73

Lentils in Pita Pockets

4 whole wheat pita breads
Lettuce
2 cups Marinated Lentil Salad (page 136), well drained

Cut pitas in half. Place a lettuce leaf inside each half, then scoop in Lentil Salad.

Serves: 4
Serving size: 1 sandwich with 1/2 cup Lentil Salad

Per serving:	Calories	Fat (g)	Cholesterol (mg)	Fiber (g)	Sodium (mg)
	156	0	0	7	19

Chicken Fajita Sandwich

Fajita Marinade (page 153)
4 skinless, boneless chicken breasts
Mary's Guacamole (page 6)

4 slices tomato
4 thin slices red onion
4 onion *or* whole wheat buns

Pour marinade over chicken breasts and marinate 1 to 2 hours. Drain and grill 5 to 10 minutes per side or until no longer pink when cut in thickest part.

Serve on buns with guacamole, tomato and red onion.

Serves 4

Per serving:	Calories	Fat (g)	Cholesterol (mg)	Fiber (g)	Sodium (mg)
	408	11	103	5	384

Grilled Eggplant Sandwiches

1 Tbsp. olive oil
1 clove garlic, minced
1 1-lb. eggplant, trimmed
1 grilled red bell pepper (page 226)

4 fresh basil leaves
4 thin slices part-skim mozzarella cheese
Freshly ground black pepper

Combine olive oil and garlic in a small bowl. Set aside for 1 to 2 hours. Slice grilled pepper into quarters and set aside.

Slice eggplant 1/4" thick. Brush 8 slices lightly with garlic olive oil mixture. Grill or broil until lightly browned, about 5 minutes per side. Place one red pepper slice on each of 4 eggplant slices, top with a basil leaf, a slice of cheese and another eggplant slice. Grill or broil until cheese begins to soften. Turn and continue cooking until cheese melts. Sprinkle with pepper and serve.

Serves 4

Per serving:	Calories	Fat (g)	Cholesterol (mg)	Fiber (g)	Sodium (mg)
	141	9	16	4	138

Chicken Club Sandwich

2 slices whole wheat *or* sourdough bread
2 tsp. HealthMark Mayonnaise (page 287)
1 tsp. Dijon mustard
2 oz. sliced chicken (*or* turkey)

1/8 avocado, sliced
1/4 tomato, sliced
Romaine *or* leaf lettuce

Spread bread with mayonnaise and mustard (if desired). Layer chicken, avocado, tomato and lettuce onto bread; top with second slice.

Serves 1

Per serving:	Calories	Fat (g)	Cholesterol (mg)	Fiber (g)	Sodium (mg)
	320	11	53	5	418

Hummus in Pita

A unique sandwich filling

1/4 cup sesame seeds *or* 2 Tbsp. tahini
1 15-oz. can garbanzo beans, rinsed
  and drained
3 to 4 Tbsp. lemon juice
1 Tbsp. olive oil

1 to 2 cloves garlic
1/2 tsp. oregano
1/4 to 1/2 tsp. cumin (to taste)
Whole wheat pita bread

In a dry skillet, toast sesame seeds, shaking the pan frequently, until golden. Combine with remaining ingredients in a food processor or blender and pulse on and off until chopped. Then process for 30 to 45 seconds until light and fluffy. If mixture is too thick, add water, 1 Tbsp. at a time, until desired consistency.

Spread in whole wheat pita bread lined with lettuce.

Yield: 2 cups
Serving size: 1 sandwich with 1/4 cup Hummus

Per serving:	Calories	Fat (g)	Cholesterol (mg)	Fiber (g)	Sodium (mg)
	230	6	0	6	6

Salmon in Pita Bread

1 7³/4-oz. can water-packed salmon, drained
1/2 cup garbanzo beans (rinsed and drained if not salt-free)
1/3 cup chopped celery (including leaves)
1/4 cup minced red onion
2 Tbsp. chopped fresh parsley

1 Tbsp. chopped black olives (rinse and drain before chopping)
1/4 cup plain non-fat yogurt
2 Tbsp. Italian dressing
Whole wheat pita bread
Shredded romaine lettuce
Sliced tomatoes

Combine first eight ingredients in a medium bowl and blend well. Fill pita bread halves loosely with shredded lettuce; spoon in salmon filling. Garnish with tomato slices.

Serves: 4 to 6

Per serving:	Calories	Fat (g)	Cholesterol (mg)	Fiber (g)	Sodium (mg)
	218	6	27	5	280

Seafood-Avocado Salad in a Pita

1 avocado, peeled, pitted and diced
1/2 English cucumber, diced
1/2 cup diced celery, including tops
2 to 3 green onions, thinly sliced
1 tomato, cored and diced
1 carrot, grated
1/4 lb. cooked small shrimp
1/4 lb. cooked bay scallops

1/2 cup plain non-fat yogurt
2 Tbsp. fat free or light, cholesterol-free mayonnaise
2 Tbsp. chopped fresh dill
1 tsp. lemon *or* lime zest
4 whole wheat pita breads
Shredded romaine lettuce

In a medium bowl, combine avocado, cucumber, celery, green onions, tomato, carrot, shrimp and scallops. In a smaller bowl, mix together yogurt, mayonnaise, dill and zest. Combine gently with avocado mixture. Cover and chill before serving.

To serve, slice pitas in half. Stuff half-full with lettuce, then spoon in salad mixture.

Serves 4 to 6

Per serving:	Calories	Fat (g)	Cholesterol (mg)	Fiber (g)	Sodium (mg)
	225	9	39	5	186

Skinny Chicken Salad

Chicken salad can be just as delicious without the high-fat mayonnaise

1 cup diced cooked chicken *or* 1 5-oz.
  can chicken (white meat) packed in water
1/4 cup diced celery

1/4 cup diced onion
2 Tbsp. chopped fresh cilantro
2 to 3 Tbsp. light dijon vinaigrette

Combine all ingredients in a small bowl and chill before serving. Use for a sandwich filling or serve as a salad.

Yield: 1 1/2 cups

Serving size: 1/2 cup

Per serving:	Calories	Fat (g)	Cholesterol (mg)	Fiber (g)	Sodium (mg)
	65	2	26	0	82

Tuna Pita

1 6 1/2-oz. can water-packed
  low-sodium tuna
2 celery stalks, chopped
2 green onions, thinly sliced
1 Tbsp. minced fresh dill *or*
  1/4 tsp. dried

1/2 cup plain non-fat yogurt
2 tsp. coarse grained mustard
1/4 tsp. celery salt
Whole wheat pita bread
Romaine lettuce
Sliced tomato

Drain and flake tuna. Combine with celery, green onion and dill. Blend together yogurt, mustard and celery salt, then mix with tuna.

Cut pita bread in half and line with lettuce and tomato slices. Add tuna and serve.

Serves 3 to 4

Per serving:	Calories	Fat (g)	Cholesterol (mg)	Fiber (g)	Sodium (mg)
	170	1	31	5	180

Zucchini Pockets

1 zucchini, shredded
1 carrot, shredded
1/2 cup sliced mushrooms
3 green onions, thinly sliced
1 tomato, cored and chopped
1 clove garlic, minced

1/4 cup grated part-skim mozzarella cheese *or*
    2 Tbsp. Parmesan cheese
3 Tbsp. chopped fresh parsley
1/4 cup Italian dressing
2 to 3 whole wheat pita breads

Combine all ingredients except pita bread. Toss vegetable mixture lightly.

Cut pita pockets in half and spoon filling into pockets.

Serves 4 to 6

Per serving:	Calories	Fat (g)	Cholesterol (mg)	Fiber (g)	Sodium (mg)
	135	7	3	3	241

Quick Pizzas

1 Tbsp. olive oil
1/2 cup minced onions
2 cloves garlic, minced
1 cup salt-free tomato sauce
1/2 tsp. dried oregano
1/2 tsp. dried basil
1/4 tsp. dried thyme
1 cup sliced mushrooms

1/2 zucchini, sliced
4 flour *or* corn tortillas
1/2 cup diced red bell pepper
1/2 cup diced green bell pepper
1/4 cup sliced black olives (rinse and
    drain before slicing)
1/2 cup grated part-skim mozzarella cheese

Heat half of oil in a medium saucepan and saute onions and garlic until soft. Stir in tomato sauce, oregano, basil and thyme. Simmer 10 to 15 minutes.

Heat remaining oil in a skillet. Saute mushrooms and zucchini until softened, about 5 minutes. Set aside.

Place tortillas on a baking sheet and bake at 350° until crisp, 4 to 5 minutes. Spread 1/4 cup sauce over each tortilla then top with mushrooms, zucchini, peppers, olives and cheese. Bake until cheese melts, about 5 minutes.

Serves 4

Per serving:	Calories	Fat (g)	Cholesterol (mg)	Fiber (g)	Sodium (mg)
	233	8	8	3	382

Add crunch to a meal with a crisp salad or make a meal of a hearty salad. Use dark green lettuces — rich in carotene — for maximum flavor and nutrition.

Delitefully HealthMark

Vegetable

Acupulco 53
Caesar 51
  Garlic Croutons 51
Chunky 52
Citrus Avocado 54
Creamy Cucumber 54
Crunchy Green Pea 59
Ensalada Escabeche 55
Firecracker Cole Slaw 60
Gazpacho Salad 56
Greek Cucumber 54
Green Beans Nicoise 57
Grilled Onion 57
Lemon Zucchini 58
Minted Tomato 58
Moroccan 59
Orange Slaw 60
Oriental Cucumbers 55
Pesto Potato 67
Pineapple Cole Slaw 61
Roasted Pepper 56
Sesame Spinach 52
Shanghi Chicken 67
Sweet Potato 61
Sweet and Sour Spinach 53

Pasta and Grains

Brown Rice and Avocado 63
Bulgur and Spinach 64
Corn and Barley 63
Couscous with Dill Vinaigrette 65
Marinated Spaghetti 62
Mediterranean 66
Tri Color Pasta 62

Chicken

Chicken Salad Pesto 69
Shanghi Chicken 67
Tossed Chicken 68

Caesar Salad

6 cups romaine lettuce, torn into
  bite-size pieces
1/4 cup olive oil
3 Tbsp. fresh lemon juice
1 tsp. white wine Worcestershire sauce

1 tsp. Dijon mustard
1 clove garlic, minced
1 anchovy, rinsed and drained, then mashed
1/4 cup Parmesan cheese
1/2 cup Garlic Croutons (recipe follows)

Place lettuce in a large bowl. In a small bowl or jar combine oil, lemon juice, Worcestershire sauce, mustard, garlic and anchovy. Mix well. Drizzle dressing over lettuce and toss to mix thoroughly. Sprinkle on cheese and mix well. Serve garnished with Garlic Croutons.

Serves 4 to 6

Per serving:	Calories	Fat (g)	Cholesterol (mg)	Fiber (g)	Sodium (mg)
	142	12	1	2	82

Garlic Croutons

1/4 cup olive oil
1 clove garlic, mashed
6 slices day-old whole grain *or* sourdough bread, cubed

Combine oil and garlic and let stand in a tightly covered jar for several hours or overnight. Drizzle over bread cubes and toss to coat well. Spread bread cubes on a baking sheet and bake at 325° for 20 to 30 minutes or until golden brown. Stir occasionally. Store in a tightly covered container.

Yield: 4 cups

Per serving:	Calories	Fat (g)	Cholesterol (mg)	Fiber (g)	Sodium (mg)
	145	10	1	2	130

Sesame Spinach Salad

Dressing:

2 Tbsp. sesame seeds
1/4 cup sherry vinegar
3 Tbsp. walnut *or* canola oil
3 Tbsp. water
1 Tbsp. honey

2 tsp. poppy seeds
1/2 tsp. white pepper
1/4 tsp. paprika
1 shallot, minced

1 lb. fresh spinach
2 cups shredded red cabbage
2 cups sliced strawberries

Prepare dressing: Toast sesame seeds in a non-stick skillet over medium heat. In a small bowl, whisk together vinegar, oil, water, honey, poppy seeds, pepper, paprika and shallots. Stir in toasted sesame seeds. Set aside.

Wash and stem spinach. Tear into bite-size pieces and place in a serving bowl. Add cabbage and strawberries; mix well. Just before serving, drizzle dressing over salad and toss thoroughly.

Variation: Substitute fresh raspberries, grapefruit segments or mandarin oranges (rinsed and drained) for strawberries.

Serves 6 to 8

Per serving:	Calories	Fat (g)	Cholesterol (mg)	Fiber (g)	Sodium (mg)
	106	7	0	4	46

Chunky Salad

1/2 lb. broccoli
1 small head cauliflower
4 carrots, sliced
4 celery stalks, sliced

1 cup cubed jicama
4 oz. part-skim mozzarella, cubed
1/2 cup Herbed Dijon Vinaigrette (page 283)

Cut broccoli and cauliflower into bite-size pieces. Steam broccoli, cauliflower and carrots until barely tender. Rinse under cold water and drain well. Combine with celery, jicama, cheese and Herbed Dijon Vinaigrette; mix well. Cover and chill 2 to 3 hours before serving.

Serves 4 to 6

Per serving:	Calories	Fat (g)	Cholesterol (mg)	Fiber (g)	Sodium (mg)
	200	13	11	4	200

Sweet and Sour Spinach Salad

1¹/₂ lbs. fresh spinach
2 oranges
¹/₂ red onion, thinly sliced
3 to 4 green onions, thinly sliced

2 Tbsp. brown sugar
¹/₄ cup cider vinegar
¹/₂ tsp. each dry mustard, celery seed and paprika
¹/₂ cup canola *or* safflower *or* olive oil

Wash spinach thoroughly, removing stems. Tear into bite-size pieces and place in a large serving bowl. Chill.

Peel oranges and cut into segments, reserving juice. Add to spinach along with onion slices.

In a small bowl, mix together sugar, vinegar, mustard, celery seed and paprika. Gradually whisk in oil. Pour half of dressing over salad, tossing to coat thoroughly. Add more dressing if needed.

Serves 6 to 8

Per serving:	Calories	Fat (g)	Cholesterol (mg)	Fiber (g)	Sodium (mg)
	181	14	0	4	62

Acapulco Salad

Colorful, crisp and full of South-of-the-Border flavor — perfect for a Mexican buffet

1 large jicama, peeled
2 carrots, peeled
1 green *or* red bell pepper,
  cored and seeded
1 yellow bell pepper, cored and seeded
¹/₄ cup fresh lime juice

2 Tbsp. olive oil
4 Tbsp. plain non-fat yogurt
1 to 2 tsp. sugar *or* honey
¹/₄ to ¹/₂ cup chopped fresh cilantro
1 *or* 2 jalapeño peppers, seeded
  and minced (optional)

Using a food processor (or by hand), slice jicama, carrots and bell peppers into thin slices, then julienne. Mix together in a large bowl.

In a small bowl, whisk together lime juice, oil, yogurt and sugar. Mix in cilantro. Pour dressing over vegetables and toss gently to blend. Add jalapeño peppers and mix well. Serve at room temperature or chill for several hours before serving.

Serves 6 to 8

Per serving:	Calories	Fat (g)	Cholesterol (mg)	Fiber (g)	Sodium (mg)
	66	4	0	1	13

Citrus-Avocado Salad

2 grapefruit
¹/2 avocado, peeled and pitted
¹/2 cup Dijon Mustard Sauce (page 290)

1 head red leaf *or* romaine lettuce
¹/2 red onion, sliced

Peel and section grapefruit, reserving juice. Slice avocado. Whisk together Mustard Sauce and grapefruit juice. Place lettuce leaves on salad plates then arrange grapefruit sections, avocado slices and onion rings on top. Drizzle with dressing and serve.

Serves 4

Per serving:	Calories	Fat (g)	Cholesterol (mg)	Fiber (g)	Sodium (mg)
	126	5	2	2	79

Creamy Cucumber Salad

1 English cucumber
1 cup plain non-fat yogurt
2 Tbsp. low-fat sour cream
2 Tbsp. chopped fresh dill

2 Tbsp. chopped fresh chives
1 tsp. lemon zest
¹/2 tsp. white pepper

Slice cucumber thinly. Combine remaining ingredients in a medium bowl. Fold in cucumber slices. Cover and chill before serving.

Variation: Greek Cucumber Salad: Add 1 clove garlic, minced, and 1 oz. feta cheese, crumbled.

Serves 3 to 4

Per serving:	Calories	Fat (g)	Cholesterol (mg)	Fiber (g)	Sodium (mg)
	49	1	4	0	48

Oriental Cucumbers

2 Tbsp. canola *or* peanut oil
4 Tbsp. rice vinegar
2 tsp. low-sodium soy sauce
1 tsp. minced fresh ginger

1/2 tsp. brown sugar
1 English cucumber, thinly sliced
Dash oriental sesame oil
1 Tbsp. toasted sesame seeds

Combine first 5 ingredients in a medium bowl, stirring until sugar dissolves. Add cucumber slices and sesame oil. Stir well. Cover and marinate in refrigerator 1 to 2 hours. Serve sprinkled with sesame seeds.

Serves 4

Per serving:	Calories	Fat (g)	Cholesterol (mg)	Fiber (g)	Sodium (mg)
	76	8	0	0	100

Ensalada Escabeche

2 cups broccoli florets
2 cups cauliflowerets
2 cups sliced green beans
2 carrots, sliced
1 small red onion, thinly sliced

3/4 cup Mexican Salsa (page 10)
2 Tbsp. olive oil
1/2 tsp. dried oregano, crushed
1/4 cup chopped fresh cilantro

Steam broccoli, cauliflower, green beans and carrots until just tender. Drain and place in a large serving bowl. Mix in sliced onion.

In a small bowl or in a jar with a screw-top lid, combine salsa, olive oil, oregano and cilantro. Mix well. Pour over warm vegetables and combine thoroughly. Serve at room temperature or cover and refrigerate until well chilled, 4 to 6 hours.

Variation: Add any one or more of the following: chopped radishes, chopped jicama, julienne red pepper, sliced celery.

Serves: 6 to 8

Per serving:	Calories	Fat (g)	Cholesterol (mg)	Fiber (g)	Sodium (mg)
	79	4	0	3	23

Gazpacho Salad

Just as good as the soup

1 English cucumber, halved
  and thinly sliced
1 green pepper, cored, seeded
  and chopped
1 red bell pepper, cored, seeded
  and chopped
3 tomatoes, cored and chopped

1 stalk celery (including leaves), thinly sliced
1/2 cup chopped red onion
2 cloves garlic, minced
1/4 cup red wine vinegar
2 Tbsp. olive oil
1/8 tsp. *each* Lite Salt™, cumin and pepper
1 avocado, seeded and diced

Combine vegetables in a serving bowl. In a small bowl, whisk together vinegar, olive oil, Lite Salt, cumin and pepper. Pour over vegetables and mix well. Cover and refrigerate overnight, stirring occasionally, to blend flavors. Gently stir in avocado just before serving. Serve chilled in soup mugs.

Variations:

• Add 1 to 2 Tbsp. tequila or vodka to dressing

• Add 1/4 cup chopped sun-dried tomatoes to vegetable mixture

Serves: 4 to 6

Per serving:	Calories	Fat (g)	Cholesterol (mg)	Fiber (g)	Sodium (mg)
	133	11	0	2	35

Roasted Pepper Salad

2 green peppers
2 red bell peppers
1/2 cup thinly sliced red onion

1/2 cup thinly sliced English cucumber
1/4 to 1/3 cup Tomato Vinaigrette (page 286)

Grill peppers according to directions on page 226, then slice thinly. Combine with onion, cucumber and dressing. Toss gently. Serve on salad plates lined with red leaf or romaine lettuce.

Serves 4 to 6

Per serving:	Calories	Fat (g)	Cholesterol (mg)	Fiber (g)	Sodium (mg)
	65	5	0	1	13

Green Beans Nicoise

1¹/₂ lbs. fresh green beans
¹/₂ cup sliced black olives (rinse and
   drain before slicing)
2 tomatoes, cored and cut into wedges
¹/₄ cup chopped walnuts

Dill dressing:
¹/₂ cup plain non-fat yogurt
1 Tbsp. olive oil
3 Tbsp. chopped fresh dill
1 tsp. lemon juice
¹/₄ tsp. Lite Salt™
¹/₄ tsp. white pepper

Steam green beans until tender crisp. Cool to room temperature. Combine in a large bowl with olives, tomato and nuts. Toss gently.

In a small bowl, whisk together yogurt, olive oil, dill, lemon juice, salt and pepper. Pour dressing over green bean mixture and toss to combine well. Serve chilled or at room temperature garnished with dill sprigs.

Serves 6 to 8

Per serving:	Calories	Fat (g)	Cholesterol (mg)	Fiber (g)	Sodium (mg)
	93	7	1	3	119

Grilled Onion Salad

Great at a barbecue

1 red onion, peeled
Olive oil
Freshly ground pepper
1 tsp. olive oil

1 tsp. fresh lime juice
¹/₄ tsp. dried oregano, crushed
Romaine *or* red leaf lettuce

Cut onion into ¹/₂" thick slices. Arrange on baking pan. Brush lightly with olive oil and sprinkle with pepper. Broil 4 to 6" from heat (or grill on barbecue) until softened and just beginning to char, 5 to 7 minutes. Turn over, sprinkle with pepper and continue to broil until beginning to char, about 2 to 3 minutes.

Place onion slices in a bowl and add remaining ingredients. Toss to blend. Cool to room temperature. Place a lettuce leaf on a salad plate and arrange onion slices on top.

Serves: 2 to 3

Per serving:	Calories	Fat (g)	Cholesterol (mg)	Fiber (g)	Sodium (mg)
	64	5	0	1	7

Lemon Zucchini Salad

The sweet-tart flavor adds new life to zucchini

3 zucchini, julienne
1 lemon, thinly sliced
2 Tbsp. minced fresh mint *or* **parsley**
1 Tbsp. sugar *or* **2 pks. Equal**

2 Tbsp. olive oil
3 Tbsp. fresh orange juice
1 tsp. orange zest
1 tsp. lemon zest

Steam zucchini for 1 minute. Drain and cool.

Cut each lemon slice into 6 wedges. In a large bowl, combine lemon wedges with mint, sugar, olive oil, orange juice and zest. Add zucchini and toss to blend with dressing. Serve garnished with fresh mint leaves and lemon wedges.

Serves 6

Per serving:	Calories	Fat (g)	Cholesterol (mg)	Fiber (g)	Sodium (mg)
	74	5	0	1	3

Minted Tomato Salad

6 tomatoes, cored and cut into wedges
6 green onions, thinly sliced
1/2 cup chopped red onion
1 Tbsp. chopped fresh mint *or*
  1 tsp. dried

1/4 cup olive oil
3 Tbsp. lemon *or* **lime juice**
1 clove garlic, minced
1 shallot, minced
Freshly ground black pepper

In a medium bowl, combine tomato wedges, onions and mint. Whisk together oil, lemon juice, garlic, shallot and pepper to taste. Pour dressing over tomatoes and toss gently to coat. Let stand, covered, at room temperature for several hours to blend flavors. Chill before serving.

Variation: Substitute fresh basil for mint.

Serves 6 to 8

Per serving:	Calories	Fat (g)	Cholesterol (mg)	Fiber (g)	Sodium (mg)
	86	7	0	1	4

Moroccan Salad

Cinnamon and orange add a new flavor twist to carrots

1 orange, peeled
4 lbs. carrots, grated
1 cup thinly sliced radishes
1/4 cup chopped fresh cilantro
1/4 cup chopped red *or* green onion
3 Tbsp. olive oil

2 Tbsp. fresh orange juice
2 Tbsp. fresh lemon juice
1/8 tsp. cinnamon
1/8 tsp. cumin (optional)
1/8 tsp. white pepper

Cut orange into bite-size pieces. Combine in a medium bowl with carrots, radishes, cilantro and onion. In a small bowl, whisk together oil, juices, cinnamon, cumin and white pepper. Pour dressing over salad and toss gently. Serve chilled.

Serves 4 to 6

Per serving:	Calories	Fat (g)	Cholesterol (mg)	Fiber (g)	Sodium (mg)
	114	7	0	2	41

Crunchy Green Pea Salad

A colorful addition to a buffet table

1 cup Dijon Mustard Sauce (page 290)
1 Tbsp. fat free or light, cholesterol-free
  mayonnaise
1/2 tsp. dried tarragon
1/4 tsp. nutmeg

3 10-oz. pkgs frozen peas, thawed
1 1/2 cups sliced mushrooms
6 green onions, thinly sliced
1 red bell pepper, cored, seeded and diced
1/4 cup unsalted sunflower seeds

In a small bowl, combine Mustard Sauce, mayonnaise, tarragon and nutmeg. Set aside.

In a large bowl, combine peas, mushrooms, onion, pepper and sunflower seeds. Pour dressing over peas and stir gently to combine. Cover and chill before serving.

Variation: Add leftover cooked brown rice or pasta.

Serves: 6 to 8

Per serving:	Calories	Fat (g)	Cholesterol (mg)	Fiber (g)	Sodium (mg)
	132	4	2	5	206

Firecracker Cole Slaw

6 cups shredded green cabbage
6 cups shredded red cabbage
2 cups grated carrots
1 to 2 jalapeño peppers, seeded
  and minced

1 cup plain non-fat yogurt
2 Tbsp. fat free or light, cholesterol-free
  mayonnaise
1/2 tsp. cumin
Fresh cilantro *or* parsley, chopped

In a large bowl, toss together cabbages, grated carrots and minced peppers. In a small bowl, combine yogurt, mayonnaise and cumin. Blend dressing with cabbage mixture and mix thoroughly. Chill before serving. Garnish with cilantro or parsley.

Serves 8

Per serving:	Calories	Fat (g)	Cholesterol (mg)	Fiber (g)	Sodium (mg)
	79	2	2	6	121

Orange Slaw

1 head green cabbage
4 oranges
1/2 cup golden raisins

1 tsp. cumin
1/2 cup chopped dry-roasted peanuts

Shred cabbage into a large serving bowl. Remove zest from 2 oranges and add to cabbage. Squeeze juice from these oranges over cabbage. Peel remaining oranges and remove white membrane from fruit. Cut oranges into segments and add to cabbage. Mix in raisins and cumin; toss well. Refrigerate until chilled. Serve garnished with chopped peanuts.

Serves 6 to 8

Per serving:	Calories	Fat (g)	Cholesterol (mg)	Fiber (g)	Sodium (mg)
	157	5	0	8	75

Pineapple Cole Slaw

1/2 cup plain non-fat yogurt
2 Tbsp. fat free or light, cholesterol-free
    mayonnaise
1 Tbsp. frozen orange juice concentrate,
    thawed
1 tsp. ground coriander
1/2 head green cabbage, shredded

1/2 head red cabbage, shredded
1 cup shredded carrots
1 cup shredded jicama
1 red apple, cored and diced
1 red *or* green bell pepper, cored and diced
1 cup chopped fresh pineapple

In a small bowl, combine yogurt, mayonnaise, orange juice concentrate and coriander. Set aside.

In a large bowl, mix together remaining ingredients. Add dressing and toss to combine well. Chill before serving.

Serves 6 to 8

Per serving:	Calories	Fat (g)	Cholesterol (mg)	Fiber (g)	Sodium (mg)
	81	1	1	5	27

Sweet Potato Salad

2 lbs. (about 4 medium) sweet potatoes
1/3 cup cream sherry
1/4 cup fresh lemon juice
1 Tbsp. honey

1 Tbsp. minced fresh ginger
1/2 cup sliced green onion
1 cup thinly sliced celery
1/4 cup sliced almonds, toasted

Scrub sweet potatoes and pierce with a fork. Microwave or bake until just tender. Let cool, then peel and cut into 1/2" cubes.

In a medium bowl, whisk together sherry, lemon juice, honey and ginger. Mix in sweet potato cubes, onion, celery and almonds. Serve at room temperature.

Tip: Sweet potatoes are easier to slice when knife is moistened.

Serves: 6 to 8

Per serving:	Calories	Fat (g)	Cholesterol (mg)	Fiber (g)	Sodium (mg)
	176	2	0	4	35

Marinated Spaghetti Salad

12 oz. spaghetti, cooked and drained
6 green onions, thinly sliced
1 red bell pepper, seeded, cored
   and chopped

1/2 cup sliced black olives (rinse and
   drain before slicing)
3/4 cup Balsamic Vinaigrette (page 279)

Combine spaghetti, green onions, pepper and olives in a large bowl; mix well. Drizzle with dressing and mix thoroughly. Serve at room temperature or cover and chill before serving.

Serves 6

Per serving:	Calories	Fat (g)	Cholesterol (mg)	Fiber (g)	Sodium (mg)
	350	2	1	1	527

Tri-Color Pasta Salad

1 lb. fresh broccoli
2 cups pasta shells (eggless)
1 15-oz. can salt-free kidney beans,
   rinsed and drained
1/3 cup olive oil

1/4 cup red wine *or* balsamic vinegar
1 Tbsp. Dijon mustard
1/2 tsp. dried basil *or* 1 Tbsp. chopped
   fresh basil

Cut broccoli into bite-size pieces and steam until tender crisp. Rinse with cold water to cool; drain well and set aside. Cook pasta in a large pot of boiling water until al dente; drain and let cool slightly. In a large bowl, combine broccoli, pasta and beans.

In a small bowl, combine oil, vinegar, mustard and basil. Add to pasta mixture and mix well. Serve at room temperature, or cover and chill 1 to 2 hours.

Serves 6 to 8

Per serving:	Calories	Fat (g)	Cholesterol (mg)	Fiber (g)	Sodium (mg)
	194	10	12	6	37

Brown Rice and Avocado Salad

1 cup raw brown rice
2¹/2 cups low-sodium chicken broth, defatted
2 tsp. dried marjoram
¹/4 tsp. Lite Salt™
1 avocado, peeled, pitted and diced
¹/2 cup minced fresh parsley

3 green onions, thinly sliced *or*
  ¹/2 cup chopped red onion
1 tomato, cored and chopped
5 Tbsp. fresh lemon juice
3 Tbsp. olive oil
Freshly ground pepper

Combine rice, chicken broth, marjoram and Lite Salt in a saucepan. Bring to a boil; reduce heat, cover and simmer 40 to 45 minutes. Cool.

In a medium bowl, combine avocado, parsley, onion, tomato, lemon juice and olive oil. Season to taste with pepper. Gently combine avocado mixture with brown rice.

Serves 6 to 8

Per serving:	Calories	Fat (g)	Cholesterol (mg)	Fiber (g)	Sodium (mg)
	194	10	0	3	40

Corn and Barley Salad

Barley is a delicious source of cholesterol-lowering fiber.

2 cups water
1 cup barley
3 Tbsp. olive oil
2 Tbsp. fresh lime juice
1 clove garlic, minced
¹/4 tsp. Lite Salt™
Freshly ground black pepper

¹/2 cup chopped red onion
2 to 3 green onions, thinly sliced
1 green *or* red bell pepper, cored, seeded and diced
1 cup cooked corn kernels
¹/4 cup chopped fresh cilantro

Bring water to a boil. Add barley; cover and simmer for 50 to 60 minutes or until tender.

While barley is cooking, whisk together oil, lime juice, garlic, salt and pepper. Add dressing to hot barley. Add remaining ingredients and mix well. Serve immediately.

Serves 4

Per serving:	Calories	Fat (g)	Cholesterol (mg)	Fiber (g)	Sodium (mg)
	177	11	0	6	73

Bulgur and Spinach Salad

Good as a main dish for a cool summer meal

1 cup boiling low-sodium chicken
  broth (defatted)
1/2 cup bulgur
1 bunch fresh spinach, washed
  and stemmed
1 15-oz. can garbanzo beans, rinsed
  and drained
1 green *or* red bell pepper, cored
  and chopped

1 carrot, sliced
1/4 cup chopped red onion
1 clove garlic, minced
1/2 cup red wine *or* balsamic vinegar
2 tsp. Dijon *or* Pommery mustard
6 Tbsp. olive oil
2 Tbsp. chopped parsley
Freshly ground black pepper

In a small bowl, combine chicken broth and bulgur. Let stand 1 hour or until broth is absorbed.

Tear spinach into bite-size pieces. In a large bowl, combine bulgur, spinach, beans, bell pepper, carrot, onion and garlic. Toss to mix well.

Mix together vinegar and mustard, then whisk in olive oil. Add parsley and mix well. Pour dressing over salad and toss. Season to taste with freshly ground pepper.

Serves 4

Per serving:	Calories	Fat (g)	Cholesterol (mg)	Fiber (g)	Sodium (mg)
	366	15	0	4	73

Couscous Salad with Dill Vinaigrette

1¹/2 cups couscous
2¹/4 cups water *or* salt-free chicken
   broth, defatted
2 cups sliced fresh spinach
1 cup sliced mushrooms
¹/2 cup frozen peas, thawed and drained
¹/2 cup diced jicama
¹/4 cup pine nuts, toasted
3 to 4 green onions, thinly sliced
2 oz. (¹/8 lb.) part-skim mozzarella
   cheese, julienne

Dill Vinaigrette:
¹/3 cup olive oil
¹/4 cup fresh lemon juice
1 Tbsp. Dijon mustard
1 tsp. lemon zest
¹/8 tsp. cumin
1 clove garlic, minced
2 Tbsp. minced fresh dill *or*
   2 tsp. dried
Fresh spinach leaves

Toast couscous in a large skillet over medium heat until lightly browned. Add water and bring to a boil. Cover, remove from heat and let stand until water is absorbed, 5 to 10 minutes.

In a large bowl, combine couscous with sliced spinach, mushrooms, peas, jicama, pine nuts, onions and cheese. Toss to combine thoroughly.

In a small bowl, whisk together oil, lemon juice, mustard, zest, cumin, garlic and dill, Pour over couscous mixture and toss gently. Line a large platter with spinach leaves and mound salad in center. Serve at room temperature.

Serves 8

Per serving:	Calories	Fat (g)	Cholesterol (mg)	Fiber (g)	Sodium (mg)
	178	12	4	2	81

Mediterranean Salad

This hearty salad is a meal in itself

Dressing:
3 Tbsp. fresh orange juice
2 Tbsp. fresh lemon juice
1/3 cup olive oil
2 Tbsp. honey
1 Tbsp. poppy seeds
1/4 tsp. white pepper

1/2 cup bulgur
1/3 cup golden raisins
Hot water
1 chicken breast, skinned and boned
11/2 cups canned garbanzo beans,
  rinsed and drained
1 cup sliced radishes
1/2 cup chopped red onion
1 orange, peeled and diced
4 oz. part-skim mozzarella cheese, cubed
1 medium head romaine, washed and
  torn into bite-size pieces

Prepare dressing: whisk together juices, oil, honey, poppy seeds and white pepper. Set aside for flavors to blend.

Place bulgur and raisins in a medium bowl and cover with hot water. Let stand for 30 to 40 minutes or until all water is absorbed.

Poach chicken breast: Pour water or salt-free chicken broth into a small skillet to a depth of 2". Bring to a boil. Reduce heat to a simmer and add chicken breast. Cover and simmer gently for 10 to 15 minutes or until chicken is done. Remove, cool and cube. (Reserve poaching liquid for another use.)

In a large bowl, toss bulgur and raisins with chicken, beans, radishes, onion, orange, cheese and lettuce. Pour dressing over the salad and toss gently to coat. Cover and chill before serving.

Serves 6 to 8

Per serving:	Calories	Fat (g)	Cholesterol (mg)	Fiber (g)	Sodium (mg)
	291	13	21	2	90

Pesto Potato Salad

2 lbs. new potatoes, scrubbed
2 tomatoes, cored and diced
1/2 cup chopped red onion *or*
　6 green onions, thinly sliced
1 cup thinly sliced celery

1/2 cup fat free or light, cholesterol-free
　mayonnaise
1/2 cup plain non-fat yogurt
1/4 cup Pesto (page 293)

Steam whole unpeeled potatoes until soft when pierced with a fork, about 30 to 40 minutes. Cool and cube. Place in a large bowl and toss gently with tomatoes, onion and celery.

In a small bowl, combine mayonnaise, yogurt and Pesto. Pour dressing over potato mixture and toss gently to combine. Chill before serving.

Serves 6 to 8

Per serving:	Calories	Fat (g)	Cholesterol (mg)	Fiber (g)	Sodium (mg)
	194	10	1	2	123

Shanghai Chicken Salad

3 cups fresh spinach
2 cups romaine lettuce
1/2 cup sliced waterchestnuts
1/2 cup thinly sliced carrots
1/2 red bell pepper, julienne
1 1/2 cups bean sprouts
2 tsp. canola *or* safflower oil
2 skinless, boneless chicken breasts
1 Tbsp. sesame seeds, toasted

Oriental dressing:
1 cup plain non-fat yogurt
1/4 cup low-sodium soy sauce
1 Tbsp. oriental sesame oil
2 Tbsp. red wine vinegar

Wash spinach and romaine; drain and tear into bite-size pieces. In a large bowl, toss together spinach, romaine, waterchestnuts, carrots and red pepper. Arrange on dinner plates and surround with bean sprouts.

Brush chicken with oil and grill until done. Slice diagonally into strips and place on top of salad. Sprinkle with toasted sesame seeds. Serve with dressing on the side.

Oriental Dressing: In a small bowl, whisk together yogurt, soy sauce, sesame oil and red wine vinegar.

Per serving:	Calories	Fat (g)	Cholesterol (mg)	Fiber (g)	Sodium (mg)
	193	7	51	3	131

Tossed Chicken Salad

1 tsp. olive oil
2 skinless, boneless chicken breasts, cubed
3 Tbsp. balsamic *or* red wine vinegar
1 red onion, thinly sliced
1 Tbsp. minced fresh thyme *or* 1/4 tsp. dried

1/2 head romaine lettuce
1/2 head red leaf lettuce
Snipped fresh chives
Freshly ground pepper

Heat oil in a skillet and saute chicken cubes until cooked through, about 5 minutes. Add vinegar and stir with a wooden spoon to deglaze bottom of pan. Stir in onion and thyme; remove from heat.

Tear lettuces into bite-size pieces and arrange on plates. Top with chicken and onion mixture. Garnish with chives and freshly ground pepper.

Serves 4

Per serving:	Calories	Fat (g)	Cholesterol (mg)	Fiber (g)	Sodium (mg)
	165	6	50	1	59

Chicken Salad Pesto

1/4 cup pine nuts
1 cup salt-free chicken broth, defatted
4 skinless, boneless chicken breasts
1 cup plain non-fat yogurt
2 Tbsp. fat free or light, cholesterol-free mayonnaise

1 Tbsp. Pesto (page 293)
1/2 cup chopped red *or* green onion
2 cups sliced fresh spinach
2 Tbsp. sliced black olives (rinse and drain before slicing) (optional)

Toast pine nuts over low heat in a small skillet until lightly browned. Watch carefully as nuts burn easily. Set aside.

Pour chicken broth into a medium skillet and bring to a boil. Reduce heat to a simmer and add chicken breasts. Cover and simmer gently until just done. (Cut in center to check that chicken is no longer pink.) Chill chicken in broth. Remove chicken and cube.

In a large bowl, combine yogurt, mayonnaise and Pesto; mix well. Add chicken, onion, spinach, olives and pine nuts; mix well. Serve at room temperature.

Variation: Mix in 2 cups cooked small pasta.

Serves 4 to 6

Per serving:	Calories	Fat (g)	Cholesterol (mg)	Fiber (g)	Sodium (mg)
	244	11	70	1	148

Boost the nutritional value of breakfast by munching a homemade muffin. Using vegetable oil, egg whites, fiber-rich whole wheat flour, oats and oat bran — and reducing sugar and salt — makes these tasty breads healthier choices than commerical varieties.

Delitefully HealthMark

Breads

Ann's 76
Banana Date 72
Cinnamon Rolls 78
Heart-y Date Loaf 73
Judy's Whole Grain 77
Pumpkin Oatmeal 75
Rocky Mountain Apple 71
Whole Wheat Raisin 74

Miscellaneous

Holiday Stuffing 91

Muffins

Aloha 79
Apple-Oatmeal 79
Applesauce Raisin Bran 80
Blueberry Ginger 81
Blueberry Oatmeal 82
Carrot Oatmeal 84
Corn 85
Cranberry Orange 82
Date Walnut 86
Jalapeño Corn 85
Maple Bran 86
Oatmeal Raisin 87
Old Fashioned Bran 83
Orange Date 88
Peanut Butter Banana 87
Pumpkin Bran 89
Raspberry Poppy Seed 89
Spiced Pumpkin Marmalade 90

Rocky Mountain Apple Bread

1 egg
4 egg whites
1 1/2 cups brown sugar
1/2 cup low-fat buttermilk
1/2 cup canola *or* safflower oil
2 tsp. vanilla
1 cup rolled oats
2 1/2 cups whole wheat flour

1/2 cup non-fat dry milk
1 tsp. baking powder
1/2 tsp. baking soda
1 tsp. cinnamon
1/2 tsp. allspice
2 green apples, cored and chopped
3/4 cup raisins

In a large bowl, beat egg, egg whites, sugar, buttermilk, oil and vanilla until smooth. In another bowl, combine rolled oats, flour, dry milk, baking powder, baking soda, cinnamon and allspice. Stir in chopped apples and raisins.

Add egg mixture to flour and stir until just combined. Pour into two 9" x 5" loaf pans coated with cooking spray. Bake at 375° for 1 hour and 10 minutes or until a cake tester inserted into center comes out clean. Cool in pans on a rack for 10 minutes then remove and cool on rack.

May also bake as muffins: spoon batter into muffin cups coated with cooking spray. Bake at 375° for about 25 minutes.

Variation: Substitute golden raisins for raisins.

Yield: 2 loaves or about 24 muffins

Per serving:	Calories	Fat (g)	Cholesterol (mg)	Fiber (g)	Sodium (mg)
	182	5	11	2	75

Banana Date Bread

2 1/2 cups whole wheat flour	4 egg whites
1 tsp. baking powder	1/4 cup canola *or* safflower oil
1 tsp. baking soda	1/2 cup non-fat milk
1 tsp. cinnamon	1 cup mashed banana
1/2 tsp. nutmeg	1 cup chopped dates
1/2 tsp. cloves	1/3 cup chopped walnuts
1/2 cup brown sugar	

In a large bowl, combine flour, baking powder, baking soda, cinnamon, nutmeg and cloves. In a medium bowl, combine sugar, egg whites, oil, milk, banana and dates. Add dry ingredients, mixing just to blend. Stir in nuts. Pour into a 9" x 5" loaf pan coated with cooking spray. Bake at 350° for 55 to 60 minutes or until cake tester inserted in center comes out clean. Cool in pan for 5 to 10 minutes then turn out onto a rack to cool completely.

Variation: Replace banana with applesauce or pumpkin.

Yield: 1 loaf (16 slices)

Per serving:	Calories	Fat (g)	Cholesterol (mg)	Fiber (g)	Sodium (mg)
	179	6	0	3	96

Heart-y Date Loaf

This moist bread is made without fat and has no cholesterol — a winner!

1 cup raisins
1 8-oz. package pitted whole dates, chopped
1 cup boiling water
1/2 cup orange juice
2 cups whole wheat flour

1 tsp. baking soda
1 tsp. baking powder
1 Tbsp. orange zest
2 egg whites
1 tsp. vanilla
1/4 cup chopped walnuts

Combine raisins and dates with boiling water and juice. Let stand until cooled slightly.

In a large bowl, combine flour, baking soda, baking powder and zest. Stir egg whites and vanilla into date mixture then stir entire mixture into flour mixture. Stir until well blended; mix in nuts.

Spread batter into a 9" x 5" loaf pan coated with cooking spray. Bake at 350° for 40 to 50 minutes or until a cake tester inserted in center comes out clean. Cool in pan 10 minutes, then remove to a rack to finish cooling.

Yield: 1 loaf (16 slices)

Per serving:	Calories	Fat (g)	Cholesterol (mg)	Fiber (g)	Sodium (mg)
	125	2	0	3	86

Whole Wheat Raisin Bread

3 cups whole wheat flour
$^1/_4$ cup wheat germ
2 tsp. baking powder
$1^1/_4$ tsp. baking soda
1 tsp. cinnamon
$^1/_2$ tsp. nutmeg

$1^1/_2$ cups low-fat buttermilk
$^1/_2$ cup honey
$^1/_4$ cup canola *or* safflower oil
$^1/_2$ cup raisins
$^1/_4$ cup chopped walnuts

In a large bowl, mix together flour, wheat germ, baking powder, baking soda, cinnamon and nutmeg. In a smaller bowl, beat together buttermilk, honey and oil. Pour into flour mixture and stir just until ingredients are combined. Mix in raisins and nuts.

Pour batter into a 9" x 5" loaf pan coated with cooking spray. Bake at 325° for about I hour and 15 minutes or until a cake tester inserted in center comes out clean. Cool in pan for 10 minutes, then remove and cool on a rack.

Yield: 1 loaf (16 slices)

Per serving:	Calories	Fat (g)	Cholesterol (mg)	Fiber (g)	Sodium (mg)
	179	5	0	3	147

Pumpkin Oatmeal Bread

2 cups unbleached flour
1 cup whole wheat flour
1 cup rolled oats
1 Tbsp. baking powder
2 tsp. cinnamon
1 tsp. ginger
1 tsp. mace
1/4 tsp. cloves

3/4 cup honey
1 Tbsp. vanilla
1/2 cup canola *or* safflower oil
1 egg
6 egg whites
2/3 cup unsweetened orange juice
1 16-oz. can pumpkin
1/3 cup chopped pecans

Combine flours, rolled oats, baking powder, cinnamon, ginger, mace and cloves in a large bowl; mix well. In a small bowl mix together honey, vanilla, oil, egg, egg whites, juice and pumpkin. Add to flour mixture and stir until just blended. Mix in nuts.

Coat two 9" x 5" loaf pans with cooking spray. Divide batter evenly between pans. Bake at 350° for I hour or until a cake tester inserted in center comes out clean. Cool in pan 10 minutes, then turn out and cool on a rack.

Variations:

• Spoon batter into muffin pans coated with cooking spray. Bake at 425° for about 20 minutes.

• Add 1/2 cup each chopped apricots and dates to batter along with nuts.

Yield: 2 loaves or 24 muffins

Per serving:	Calories	Fat (g)	Cholesterol (mg)	Fiber (g)	Sodium (mg)
	176	6	9	2	67

Delitefully HealthMark

Ann's Bread

A HealthMark graduate shared a loaf of this wonderful bread with her class
and the recipe was voted right into the cookbook

3 cups rolled oats
4 cups very hot water
1/2 cup wheat germ
1/2 cup sunflower seeds (unsalted)
1/4 cup canola *or* safflower oil
1/4 cup honey
1/4 cup molasses (Grandma's™ is
   recommended)

1 Tbsp. Lite Salt™
1¹/2 Tbsp. dry yeast
1 cup whole wheat flour
3 to 5 cups unbleached flour
1 egg white, beaten (may also use oil
   or non-fat milk)
Sesame seeds

In a large bowl, combine oats and hot water. Let stand until temperature reaches 110° to 115°, then add wheat germ, sunflower seeds, oil, honey, molasses, Lite Salt and yeast. Let stand, uncovered, and allow to "bubble" about 5 minutes. Add whole wheat flour and enough unbleached flour to make a firm dough. (Start with the smaller amount of unbleached flour, adding more only if necessary. Amount needed will vary with the weather, humidity, etc. Add just enough so that dough is not sticky.) Knead until smooth and elastic, about 15 to 20 minutes. (No, this is not aerobic exercise.)

Brush a large bowl lightly with oil. Place dough smooth side down in bowl then turn over so top side is coated with oil. Let stand about 30 minutes or until doubled in volume. Punch down.

Coat three 9" x 5" bread pans with cooking spray or brush lightly with oil. Divide dough into three portions, form into loaves and place in pans. Brush loaves with beaten egg white and sprinkle with sesame seeds. Allow to rise just to top of pans, 20 to 30 minutes.

Bake at 350° for 40 to 50 minutes. To test for doneness, remove loaf from pan and tap on bottom. Bread is done when tapping produces a hollow sound. If not, return to oven to finish baking. When done, remove from pans and cool completely on wire rack before slicing. Wrap in foil. Freezes well. Recipe can be doubled.

Yield: 3 loaves (12 slices each)

Per serving:	Calories	Fat (g)	Cholesterol (mg)	Fiber (g)	Sodium (mg)
	123	3	0	2	84

Judy's Whole Grain Loaf

An import from South Africa, this delicious bread disappears fast

2 cups whole wheat flour
1 cup white bread flour
1 cup Four Grain cereal (e.g. Stone-Buhr)
1/2 cup cracked wheat (e.g. Manna)
1/2 cup wheat germ
1/2 cup bran

1 tsp. Lite Salt™
2 tsp. dry yeast
13/4 cups warm water
4 Tbsp. honey (*or* 2 Tbsp. honey
and molasses)
1/2 cup canola *or* safflower oil

In a large bowl, mix together flours, cereal, cracked wheat, wheat germ, bran and salt. In a smaller bowl, combine yeast with water and honey. Stir in oil. Add to dry ingredients and mix well.

Turn dough into a 9" x 5" loaf pan coated with cooking spray. Bake at 150° for 50 minutes, then increase temperature to 350° and bake for 50 to 60 minutes. Cool in pan 10 minute then remove to a rack to finish cooling.

Yield: 1 loaf (16 slices)

Per serving:	Calories	Fat (g)	Cholesterol (mg)	Fiber (g)	Sodium (mg)
	192	8	0	4	119

Cinnamon Rolls

These delicious rolls minimize fat and cholesterol without
sacrificing taste — but watch the calories!

1 pkg. yeast
1/4 cup warm (115°) water
1/4 cup warm (115°) non-fat milk
1/2 cup whole wheat flour
1/2 cup rolled oats
1 1/4 to 1 1/2 cups unbleached flour

1 Tbsp. sugar
1/4 tsp. Lite Salt™
1 to 2 tsp. cinnamon
1 Tbsp. liquid margarine
2 egg whites

Caramel Topping:
1/3 cup liquid margarine
1/2 cup brown sugar

2 Tbsp. light corn syrup *or* honey
1 Tbsp. non-fat milk

Filling:
1 to 2 Tbsp. liquid margarine
1/2 cup sugar (brown *or* white)
1 to 2 tsp. cinnamon

Dissolve yeast in warm water; let stand 10 minutes. Add warm milk. In a food processor, combine whole wheat flour, rolled oats, 1 1/4 cups unbleached flour, 1 Tbsp. sugar, salt, cinnamon, margarine and egg whites. With motor running, pour in yeast mixture. Let motor run until dough forms a loose ball. Add remaining 1/4 cup flour as needed if dough is sticky.

Remove to a greased bowl or plastic bag. Cover bowl loosely or seal end of bag loosely. Let rise until doubled, 46 to 60 minutes.

Prepare topping while dough rises. Combine topping ingredients in a small saucepan. Cook and stir over medium heat until well blended. Set aside.

Punch dough down. Roll out into a 10" x 20" rectangle. Spread with liquid margarine, then sprinkle with sugar and remaining cinnamon. Roll up jellyroll fashion; pinch ends and seam to seal. Cut into 12 pieces. Spray a 12" x 7" baking pan with cooking spray and pour in caramel mixture. Arrange rolls over caramel. Cover and let rise in a warm place until doubled, 30 to 45 minutes.

Bake at 375° for 20 minutes.

Yield: 12 rolls

Per serving:	Calories	Fat (g)	Cholesterol (mg)	Fiber (g)	Sodium (mg)
	226	9	0	1	144

Aloha Muffins

1 cup whole wheat flour
1 cup unbleached flour
1/3 cup brown sugar
2 tsp. baking powder
1/2 tsp. baking soda

1 cup plain non-fat yogurt
2 egg whites
1/4 cup canola *or* safflower oil
2 tsp. coconut extract
1 cup crushed pineapple (juice pack), well
    drained

In a medium bowl, combine flours, sugar, baking powder and baking soda. Combine yogurt, egg whites, oil and coconut extract. Mix into flour mixture stirring until just blended. Fold in pineapple.

Spoon batter into muffin cups coated with cooking spray. Bake at 400° for 20 to 25 minutes.

Yield: about 12 muffins

Per serving:	Calories	Fat (g)	Cholesterol (mg)	Fiber (g)	Sodium (mg)
	164	5		1	1 126

Apple-Oatmeal Muffins

1 cup non-fat milk, warmed
1 cup rolled oats
1/4 cup honey
1/4 cup canola *or* safflower oil
1 1/2 cups whole wheat flour
2 1/2 tsp. baking powder

1 tsp. cinnamon
1/2 tsp. nutmeg
1/4 tsp. cloves
1 apple (unpeeled), cored and diced
1/4 cup chopped walnuts (optional)
3 egg whites

Combine milk, oats, honey and oil in a medium bowl. Mix well, then let cool. Add remaining ingredients and stir until just mixed. Spoon batter into muffin cups coated with cooking spray. Bake at 425° for 20 to 25 minutes.

Yield: 12 to 14 muffins

Per serving:	Calories	Fat (g)	Cholesterol (mg)	Fiber (g)	Sodium (mg)
	169	7	0	3	109

Applesauce Raisin Bran Muffins

1 1/2 cups bran cereal (flakes)
1 cup low-fat buttermilk
1 cup whole wheat flour
1 cup unbleached flour
1/3 cup brown sugar
2 tsp. baking powder
1 tsp. baking soda
1 tsp. cinnamon

1 tsp. lemon zest
1/2 tsp. nutmeg
1/4 tsp. cloves
2 egg whites
1/4 cup canola *or* safflower oil
1 cup unsweetened applesauce *or*
   2 bananas, mashed
1/2 cup raisins

In a small bowl, combine cereal and buttermilk; let stand 5 to 10 minutes.

In a medium bowl, combine flours, brown sugar, baking powder, baking soda, cinnamon, zest, nutmeg and cloves. Mix together egg whites and canola or safflower oil; add to flour mixture along with cereal mixture and applesauce. Stir in raisins.

Spoon batter into muffin cups coated with cooking spray. Bake at 400° for 20 to 25 minutes.

Yield: about 12 muffins

Per serving:	Calories	Fat (g)	Cholesterol (mg)	Fiber (g)	Sodium (mg)
	184	5	0	2	221

Blueberry Ginger Muffins

1¹/2 cups whole wheat flour
1 cup unbleached flour
¹/4 cup brown sugar
1 Tbsp. baking powder
¹/2 tsp. baking soda
¹/2 tsp. cinnamon

1 tsp. ginger
2 egg whites
1 cup low-fat buttermilk
¹/4 cup canola *or* safflower oil
¹/2 cup molasses
1 cup fresh *or* frozen blueberries*

In a medium bowl, combine flours, brown sugar, baking powder, baking soda, cinnamon and ginger. In a smaller bowl, mix together egg whites, buttermilk, oil and molasses. Add to dry ingredients and mix until just blended. Fold in blueberries.

Spoon batter into muffin cups coated with cooking spray, filling 2/3 full. Bake at 400° for about 20 minutes or until done.

***Note:** If frozen berries are used, do not thaw before using

Yield: about 18 muffins

Per serving:	Calories	Fat (g)	Cholesterol (mg)	Fiber (g)	Sodium (mg)
	130	3	0	1	116

Blueberry Oatmeal Muffins

1 cup low-fat buttermilk
1 cup rolled oats
1 cup whole wheat flour
1/3 cup brown sugar
1 tsp. cinnamon
1/2 tsp. nutmeg

1 tsp. baking powder
1/2 tsp. baking soda
2 egg whites
1/4 cup canola *or* safflower oil
1 cup fresh *or* frozen (unthawed) blueberries

In a small bowl, combine buttermilk and oats; let stand 5 to 10 minutes.

In a medium bowl, combine flour, sugar, cinnamon, nutmeg, baking powder and baking soda. Mix in egg whites, oil and oat mixture. Stir until just combined. Gently fold in blueberries.

Spoon batter into muffin cups coated with cooking spray. Bake at 400° for 20 to 25 minutes.

Variation: Substitute raspberries or sliced strawberries for blueberries.

Yield: about 12 muffins

Per serving:	Calories	Fat (g)	Cholesterol (mg)	Fiber (g)	Sodium (mg)
	139	5	0	2	105

Cranberry Orange Muffins

These sweet-tart muffins are a nice addition to any holiday table

2 cups whole wheat flour
1/2 cup brown sugar
2 1/2 tsp. baking powder
1/2 tsp. baking soda
1 tsp. orange zest
1 tsp. cinnamon

1/4 tsp. cloves
1 1/2 cups cranberries
2 egg whites
1/4 cup honey
1/4 cup canola *or* safflower oil
3/4 cup orange juice

Place flour, sugar, baking powder, baking soda, zest, cinnamon, cloves and cranberries in the bowl of a food processor. Pulse 6 to 8 times to mix and chop cranberries.

Add remaining ingredients, then pulse 6 to 8 times to thoroughly combine ingredients (do not overmix). Spoon batter into muffin cups coated with cooking spray. Bake at 400° for 20 to 25 minutes.

Yield: 14 to 16 muffins

Per serving:	Calories	Fat (g)	Cholesterol (mg)	Fiber (g)	Sodium (mg)
	134	4	0	2	41

Old-Fashioned Bran Muffins

1 cup bran cereal
2/3 cup low-fat buttermilk
1 cup whole wheat flour
1/4 cup brown sugar
2 1/2 tsp. baking powder
1/2 tsp. baking soda
1/2 tsp. cinnamon

1/2 tsp. nutmeg
1/4 tsp. ginger
2 egg whites
1/4 cup molasses
1/4 cup canola *or* safflower oil
1/3 cup raisins

In a small bowl, combine bran cereal and buttermilk. Let stand for 5 to 10 minutes to soften cereal.

In a medium bowl, mix together flour, brown sugar, baking powder, baking soda, cinnamon, nutmeg and ginger. Beat together egg whites, molasses and oil. Add to dry ingredients along with cereal mixture and raisins; stir until just blended. Spoon batter into muffin cups coated with cooking spray. Bake at 400° for 20 to 25 minutes.

Yield: about 12 muffins

Per serving:	Calories	Fat (g)	Cholesterol (mg)	Fiber (g)	Sodium (mg)
	138	5	0	2	179

Carrot Oatmeal Muffins

1 cup rolled oats
1 cup low-fat buttermilk
1 cup whole wheat flour
$^1/_3$ cup brown sugar
1 Tbsp. baking powder
$^1/_2$ tsp. baking soda
1 tsp. allspice
1 tsp. orange zest

$^1/_4$ tsp. ginger
2 egg whites
$^1/_4$ cup canola *or* safflower oil
$^3/_4$ cup grated carrot
2 Tbsp. honey
1 tsp. vanilla
$^1/_3$ cup raisins

In a small bowl, combine oats and buttermilk; let stand 5 to 10 minutes. In a larger bowl, combine flour, brown sugar, baking powder, baking soda, allspice, orange zest and ginger. Add egg whites, oil, carrot, honey and vanilla to oats and mix well. Add raisins. Combine with dry ingredients until just blended.

Spoon batter into muffin cups coated with cooking spray. Bake at 400° for 20 to 25 minutes.

Variation: Substitute well-drained crushed pineapple for grated carrots.

Yield: about 12 muffins

Per serving:	Calories	Fat (g)	Cholesterol (mg)	Fiber (g)	Sodium (mg)
	155	5	0	2	178

Corn Muffins

1 cup cornmeal (yellow *or* blue)
1/2 cup whole wheat flour
1/2 cup unbleached flour
1/4 cup brown sugar *or* honey*
2 1/2 tsp. baking powder
1/2 tsp. baking soda

1/2 to 1 tsp. crushed dried red
   pepper flakes (optional)
2 egg whites
1/4 cup corn *or* canola *or* safflower oil
1/2 cup low-fat buttermilk
1 17-oz. can creamed corn

In a medium bowl, combine cornmeal, flours, sugar, baking powder, baking soda and red pepper flakes. Beat together egg whites, oil, buttermilk and creamed corn. Add to flour mixture, stirring until just blended.

Spoon batter into muffin cups coated with cooking spray. Bake at 400° for 20 to 25 minutes.

*Note: if honey is used, add with liquid ingredients.

Variation: Jalapeño Corn Muffins — add 1 to 2 seeded and diced jalapeño peppers or 1 4-oz. can diced green chiles.

Yield: about 12 muffins

Per serving:	Calories	Fat (g)	Cholesterol (mg)	Fiber (g)	Sodium (mg)
	121	5	0	2	230

Date-Walnut Muffins

1 cup whole wheat flour
1 cup unbleached flour
1/4 cup brown sugar
2 1/2 tsp. baking powder
1 tsp. cinnamon
1/2 tsp. nutmeg

1/2 tsp. orange zest
3/4 cup non-fat milk
1/4 cup canola *or* safflower oil
2 egg whites
1/2 cup chopped dates
1/4 cup chopped walnuts

In a medium bowl, combine flours, sugar, baking powder, cinnamon, nutmeg and orange zest. Mix together milk, oil and egg whites. Stir into flour mixture until just blended. Stir in dates and walnuts.

Spoon batter into muffin cups coated with cooking spray. Bake at 400° for 20 to 25 minutes.

Yield: about 12 muffins

Per serving:	Calories	Fat (g)	Cholesterol (mg)	Fiber (g)	Sodium (mg)
	173	7	0	2	103

Maple Bran Muffins

1 1/2 cups bran cereal (flakes)
1 1/4 cups low-fat buttermilk
1 cup whole wheat flour
1 cup unbleached flour
2 tsp. baking powder
1/2 tsp. baking soda
1 tsp. cinnamon

1/2 tsp. nutmeg
1/4 tsp. cloves
2 egg whites
1/4 cup canola *or* safflower oil
1/2 cup pure maple syrup
1 tsp. maple extract
1/4 cup chopped pecans (optional)

Combine bran cereal and buttermilk; let stand for 5 to 10 minutes.

In a medium bowl, mix together flours, baking powder, baking soda, cinnamon, nutmeg and cloves. Beat together egg whites, oil, syrup and maple extract. Add to flour mixture along with cereal mixture and nuts. Stir until just combined.

Spoon batter into muffin cups coated with cooking spray. Bake at 400° for 20 to 25 minutes.

Yield: about 12 muffins

Per serving:	Calories	Fat (g)	Cholesterol (mg)	Fiber (g)	Sodium (mg)
	189	7	1	2	191

Oatmeal Raisin Muffins

1 cup whole wheat flour
1 cup rolled oats
1/4 cup brown sugar
2 tsp. baking powder
1/2 tsp. baking soda
1 tsp. cinnamon

1/2 tsp. nutmeg
1/3 cup raisins
2 egg whites
3/4 cup low-fat buttermilk
1/3 cup canola *or* safflower oil
2 tsp. vanilla

In a medium bowl, mix together flour, rolled oats, brown sugar, baking powder, baking soda, cinnamon and nutmeg. Stir in raisins.

In a small bowl, combine egg whites, buttermilk, oil and vanilla. Add to dry ingredients and stir until just blended. Spoon batter into muffin cups coated with cooking spray, filling 2/3 full. Bake at 400° for 20 minutes or until lightly browned.

Variation: Replace raisins with 1/3 cup chopped dates or dried fruit of your choice.

Yield: about 12 muffins

Per serving:	Calories	Fat (g)	Cholesterol (mg)	Fiber (g)	Sodium (mg)
	147	7	0	2	133

Peanut Butter Banana Muffins

1/2 cup natural-style peanut butter
1/3 cup brown sugar *or* honey
1/4 cup canola *or* safflower oil
2 egg whites
1 tsp. vanilla
3 bananas, broken into pieces

1 cup whole wheat flour
1/2 cup rolled oats
1 1/2 tsp. baking powder
1/2 tsp. baking soda
1 tsp. cinnamon (optional)

In a food processor, combine peanut butter, sugar, oil, egg whites, vanilla and bananas. Process until smoothly mixed. Add remaining ingredients and pulse 5 or 6 times until well blended.

Spoon batter into muffin cups coated with cooking spray. Bake at 400° for 20 to 25 minutes.

Yield: about 12 muffins

Per serving:	Calories	Fat (g)	Cholesterol (mg)	Fiber (g)	Sodium (mg)
	199	10	0	3	159

Orange Date Muffins

1 cup low-fat buttermilk	1/2 tsp. baking soda
1/2 cup chopped dates	1 tsp. cinnamon
1 Tbsp. orange zest	1/2 tsp. nutmeg
11/2 cups whole wheat flour	1/2 tsp. mace
11/2 cups unbleached flour	2 egg whites
1/3 cup brown sugar	1/4 cup canola *or* safflower oil
21/2 tsp. baking powder	1/2 cup orange juice

In a small bowl, combine buttermilk, dates and zest. Let stand for 1 hour.

In a medium bowl, combine flours, sugar, baking powder, baking soda, cinnamon, nutmeg and mace. Mix together egg whites, oil and orange juice; add to flour mixture along with buttermilk and dates. Mix until just combined.

Spoon batter into muffin cups coated with cooking spray. Bake at 400° for 20 to 25 minutes.

Yield: 12 to 14 muffins

Per serving:	Calories	Fat (g)	Cholesterol (mg)	Fiber (g)	Sodium (mg)
	202	5	0	2	156

Pumpkin Bran Muffins

2 1/2 cups bran cereal (flakes)
1/2 cup rolled oats *or* oat bran
3/4 cup non-fat milk
1 1/4 cups whole wheat flour
2 tsp. baking powder
1 tsp. allspice

2 egg whites
1/3 cup brown sugar
1/4 cup canola *or* safflower oil
1 cup pumpkin
1/2 cup chopped dates
1/4 cup chopped walnuts *or* pecans (optional)

In a medium bowl, combine bran flakes and oats with milk. Let stand 2 to 3 minutes to soften.

In another bowl, mix together flour, brown sugar, baking powder and allspice. In a small bowl, beat egg whites, oil and pumpkin together. Stir into cereal mixture. Add flour mixture, stirring until just combined. Mix in dates and nuts.

Spoon batter into muffin cups coated with cooking spray. Bake at 400° for 20 minutes.

Yield: about 12 muffins

Per serving:	Calories	Fat (g)	Cholesterol (mg)	Fiber (g)	Sodium (mg)
	194	7	0	3	162

Raspberry Poppy Seed Muffins

1 cup whole wheat flour
1 cup unbleached flour
1/4 cup brown sugar
2 Tbsp. poppy seeds
2 1/2 tsp. baking powder
1/2 tsp. lemon zest

3/4 cup non-fat milk
1/4 cup canola *or* safflower oil
2 Tbsp. honey
2 egg whites
1 tsp. almond extract
1 1/2 cup fresh *or* frozen (unthawed) raspberries

In a medium bowl, combine flours, brown sugar, poppy seeds, baking powder and zest. Mix together milk, oil, honey, egg whites and almond extract then stir into flour mixture until just blended. Gently fold in berries.

Spoon batter into muffin cups coated with cooking spray. Bake at 400° for 20 to 25 minutes.

Variation: Substitute strawberries for raspberries.

Yield: about 12 muffins

Per serving:	Calories	Fat (g)	Cholesterol (mg)	Fiber (g)	Sodium (mg)
	186	6	0	3	103

Spiced Pumpkin Marmalade Muffins

1 cup whole wheat flour
1 cup unbleached flour
1/3 cup brown sugar
1 tsp. baking powder
1 tsp. baking soda
1 tsp. cinnamon
1 tsp. orange zest
1/2 tsp. ginger
1/2 tsp. nutmeg

1/8 tsp. cloves
2 egg whites
1/4 cup canola *or* safflower oil
1/3 cup plain *or* vanilla non-fat yogurt
1 cup pumpkin
1/4 cup low-sugar orange marmalade
   or apricot conserves
1/2 cup raisins

In a medium bowl, combine flours, sugar, baking powder, baking soda, zest and spices.

Combine remaining ingredients, except raisins, in a small bowl and beat well. Add to dry mixture, stirring until just blended. Stir in raisins.

Spoon batter into muffin cups coated with cooking spray. Bake at 400° for 20 to 25 minutes.

Yield: about 12 muffins

Per serving:	Calories	Fat (g)	Cholesterol (mg)	Fiber (g)	Sodium (mg)
	173	5	0	2	120

Holiday Stuffing

This flavorful dressing is moistened by fresh vegetables rather than butter

1 Tbsp. liquid margarine
1 onion, chopped
4 stalks celery (including tops), chopped
4 to 6 green onions, thinly sliced
1/2 lb. mushrooms, chopped
6 cups bread crumbs (from day old bread)
2 tsp. dried sage

1 tsp. dried marjoram
1/2 tsp. celery salt
1/2 tsp. dried oregano
1/4 tsp. dried thyme
1/2 cup chopped fresh parsley
1/2 cup bourbon (optional)

In a large non-stick skillet, heat margarine. Add chopped vegetables. Cover and cook 5 to 10 minutes or until onions are soft and mushrooms have released some juice. Remove from heat and mix in remaining ingredients. Use to stuff turkey or place in a casserole dish coated with cooking spray and bake at 325° for 30 to 45 minutes. Moisten with salt-free chicken broth as needed during cooking.

Serves 8 to 10

Per serving:	Calories	Fat (g)	Cholesterol (mg)	Fiber (g)	Sodium (mg)
	250	4	0	2	496

*Power your way through the day
with a "jet fuel" start — a nutritious breakfast!*

Beverages

Banana Smoothie 96
OJ Shake 95
Peachy Frappe 95
Tropical Shake 96

Cereals

CranApple Oatmeal 98
Grape Nutty Oatmeal 99
Mom's Best Oats 99
Spiced Oatmeal with Dates 98
Swiss Breakfast Combo 100

Eggs

Basic Omelette 109
Cheese Omelette 109
Chile Relleno Brunch Casserole 110
Florentine Omelette 109
Green Chile Omelette 110
Herb Omelette 109
Italian Omelette 109
Mushroom Omelette 109
New Eggs 108
Pizza Omelette 109
Seafood Omelette 109
Smoked Salmon Omelette 109
Spinach Omelette 109
Tomato and Basil Omelette 109
Veggie Omelette 109

Pancakes, Waffles, etc.

Banana Oatmeal 102
Buttermilk Oatmeal 102
Cinnamon French Toast 104
Cottage Cakes 103
Oat Cornmeal Waffles 103
Spiced Waffles 104
Sunshine Breakfast Cake 108
Whole Wheat Buttermilk Pancakes 100
Whole Wheat Raisin Pancakes 101

Miscellaneous

Breakfast Split 97
Golden Fruit Compote 97
Yogurt Parfait 96

Toppings

Banana Honey Cream 105
Creamy Orange Topping 105
Creole Syrup 106
Orange Honey Creamed Cheese 107
Peachy Syrup 106
Spiced Honey 107

OJ Shake

This quick shake gets you off to a good start for the day

1 6-oz. can frozen orange juice
  concentrate, thawed
1 cup plain non-fat yogurt
1/2 cup non-fat milk

2 Tbsp. non-fat dry milk
1 to 2 Tbsp. wheat germ (optional)
1 tsp. vanilla

Combine all ingredients in a blender and blend until frothy. Serve immediately.

Serves 2

Per serving:	Calories	Fat (g)	Cholesterol (mg)	Fiber (g)	Sodium (mg)
	282	0-3	10	0	154

Peachy Frappe

1 peach, peeled and sliced
1 cup raspberry non-fat yogurt
1/2 cup non-fat milk

2 Tbsp. non-fat dry milk
1/2 tsp. vanilla
2 to 3 ice cubes

Place peach slices on a shallow dish and freeze for 30 minutes. Combine frozen peach slices, yogurt, milk and vanilla in a blender or food processor and process until well blended. Add ice cubes and continue blending until smooth and frothy.

Serves 1 to 2

Per serving:	Calories	Fat (g)	Cholesterol (mg)	Fiber (g)	Sodium (mg)
	173	1	10	1	152

Tropical Shake

¹/₂ cup unsweetened pineapple juice
1 cup plain non-fat yogurt
1¹/₂ cups frozen, unsweetened strawberries
1 tsp. coconut extract (optional)

Combine juice and yogurt in blender or food processor. Turn on motor and gradually add strawberries blending until thick and smooth. Blend in extract.

Yield: 3 cups

Per serving:	Calories	Fat (g)	Cholesterol (mg)	Fiber (g)	Sodium (mg)
	146	2	7	0	82

Banana Smoothie

1 cup orange *or* pineapple juice   **¹/₂ cup plain non-fat yogurt**
1 banana, sliced   **3 ice cubes *or* 3 large frozen strawberries**

Combine all ingredients in a blender or food processor. Blend until smooth.

Serves 1

Per serving:	Calories	Fat (g)	Cholesterol (mg)	Fiber (g)	Sodium (mg)
	370	1	14	2	163

Yogurt Parfait

2 8-oz. cartons vanilla non-fat yogurt
2 cups sliced fresh fruit (your choice)
1 cup granola (without coconut)

In a parfait or other tall glass, layer yogurt, fruit and granola ending with a layer of granola.

Serves 4

Per serving:	Calories	Fat (g)	Cholesterol (mg)	Fiber (g)	Sodium (mg)
	187	6	7	1	124

Breakfast Split

Fun for kids or the kid in you

1 banana
1/2 cup 1% cottage cheese *or*
  non-fat yogurt

Fresh blueberries, raspberries *or*
  sliced strawberries
1/4 cup granola (without coconut)

Peel banana and slice in half lengthwise. Place in a serving dish. Mound cottage cheese in center and sprinkle with berries and granola. Enjoy!

Serves 1

Per serving:	Calories	Fat (g)	Cholesterol (mg)	Fiber (g)	Sodium (mg)
	322	5	5	5	505

Golden Fruit Compote

1 cup dried apricots
1 cup dried apples
1/2 cup golden raisins
1 cup orange juice

1 cinnamon stick
4 cloves
2 oranges, peeled

Slice apricots and apples in half. Combine with raisins, juice, cinnamon stick and cloves in a medium saucepan. Bring to a boil over medium heat then reduce heat and simmer for 15 minutes. Cover and refrigerate overnight.

Slice oranges, then cut into bite-size pieces. Add to compote and stir well. Remove cinnamon stick and cloves before serving.

Serves 4 to 6

Per serving:	Calories	Fat (g)	Cholesterol (mg)	Fiber (g)	Sodium (mg)
	172	1	0	6	11

Spiced Oatmeal with Dates

3 cups water
1 tsp. cinnamon
1/4 tsp. nutmeg
1/4 tsp. allspice

1/3 cup raisins
1/2 cup chopped dates
1 1/3 cups rolled oats

Combine water with spices, raisins and dates. Bring to a boil; stir in rolled oats. Cover and simmer until water is absorbed, about 8 to 10 minutes.

Serves 4

Per serving:	Calories	Fat (g)	Cholesterol (mg)	Fiber (g)	Sodium (mg)
	179	2	0	5	4

CranApple Oatmeal

2 cups cranberry-apple juice
2 cups water
1 3/4 cups rolled oats

1 tsp. cinnamon
1 tsp. lemon zest
1 apple, cored and chopped (unpeeled)

Combine juice and water; bring to a boil. Stir in rolled oats, cinnamon and lemon rind. Cook 8 to 10 minutes, stirring occasionally. Remove from heat. Add chopped apple; cover and let stand for 5 minutes before serving.

Serves 4 to 6

Per serving:	Calories	Fat (g)	Cholesterol (mg)	Fiber (g)	Sodium (mg)
	131	1	0	3	2

Mom's Best Oats

1³/₄ cups water
¹/₄ to ¹/₃ cup raisins
¹/₃ cup rolled oats

¹/₃ cup non-fat dry milk
¹/₃ cup oat bran

Combine water and raisins in a small saucepan and bring to a boil. Reduce heat to simmer; add rolled oats and dry milk, stirring to mix well. Slowly stir in oat bran; stir constantly to prevent lumping. Simmer 5 to 7 minutes.

Variations:

• Add ¹/₂ tsp. cinnamon or nutmeg.

• Soak raisins overnight in cooking water for sweetness without added sugar.

Serves 2 to 3

Per serving:	Calories	Fat (g)	Cholesterol (mg)	Fiber (g)	Sodium (mg)
	156	1	3	4	75

Grape-Nutty Oatmeal

1 cup water
¹/₃ cup rolled oats
¹/₃ cup non-fat dry milk (optional)

1 tsp. cinnamon
1 Tbsp. brown sugar *or* honey (optional)
¹/₃ cup Grape Nuts™

Combine water, oats, dry milk, cinnamon and sugar in a small saucepan. Bring to a boil over medium heat and simmer for 5 minutes. Add Grape Nuts and simmer 1 to 2 minutes, adding water or milk as necessary for desired consistency.

Serves 1

Per serving:	Calories	Fat (g)	Cholesterol (mg)	Fiber (g)	Sodium (mg)
	415	2	8	5	478

Swiss Breakfast Combo

Made ahead, this wholesome blend of fruit, yogurt
and whole grains is a quick, filling breakfast

¹/₄ cup bulgur
¹/₄ cup boiling water *or* apple juice
¹/₂ cup rolled oats
¹/₂ cup raisins, chopped dates,
  prunes *or* apricots

¹/₄ cup chopped walnuts *or* almonds
1 cup plain non-fat yogurt
1 cup vanilla *or* fruit flavored non-fat yogurt
Sliced fresh fruit

Combine bulgur and boiling water; let stand 30 minutes or until all water is absorbed. Mix with oats, raisins, nuts and yogurt. Cover and refrigerate overnight.

To serve, top with fresh fruit

Serves 4

Per serving:	Calories	Fat (g)	Cholesterol (mg)	Fiber (g)	Sodium (mg)
	266	7	7	3	85

Whole Wheat Buttermilk Pancakes

1¹/₄ cups whole wheat flour
2 tsp. baking powder
¹/₂ tsp. baking soda
1 Tbsp. honey *or* brown sugar

2 egg whites
1 cup low-fat buttermilk
2 Tbsp. canola *or* safflower oil

In a medium bowl, combine flour, baking powder, baking soda and honey. In a smaller bowl, beat together egg whites, buttermilk and oil. Add to dry ingredients and stir until just mixed. Batter will be slightly lumpy.

Coat a non-stick griddle with cooking spray. Spoon batter onto griddle and cook until bubbles form and top is slightly dry. Turn and continue cooking 1 to 2 minutes more.

Yield: 8 to 10 pancakes

Per pancake:	Calories	Fat (g)	Cholesterol (mg)	Fiber (g)	Sodium (mg)
	92	3	1	1	165

Whole Wheat Raisin Pancakes

1 cup boiling water	3/4 cup whole wheat flour
1/2 cup raisins	1 Tbsp. brown sugar *or* honey
2 egg whites	1 tsp. cinnamon
1 cup non-fat buttermilk	1 tsp. baking powder
2 Tbsp. canola *or* safflower oil	1/2 tsp. baking soda

In a small bowl, pour boiling water over raisins and let stand 1 to 2 hours (or overnight). Drain well.

In a large bowl, beat egg whites slightly. Add buttermilk, oil, flour, sugar, cinnamon, baking powder and baking soda. Mix until smooth. Stir in raisins.

Coat a non-stick griddle with cooking spray. Cook as directed for Whole Wheat Buttermilk Pancakes (page 100).

Variation: Omit raisins. Stir 1 ripe banana, mashed, and/or 1 cup blueberries into batter

Yield: 10 pancakes

Per pancake:	Calories	Fat (g)	Cholesterol (mg)	Fiber (g)	Sodium (mg)
	92	3	1	1	126

Banana Oatmeal Pancakes

These delicious pancakes are sweetened naturally with bananas — no added sugar!

3/4 cup rolled oats
2/3 cup whole wheat flour
1 tsp. baking powder
1/2 tsp. baking soda
1 ripe banana

2 egg whites
3/4 cup non-fat buttermilk
2 Tbsp. canola *or* safflower oil
1 tsp. vanilla

In a medium bowl, combine oats, flour, baking powder and baking soda. In a smaller bowl, mash the banana. Add egg whites, buttermilk, oil and vanilla; beat until well blended. Add to dry ingredients and mix until smooth.

Coat a non-stick griddle with cooking spray. Cook as directed for Whole Wheat Buttermilk Pancakes (page 100).

Yield: 10 pancakes

Per pancake:	Calories	Fat (g)	Cholesterol (mg)	Fiber (g)	Sodium (mg)
	91	3	0	2	116

Buttermilk Oatmeal Pancakes

1 1/2 cups rolled oats *or* 1 1/4
  cups rolled oats plus 1/4 cup oat bran
2 cups non-fat buttermilk
3 egg whites

1 cup whole wheat flour
2 Tbsp. brown sugar *or* honey
2 tsp. baking soda

Combine oats, buttermilk and egg whites. Let stand for 1/2 hour or refrigerate overnight. Add flour, brown sugar and baking soda. Stir just until dry ingredients are moist.

Coat a non-stick griddle with cooking spray and cook pancakes according to directions in Whole Wheat Buttermilk Pancakes (page 100).

Yield: 14 to 16 pancakes

Per pancake:	Calories	Fat (g)	Cholesterol (mg)	Fiber (g)	Sodium (mg)
	73	1	1	2	163

Cottage Cakes

¹/₂ cup whole wheat flour
¹/₂ cup unbleached flour
2 Tbsp. wheat germ
1 tsp. baking powder
1 tsp. orange *or* lemon zest
¹/₂ tsp. baking soda

¹/₄ tsp. Lite Salt™ (optional)
1 cup 1% cottage cheese
2 egg whites
1 cup non-fat buttermilk
1 Tbsp. honey *or* brown sugar

In a medium bowl, combine flours, wheat germ, baking powder, zest, baking soda and Lite Salt. In a smaller bowl, beat together cottage cheese, egg whites, buttermilk and honey. Add to dry ingredients, stirring until just mixed.

Coat a non-stick griddle with cooking spray. Cook pancakes as directed in Whole Wheat Buttermilk Pancakes (page 100).

Yield: 10 to 12 pancakes

Per pancake:	Calories	Fat (g)	Cholesterol (mg)	Fiber (g)	Sodium (mg)
	67	0	1	1	200

Oat-Cornmeal Waffles

2 egg whites
2²/₃ cups non-fat buttermilk
1¹/₄ cups whole wheat flour
²/₃ cup rolled oats

²/₃ cup yellow *or* blue cornmeal
1¹/₄ tsp. baking soda
3 Tbsp. brown sugar *or* honey
¹/₃ cup liquid margarine

In a medium bowl, beat together egg whites and buttermilk. Combine flour, oats, cornmeal, baking soda and sugar in another bowl. Add flour mixture and margarine to buttermilk mixture and stir until well mixed.

Heat a waffle iron on medium-high heat. Coat well with cooking spray. Fill half-full with batter and close iron. Bake 6 to 8 minutes or until waffle is golden brown. Repeat with remaining batter.

Yield: 5-6″ waffles

Per waffle:	Calories	Fat (g)	Cholesterol (mg)	Fiber (g)	Sodium (mg)
	394	14	2	4	550

Cinnamon French Toast

1 recipe New Eggs (page 108)
1 tsp. cinnamon
1/2 tsp. nutmeg

1/2 tsp. vanilla
6 slices whole wheat bread

In a shallow dish, beat together New Eggs, cinnamon, nutmeg and vanilla. Dip bread slices into egg mixture coating both sides; drain briefly.

Coat a large non-stick skillet or griddle liberally with cooking spray. Cook French toast over medium heat, turning once, until browned on both sides.

Serves 4 to 6

Per serving:	Calories	Fat (g)	Cholesterol (mg)	Fiber (g)	Sodium (mg)
	85	2	1	2	164

Spiced Waffles

1 1/4 cups whole wheat flour
1/4 cup non-fat dry milk
2 Tbsp. brown sugar
2 tsp. baking powder
1 tsp. cinnamon
1/2 tsp. nutmeg

1/8 tsp. cloves
3 egg whites
1 cup non-fat milk
1/4 cup canola *or* safflower oil
1/4 cup chopped almonds *or*
    2 Tbsp. toasted sesame seeds

In a large bowl, combine flour, dry milk, sugar, baking powder, cinnamon, nutmeg and cloves. In a small bowl, beat egg whites until they form stiff, moist peaks. In another small bowl, combine milk and oil.

Stir liquid mixture into flour mixture until blended. Fold in egg whites and nuts.

Heat a waffle iron to medium-high; coat thoroughly with cooking spray. Spoon in batter until half-full. Close iron and bake until golden brown.

Yield: 6-8" waffles

Per serving:	Calories	Fat (g)	Cholesterol (mg)	Fiber (g)	Sodium (mg)
	255	12	2	3	219

Banana-Honey Cream

Serve as a topping for pancakes, french toast or waffles

3 ripe bananas, mashed
2 Tbsp. honey *or* brown sugar
1 Tbsp. liquid margarine

1 tsp. cinnamon
1/2 tsp. nutmeg
1/2 tsp. vanilla

In a small bowl, combine all ingredients mixing well. Serve immediately. Does not keep well.

Yield: about 1½ cups

Per serving:	Calories	Fat (g)	Cholesterol (mg)	Fiber (g)	Sodium (mg)
	92	2	0	1	26

Creamy Orange Topping

1 cup evaporated non-fat milk
1/4 cup frozen orange juice concentrate, thawed

1 Tbsp. brown sugar *or* honey
1 tsp. orange zest
1 tsp. vanilla

Combine all ingredients in a small saucepan and simmer until slightly thickened. Serve over pancakes, french toast or waffles.

Yield: 1¼ cups

Per serving:	Calories	Fat (g)	Cholesterol (mg)	Fiber (g)	Sodium (mg)
	58	0	2	0	50

Creole Syrup

1/2 cup molasses
3/4 cup evaporated non-fat milk
1 Tbsp. liquid margarine

Combine all ingredients in a small saucepan and simmer until warm. Serve over pancakes, french toast or waffles. Also good over frozen yogurt.

Yield: 1 1/4 cups

Per serving:	Calories	Fat (g)	Cholesterol (mg)	Fiber (g)	Sodium (mg)
	127	4	10	0	62

Peachy Syrup

1 15-oz. can sliced peaches (juice pack)   **1/2 tsp. cinnamon**
Orange juice   **1/4 tsp. nutmeg**
1/4 cup brown sugar *or* honey   **1/4 tsp. ginger**
1 Tbsp. cornstarch

Drain juice from peaches into a 1 cup measure. If needed, add orange juice to measure one cup.

Divide peaches in half and puree one half in food processor. Add juice. In a small saucepan, combine sugar, cornstarch and spices. Gradually blend into juice mixture. Bring to a boil over medium heat, stirring frequently. Reduce heat and simmer until thickened. Add remaining peach slices. Serve over pancakes, french toast or waffles.

Yield: about 2 cups

Per serving:	Calories	Fat (g)	Cholesterol (mg)	Fiber (g)	Sodium (mg)
	56	0	0	6	6

Spiced Honey

Delicious spread on toast, muffins, bagels or warmed and drizzled over frozen yogurt. Makes a peanut butter sandwich special!

1 cup honey
1 tsp. cinnamon
1 tsp. cardamom

1 tsp. nutmeg
1/4 tsp. cloves

Blend honey with spices (easier when honey is warmed). Store in a tightly covered container.

Yield: l cup

Per serving:	Calories	Fat (g)	Cholesterol (mg)	Fiber (g)	Sodium (mg)
	66	0	0	0	1

Orange-Honey Creamed Cheese

1 1/2 cups 1% cottage cheese
2 Tbsp. honey
1 Tbsp. orange zest

Place cottage cheese and honey in blender or food processor and process until very smooth, about 2 to 3 minutes. Add orange zest and process just to blend.

Cover and chill before serving. Use as a spread for toast, muffins or bagels.

Yield: about 1 1/2 cups.

Per serving:	Calories	Fat (g)	Cholesterol (mg)	Fiber (g)	Sodium (mg)
	31	0	1	0	115

Sunshine Breakfast Cake

Who says you can't eat cake for breakfast?!

1¹/2 cups whole wheat flour
1 tsp. baking soda
1 Tbsp. orange zest
1¹/2 cups orange juice concentrate

1 Tbsp. vinegar
1 tsp. vanilla
6 Tbsp. canola *or* safflower oil

Mix together flour, baking soda, orange zest and ¹/2 cup orange juice concentrate. Make 3 indentations in batter then pour in vinegar, vanilla and oil. Pour remaining orange juice concentrate over batter and mix well. Pour into a 8 or 9 inch square baking pan coated with cooking spray. Bake at 350° for 30 minutes or until a cake tester inserted in the center comes out clean.

Variation: Add ¹/2 cup raisins or well-drained pineapple

Yield: One 8" cake

Per serving:	Calories	Fat (g)	Cholesterol (mg)	Fiber (g)	Sodium (mg)
	154	7	0	1	70

New Eggs

4 egg whites
1 tsp. canola *or* safflower oil *or* liquid margarine
Pinch turmeric

In a small bowl, beat together egg whites and oil. Sprinkle in turmeric a little at a time, beating well after each addition.

Use as an egg replacement for omelettes and scrambled eggs

Yield: equivalent of 2 eggs

Per serving:	Calories	Fat (g)	Cholesterol (mg)	Fiber (g)	Sodium (mg)
	100	5	0	0	200

Basic Omelette

Egg white omelettes can be just as tasty as the high cholesterol version — but use a gentle touch and a low temperature to prevent the omelette from drying out

Cooking Spray
One recipe New Eggs (page 108)

Coat a small non-stick skillet with cooking spray. Heat pan over medium heat. Pour in New Eggs. Cook over low heat until about half cooked. Add filling of your choice. Cover and continue cooking over low heat until eggs are set and filling is warm. (Total cooking time will be 5 to 10 minutes.) Fold omelette in half and serve

Yield: 1 omelette

Filling suggestions:

• Grated, low-fat cheese, 2 Tbsp. per serving.

• Mushrooms: saute sliced mushrooms in a small amount of olive oil or cook, covered in microwave until wilted.

• Spinach: steam in microwave 1 to 2 minutes.

• Smoked salmon: use sparingly as it is high in sodium. Steamed asparagus is a tasty addition.

• Veggie: your choice of sprouts, diced tomato, avocado slices, thinly sliced zucchini, steamed broccoli or asparagus.

• Italian: sauteed red or green pepper, onion, zucchini, diced tomato.

• Tomato and basil: diced tomato and chopped fresh basil. Top with a sprinkle of Parmesan cheese.

• Herb: chopped fresh herbs: basil, oregano, parsley or, for a Mexican flavor, cilantro and chopped green chiles.

• Seafood: shrimp (1 to 2 oz. per serving) and/or crab. Season with chopped fresh dill.

• Pizza: fill with Quick Tomato Sauce (page 294) and top with grated part-skim mozzarella cheese.

• Florentine: fill with Creamed Spinach (page 229).

Green Chile Omelette

One recipe New Eggs (page 108)
1 to 2 Tbsp. chopped green chile *or*
  1 jalapeño pepper, seeded and diced
1 corn tortilla

1/4 cup vegetarian refried beans
1 to 2 Tbsp. grated low-fat Monterey Jack
  cheese (optional)
Mexican Salsa (page 10)

Beat together New Eggs and chile. Coat a non-stick skillet with cooking spray. Heat over medium heat. Pour in eggs. Reduce heat to low and cook until halfway set. Spread tortilla with beans and place on top of eggs. Add cheese, if desired. Cover and continue to cook over low heat until eggs are set and filling is warm. Fold in half and serve topped with Salsa.

Serves 1

Per serving:	Calories	Fat (g)	Cholesterol (mg)	Fiber (g)	Sodium (mg)
	320	16	0	4	527

Chile Relleño Brunch Casserole

1/2 cup non-fat dry milk
2 cups non-fat milk
1 lb. turkey sausage
1/2 cup chopped onion

1/2 cup chopped red bell pepper
Egg substitute equivalent to 12 eggs
1 4-oz. can chopped green chiles
4 oz. low-fat sharp cheddar cheese, grated

In a large bowl, combine dry milk, and liquid milk; mix well to dissolve dry milk. Set aside.

Crumble sausage into a skillet. Add onion and red pepper; cook until browned, draining fat as it accumulates. Drain cooked sausage well on paper towels.

Add sausage and remaining ingredients to milk mixture and stir to combine. Pour into a 9" x 13" baking dish coated with cooking spray. Bake at 325° for 1 hour or until eggs are set.

Variation: Add 1 12-oz. can salt-free whole kernel corn, well drained.

Serves 10 to 12

Per serving:	Calories	Fat (g)	Cholesterol (mg)	Fiber (g)	Sodium (mg)
	104	3	31	0	145

Rich in complex carbohydrates, B vitamins and iron, pastas and whole grains should comprise at least 50 percent of our caloric intake. Trade in the high-fat, high-cholesterol foods for low-fat, cholesterol-free pasta — be sure to buy the eggless varieties — for meals that fill you up but not out.

Delitefully HealthMark

Grains

Citrus Rice 128
Couscous Primavera 130
Lemony Barley Pilaf 130
Mexican Brown Rice 129
Rice Florentine 129

Pasta

Entrees
   Chunky Vegetable Marinara Sauce 128
   Creamy Seafood Pasta 125
   Fettuccine with Fresh Herbs 127
   Fresca with Basil 127
   Garden Linguine 123
   Mexicali   122
   Mexican Lasagne 118
   Neptune 125
   Primavera in Cheese Sauce 124
   Provencal 126
   Sesame Noodles 119
   Tomato Fettucine
      with Piñon Vinaigrette 126
   Year of the Snake Noodles 120

Salads
   Dill Pasta Salad with Shrimp 116
   Garden Pasta Salad 116
   Golden Pasta Salad 113
   Greek Pasta Salad 115
   Hot Pasta Salad with Tuna 121
   Mexican Pasta Salad 117
   Oriental Asparagus Salad 114

Golden Pasta Salad

4 ounces small pasta (eggless) e.g. seashell
2 carrots, peeled and sliced
1/4 cup golden raisins
3/4 cup plain non-fat yogurt
1/4 cup chutney (e.g. Major Grey's)

2 Tbsp. orange juice concentrate
1 tsp. orange zest
1/4 cup chopped peanuts *or* cashews
  (dry roasted, unsalted)

Cook pasta according to package directions, omitting salt. Add carrots during last five minutes of cooking. Drain pasta and carrots; cool. In a medium bowl toss raisins with pasta mixture.

In a small bowl, combine yogurt, chutney, orange juice concentrate and orange zest. Add to pasta and blend well. Cover and chill. Serve garnished with chopped peanuts.

Variations:

• Add 1/2 tsp. curry powder to yogurt mixture.

• 1 cup canned garbanzo beans (rinsed and drained).

• 4 oz. cooked small shrimp, cooked bay scallops and/or crab.

Serves 4

Per serving:	Calories	Fat (g)	Cholesterol (mg)	Fiber (g)	Sodium (mg)
	322	8	3	3	53

Oriental Asparagus Salad

8 oz. udon (Japanese noodles) *or* spaghetti
1/2 lb. scallops, rinsed and drained
1 lb. asparagus, trimmed
2 Tbsp. canola *or* safflower oil
3 Tbsp. water
1 clove garlic, minced

1 Tbsp. minced fresh ginger
1/2 cup rice vinegar (*or* white wine
   vinegar plus 1 tsp. sugar)
2 tsp. sugar
1 tsp. low-sodium soy sauce
1 tsp. oriental sesame oil

Cook noodles in a large pot of boiling water until al dente. Drain and rinse with cold water until cool. Place noodles in a shallow serving dish.

Cut scallops into 1/2" pieces; set aside.

Slice asparagus on the diagonal. Heat 1 Tbsp. oil in a wok or large skillet. Add asparagus and stir-fry 1 minute. Add water, cover and steam until just tender-crisp, 2 to 3 minutes. Remove asparagus and arrange over noodles.

Add remaining oil to wok and heat. Add garlic, ginger and scallops. Stir-fry until scallops are opaque in the center, 2 to 3 minutes. Add rice vinegar, sugar, soy sauce and sesame oil. Stir just until sugar dissolves. Pour over noodles. Serve immediately or cover and chill 2 to 4 hours before serving.

Serves 4 to 6

Per serving:	Calories	Fat (g)	Cholesterol (mg)	Fiber (g)	Sodium (mg)
	246	7	21	1	137

Greek Pasta Salad

Dressing:
3/4 cup fresh dill
1/3 cup fresh mint
2 cloves garlic
1/2 cup chopped red onion
1/2 cup olive oil
3 Tbsp. fresh lemon *or* lime juice
1/4 tsp. Lite Salt™

1/4 lb. cooked small shrimp
1/2 lb. cooked bay scallops
8 oz. fusilli pasta (eggless)
15 cherry tomatoes, halved
1/4 cup sliced black olives (rinse and
   drain before slicing)
1/2 cup thinly sliced English cucumber
2 oz. feta cheese, crumbled

Prepare dressing: Combine all ingredients in food processor and pulse until well combined. Toss shrimp and scallops with 1/4 cup dressing. Refrigerate 4 hours or overnight. Chill remaining dressing separately.

Cook pasta according to package directions, omitting salt. Drain well. In a large bowl, toss pasta with seafood mixture and remaining ingredients. Add dressing as needed to moisten. Serve at room temperature.

Serves 4

Per serving:	Calories	Fat (g)	Cholesterol (mg)	Fiber (g)	Sodium (mg)
	417	13	84	1	534

Dill Pasta Salad with Shrimp

4 oz. eggless small pasta (e.g. seashell)
1 10-oz. pkg. frozen peas, thawed
    and drained
4 to 6 green onions, thinly sliced *or*
    1/2 cup chopped red onion
2 to 3 stalks celery, sliced
1/4 lb. cooked small shrimp
1/4 lb. cooked bay scallops
1/2 cup dry-roasted cashews,
    coarsely chopped

Dill dressing:
1 cup plain non-fat yogurt
1/4 cup fat-free or light, cholesterol-free
    mayonnaise
2 Tbsp. chopped fresh dill
1 tsp. lemon zest

Cook pasta according to package directions, omitting salt. Drain and cool. In a medium bowl combine with peas, onion, celery, shrimp, scallops and cashews.

Dill dressing: Blend all ingredients in a small bowl. Combine with pasta mixture and toss gently until well mixed. Cover and chill 2 to 4 hours before serving.

Serves 4 to 6

Per serving:	Calories	Fat (g)	Cholesterol (mg)	Fiber (g)	Sodium (mg)
	309	14	39	3	306

Garden Pasta Salad

1/2 lb. eggless rotini *or* seashell pasta,
    cooked and drained
1/2 cup Italian dressing
1 15-oz. can garbanzo beans,
    rinsed and drained
1 zucchini, halved and sliced
1 cup sliced mushrooms
1 cup sliced celery
1 cup broccoli florets

1 cup cauliflower, cut into bite-sized pieces
1/2 green *or* red bell pepper, cored
    and diced
2 carrots, sliced
1/2 cup frozen peas, thawed
4 green onions, thinly sliced
1 tomato, cored and diced
1 Tbsp. salt-free herb seasoning

Combine all ingredients in a large bowl and mix well. Chill 1 to 2 hours before serving.

Serves 6 to 8

Per serving:	Calories	Fat (g)	Cholesterol (mg)	Fiber (g)	Sodium (mg)
	216	10	1	3	362

Mexican Pasta Salad

Great for a buffet or pot-luck

8 oz. eggless fusilli (long curly pasta)
1¹/2 cups Mexican Salsa (page 10)
3/4 cup chopped red onion
2 tomatoes, cored and chopped
1 red bell pepper, chopped
1 green pepper, chopped

1 cup cooked black beans (if canned, rinsed and drained)
1 cup cooked fresh corn
1 cup diced jicama
1/2 avocado, diced
Fresh cilantro

Cook pasta according to package directions, omitting salt. Drain and cool to room temperature. Mix with about ¹/2 of Salsa and remaining ingredients.

Serve garnished with fresh cilantro sprigs and red onion rings. Pass remaining Salsa.

Variations:

- Add ¾ cup of HealthMark Sour Cream (page 287) and mix thoroughly.

- Garnish with ¼ cup sunflower seeds.

- Add two grilled chicken breasts (skinless), diced

Serves 4 to 6

Per serving:	Calories	Fat (g)	Cholesterol (mg)	Fiber (g)	Sodium (mg)
	287	4	0	4	37

Mexican Lasagne

This unique version of lasagne appeals to our love of Mexican flavors.
Preparation is a breeze — double it to feed a crowd

1 Tbsp. olive oil
1 onion, chopped
2 cloves garlic, minced
1 red bell pepper, diced
2 Anaheim chiles, seeded and diced
2 16-oz. jars salsa (hot *or* mild)
1 tsp. cumin
1/2 tsp. pepper

1 8-oz. pkg lasagne noodles (eggless)
   or 12 corn tortillas

Cheese filling:
1 cup low-fat ricotta cheese
1 cup 1% cottage cheese
1/3 cup Parmesan cheese
2 egg whites
1/2 cup chopped cilantro
1 4-oz. can chopped green chiles

3 boneless, skinless chicken breasts,
   cooked and cubed

1/2 cup grated low-fat Monterey Jack cheese
   or part-skim mozzarella

Heat oil in a large skillet; saute onion, garlic, bell pepper and chiles until soft. Add salsa, cumin and pepper. Bring to a boil; reduce heat and simmer for 10 to 15 minutes. Cook noodles al dente according to package directions, omitting salt.

Make cheese filling: Combine cheeses, egg whites, cilantro and green chiles.

To assemble lasagne: Coat a 9" x 13" baking dish with cooking spray. Spread half the sauce on the bottom. Cover with half the noodles (or tortillas) then spread with the cheese filling. Spread cubed chicken over the cheese filling. Cover with remaining noodles, then spread with remaining sauce. Sprinkle with remaining 1/2 cup grated cheese. Cover with foil and bake at 375° for 45 to 50 minutes or until heated through. Let stand 5 to 10 minutes before serving.

Serves 10–12

Per serving:	Calories	Fat (g)	Cholesterol (mg)	Fiber (g)	Sodium (mg)
	248	6	37	2	263

Sesame Noodles

3 skinless, boneless chicken breasts
1 lb. spaghettini (eggless)
1/4 cup sesame seeds
6 Tbsp. low-sodium soy sauce
5 Tbsp. Tahini (sesame seed paste)
3 Tbsp. brown sugar

3 Tbsp. white wine vinegar
4 Tbsp. dry white wine *or*
    3 Tbsp. salt-free chicken broth, defatted
2 cloves garlic, minced
Shredded romaine lettuce

Bring a large pot of water to a boil. Reduce heat and add chicken breasts. Simmer until done, about 10 to 15 minutes. Remove, cool and cut into strips.

Return water to a boil and add spaghetti. Cook until al dente. Drain and set aside.

Toast sesame seeds in a small skillet over medium heat until light brown, about 5 minutes. Stir frequently. Let cool. In a small bowl combine soy sauce, Tahini, brown sugar, vinegar, wine, garlic and sesame seeds.

Divide spaghetti among plates and top with shredded lettuce and chicken strips. Drizzle dressing over each salad. Garnish with additional sesame seeds.

Variation: Toss spaghetti with julienne red and/or green pepper, julienne carrots and sliced water chestnuts.

Serves 6

Per serving:	Calories	Fat (g)	Cholesterol (mg)	Fiber (g)	Sodium (mg)
	504	12	50	1	659

Year of the Snake Noodles

In honor of the Year of the Snake (1989) on the Chinese calendar, try this tasty dish

1/2 lb. eggless spaghetti
1/2 lb. eggless whole wheat spaghetti
4 tsp. cornstarch
1/4 cup low-sodium soy sauce
3 Tbsp. dry sherry
1 cup salt-free chicken broth,
   defatted *or* water
2 tsp. oriental sesame oil
3/4 lb. ground turkey

6 green onions, thinly sliced
   on the diagonal
1/2 cup thinly sliced onion
1 cup sliced mushrooms
2 Tbsp. minced fresh ginger
2 cloves garlic, minced
1/2 tsp. crushed red pepper flakes
1/4 lb. cooked baby shrimp, rinsed and drained

Cook spaghetti according to package directions, omitting salt. Drain and keep warm.

Measure cornstarch into a small bowl, then blend in soy sauce, sherry and chicken broth. Set aside.

Heat a wok or large skillet. Add sesame oil and stir-fry turkey, onions, mushrooms, ginger, garlic and red pepper until turkey is done. Add a small amount of water if mixture sticks to pan. Add soy sauce mixture; cook and stir until mixture boils and thickens slightly. Stir in shrimp.

Pour sauce over spaghetti and toss to combine well

Variation: Add 2 cups shredded cabbage or bok choy to wok along with turkey and vegetables.

Serves 6

Per serving:	Calories	Fat (g)	Cholesterol (mg)	Fiber (g)	Sodium (mg)
	411	5	63	1	507

Hot Pasta Salad with Tuna

12 oz. eggless pasta shells

Chili dressing:
1/4 cup olive oil
3 Tbsp. balsamic *or* red wine vinegar
1 Tbsp. capers, rinsed and drained
2 cloves garlic, minced
1/2 tsp. crushed dried red chiles

1 tsp. olive oil
1 red bell pepper, seeded and chopped
1/3 cup chopped parsley
1 3 1/2-oz. can pitted black olives,
  rinsed and drained
1 6-oz. can low-sodium,
  water-packed tuna, drained
2 tomatoes, cored and diced

Cook pasta al dente according to package directions, omitting salt. Drain. Prepare dressing: whisk together 1/4 cup olive oil and vinegar in a small bowl until well combined. Add capers, garlic and chiles.

Heat 1 tsp. olive oil in a large skillet and saute red pepper until soft, about 5 minutes. Add parsley, olives and tuna. Stir gently until heated through, about 2 minutes. Add half of dressing and set aside.

Combine diced tomatoes and remaining dressing with pasta and mix well. Pour into a serving bowl. Spoon tuna mixture into center of pasta and toss gently to combine.

Serves 6

Per serving:	Calories	Fat (g)	Cholesterol (mg)	Fiber (g)	Sodium (mg)
	352	14	18	2	377

Mexicali Pasta

*Rich in complex carbohydrates and full of flavor, this quick
and easy dish is a favorite for pot lucks and parties*

1 16-oz. can salt-free pinto beans,
  well drained
1 tsp. olive oil
1 onion, chopped
1 green pepper, cored, seeded and chopped
2 cloves garlic, minced
2 15-oz. cans Mexican-style stewed
  tomatoes, undrained
1 4-oz. can chopped green chiles

1/4 cup chopped fresh cilantro
1/2 tsp. chili powder
1/2 tsp. brown sugar
1/4 tsp. dried oregano, crushed
1 8-oz. can salt-free corn, drained *or*
  1 cup cooked fresh corn kernels
8 oz. eggless rotelli pasta *or* spaghetti
Chopped fresh cilantro

Pour beans into a medium bowl and mash slightly. Set aside.

Heat olive oil in a medium skillet. Saute onion, green pepper and garlic until soft. Add tomatoes, green chiles, cilantro, chili powder, brown sugar and oregano. Simmer 15 to 20 minutes, stirring occasionally. Stir mashed beans and corn into mixture. Keep warm over low heat.

Cook pasta according to package directions, omitting salt. Drain well. Serve sauce over hot pasta garnished with chopped cilantro.

Serves 4

Per serving:	Calories	Fat (g)	Cholesterol (mg)	Fiber (g)	Sodium (mg)
	453	3	0	15	250

Garden Linguine

(Adapted from *Creme de Colorado*)

Lots of ingredients, but easy to make

1 10-oz. can salt-free chicken broth, defatted
1/2 cup dry white wine
1 1/2 cups broccoli florets
2 carrots, sliced
1 lb. asparagus, trimmed and sliced
1 Tbsp. olive oil
6 green onions, thinly sliced
2 cloves garlic, minced
1/2 lb. mushrooms, sliced
1 zucchini, julienne

1 small red bell pepper, julienne
1 cup snow peas, julienne
1 cup evaporated non-fat milk
2 Tbsp. minced fresh basil *or*
   1 tsp. dried
1/2 tsp. dried oregano
1/4 cup minced fresh parsley
1/4 tsp. Lite Salt™
Freshly ground black pepper
8 oz. eggless linguine
1/4 cup Parmesan cheese

In a small saucepan, combine broth and wine. Boil until reduced to about 1/2 cup. Place broccoli, carrots and asparagus in a covered microwave-safe container and microwave 1 to 2 minutes or until just tender.

In a large skillet, heat olive oil and saute green onion, garlic, mushrooms, zucchini, red pepper, snow peas, broccoli, carrots and asparagus until soft. Add reduced broth, milk, basil, oregano, parsley, salt and pepper. Simmer for 10 to 15 minutes.

Cook pasta according to package directions, omitting salt. Drain well. Place in a large serving bowl. Pour vegetables over pasta and toss gently to combine. Sprinkle with Parmesan cheese and serve.

Serves 4

Per serving:	Calories	Fat (g)	Cholesterol (mg)	Fiber (g)	Sodium (mg)
	452	7	8	1	327

Pasta Primavera in Cheese Sauce

A creamy low-fat cheese sauce marries crisp vegetables with pasta

1/3 cup non-fat dry milk
Non-fat milk
1 package Butter Buds™
1/4 cup hot water
1 Tbsp. liquid margarine
1 1/2 Tbsp. unbleached flour
1/4 tsp. dry mustard *or* white pepper

1 cup grated low-fat cheddar cheese (4 oz.)
1/4 cup Parmesan cheese
1 cup frozen peas, thawed
1 lb. eggless spaghettini
1/2 lb. asparagus spears,
   trimmed and sliced into 1" pieces
3 carrots, peeled and sliced

Pour non-fat dry milk into a 2 cup measure and add non-fat milk to measure 2 cups. Stir well to dissolve and set aside. Dissolve Butter Buds in hot water; set aside.

Melt margarine in a medium saucepan. Stir in flour and cook over medium heat one minute or until bubbly; do not brown. Remove from heat and gradually stir in milk mixture (stir before using to dissolve non-fat dry milk). Return to heat and stir in Butter Buds, dry mustard and cheeses. Cook and stir over medium heat until thickened. Stir in peas. Keep warm over low heat, stirring occasionally.

Cook pasta according to package directions, omitting salt. Add asparagus and carrot slices during last 5 minutes of cooking. Drain well and place pasta in a large serving bowl. Pour sauce over and toss gently until well mixed. Serve immediately.

Serves 4 to 6

Per serving:	Calories	Fat (g)	Cholesterol (mg)	Fiber (g)	Sodium (mg)
	443	8	17	2	274

Creamy Seafood Pasta

1 Tbsp. olive oil *or* liquid margarine
1/2 lb. mushrooms, sliced
1/2 red bell pepper, cored and chopped
6 green onions, thinly sliced
1 1/2 cups Bechamel Sauce (page 288)

8 oz. eggless spaghettini *or* linguine
1 cup frozen peas, thawed
1/4 lb. cooked small shrimp
1/2 lb. crab meat
1/4 cup Parmesan cheese

Heat oil in a large skillet; saute mushrooms, red pepper and onions until soft. Stir in Bechamel Sauce and set aside.

Cook pasta according to package directions, omitting salt. Drain well then mix with peas, seafood and sauce mixture. Spoon into an 11" by 7" baking dish coated with cooking spray. Sprinkle with cheese. Bake at 350° for 20 to 30 minutes or until heated through.

Serves 4 to 6

Per serving:	Calories	Fat (g)	Cholesterol (mg)	Fiber (g)	Sodium (mg)
	345	10	52	3	418

Pasta Neptune

1 Tbsp. olive oil
1 1/2 Tbsp. fresh lemon juice
1 clove garlic, minced
1/4 tsp. dried thyme
1/2 tsp. lemon zest

1/4 tsp. white pepper
1 lb. swordfish *or* tuna
1 lb. pasta (eggless)
2 cups Quick Tomato Sauce (page 294)

Whisk together olive oil and lemon juice. Stir in garlic, thyme, zest and pepper. Brush over fish and marinate, refrigerated, 1 to 2 hours. Grill or broil until fish flakes easily with a fork, about 4 to 5 minutes per side. Cool and cube. Set aside.

Cook pasta according to package directions, omitting salt. Drain well. Combine pasta, Tomato Sauce and cubed fish. Toss to mix well and serve.

Serves 4

Per serving:	Calories	Fat (g)	Cholesterol (mg)	Fiber (g)	Sodium (mg)
	677	13	50	4	311

Pasta Provencal

1 large eggplant, unpeeled
2 Tbsp. olive oil
1 onion, sliced
1 red bell pepper, cored,
  seeded and thinly sliced
1 green pepper, cored,
  seeded and thinly sliced

2 cloves garlic, minced
1 tsp. dried rosemary
8 oz. eggless penne (tube shaped) pasta
1/2 cup Tomato Vinaigrette (page 286)
1/2 cup chopped fresh basil

Dice eggplant into 1" cubes. Toss with 1 Tbsp. olive oil and spread on a non-stick baking sheet. Bake at 400° until soft, but not mushy. (Cubes should hold their shape.) Set aside to cool.

Heat remaining olive oil in a large skillet and saute onion, peppers, garlic and rosemary until tender but not browned. Keep warm.

Cook pasta according to package directions, omitting salt. Drain and toss with eggplant, onion mixture, tomato vinaigrette and basil. Serve at room temperature garnished with fresh basil leaves.

Serves 4 to 6

Per serving:	Calories	Fat (g)	Cholesterol (mg)	Fiber (g)	Sodium (mg)
	289	14	0	3	12

Tomato Fettucini with Piñon Vinaigrette

2 Tbsp. piñon nuts
2 Tbsp. olive oil
2 Tbsp. red wine vinegar
1 clove garlic, minced
1 shallot, minced

1 Tbsp. fresh tarragon, minced
  or 1 tsp. dried
1 lb. eggless tomato fettucini
Freshly ground black pepper
Chopped fresh parsley

Toast piñon nuts at 325° for 10 to 15 minutes or until light golden brown. Whisk together olive oil, vinegar, garlic, shallot and tarragon. Stir in nuts. Set aside.

Cook fettucini al dente. Drain well and cool slightly. Mix with vinaigrette, add pepper to taste; sprinkle with parsley. May be served at room temperature or chilled.

Serves 4

Per serving:	Calories	Fat (g)	Cholesterol (mg)	Fiber (g)	Sodium (mg)
	492	11	0	0	13

Fettucini with Fresh Herbs

Grow basil and parsley on your window sill for this simple dish

4 oz. eggless fettucini
1 clove garlic, minced
1 Tbsp. olive oil
1/4 cup chopped fresh parsley

1/3 cup chopped fresh basil
2 tomatoes, cored and chopped
Freshly ground black pepper

Cook pasta according to package directions, omitting salt. Drain. Saute garlic in olive oil and until golden. Add pasta, herbs and chopped tomato. Season to taste with black pepper.

Yield: Serves 4 as a side dish

Per serving:	Calories	Fat (g)	Cholesterol (mg)	Fiber (g)	Sodium (mg)
	140	4	0	1	6

Pasta Fresca with Basil

Serve with a salad, whole wheat french bread and fresh fruit for a quick and easy meal

8 oz. eggless rainbow pasta (rotini *or* shells)
1 tsp. olive oil
1/3 cup chopped onion
2 cloves garlic, minced
11/2 lbs. tomatoes, cored and diced *or*
 1 28-oz. can Italian-style whole tomatoes,
 chopped

1/4 cup chopped fresh parsley
3 Tbsp. chopped fresh basil *or* 2 tsp. dried
4 oz. part-skim mozzarella cheese, grated
Freshly ground black pepper

Cook pasta according to package directions, omitting salt. While pasta is cooking, prepare sauce.

Heat olive oil in a large saucepan. Saute onion and garlic until just tender. Add tomatoes, parsley and basil; simmer 15 to 20 minutes.

Drain pasta. Mix with tomato sauce and cheese. Toss until cheese is melted. Sprinkle generously with freshly ground pepper.

Serves: 4 to 6

Per serving:	Calories	Fat (g)	Cholesterol (mg)	Fiber (g)	Sodium (mg)
	212	5	11	1	97

Chunky Vegetable Marinara Sauce

A hearty sauce without meat. Also good with kidney or garbanzo beans added

1 tsp. olive oil
1 onion, chopped
1 clove garlic, minced
2 tsp. *each* dried basil, oregano,
   tarragon and fennel seed
2 zucchini, sliced
2 cups sliced mushrooms
1 green *or* red bell pepper,
   seeded and diced

2 carrots, grated
1 cup dry red wine
2 lbs. ripe tomatoes, cored and chopped
1 12-oz. can salt-free tomato paste
1/2 tsp. Lite Salt™
1 bay leaf
Freshly ground black pepper

Heat olive oil in a large skillet and saute onion, garlic, basil, oregano, tarragon and fennel until onion is soft, 5 to 10 minutes. Add zucchini, mushrooms, green pepper and grated carrots. Continue cooking until vegetables are soft, 10 to 15 minutes.

Add wine, tomatoes, tomato paste, Lite Salt and bay leaf. Simmer, covered, until sauce is thick, about 45 minutes. Stir occasionally. Season to taste with freshly ground black pepper. Serve over hot pasta.

Variation: Add 1 to 2 Tbsp. pesto. (will increase fat)

Yield: 6 to 7 cups

Per serving:	Calories	Fat (g)	Cholesterol (mg)	Fiber (g)	Sodium (mg)
	55	1	0	2	58

Citrus Rice

3 cups salt-free chicken broth, defatted
1 clove garlic, cut in half
1 cup raw brown rice *or*
   1/2 cup *each* raw brown rice and barley

1 Tbsp. lemon zest
1 Tbsp. fresh lemon juice
2 Tbsp. chopped fresh dill

In a medium saucepan, bring broth to a boil. Add garlic, rice, lemon zest and lemon juice. Reduce heat, cover and simmer for 45 to 50 minutes or until rice is done. Stir in dill and serve.

Serves 4 to 6

Per serving:	Calories	Fat (g)	Cholesterol (mg)	Fiber (g)	Sodium (mg)
	121	1	0	2	7

Rice Florentine

1/4 cup walnuts
1 Tbsp. olive oil
1 onion, chopped
2 cloves garlic, minced

1 cup sliced fresh mushrooms
1 1/2 cups raw brown rice
3 cups salt-free beef broth, defatted
8 cups fresh spinach, coarsely chopped

Toast walnuts in a dry skillet over medium heat for 5 to 10 minutes, stirring frequently, until golden brown. Set aside.

Heat oil in a large saucepan. Saute onion and garlic until soft, 2 to 3 minutes. Add mushrooms and rice, and cook 2 to 3 minutes more. Add beef broth and bring to a boil. Cover and cook over low heat for 40 to 45 minutes. When rice is nearly done, add spinach. Stir well, cover and cook an additional 5 to 10 minutes or until rice is done. Serve garnished with toasted walnuts.

Serves: 6 to 8

Per serving:	Calories	Fat (g)	Cholesterol (mg)	Fiber (g)	Sodium (mg)
	196	5	0	5	49

Mexican Brown Rice

Serve this as a main dish with corn muffins (page 85) and Acapulco Salad (page 53)

3 cups cooked brown rice
1 cup non-fat yogurt
1 4-oz. can chopped green chiles

1/4 cup Mexican Salsa (page 10)
1/4 cup chopped fresh cilantro
4 oz. shredded low-fat Monterey Jack cheese

In a medium bowl, combine all ingredients except cheese. Spoon into a 8" x 8".baking dish coated with cooking spray. Sprinkle with cheese. Bake at 350° for 30 minutes. Serve with additional salsa, if desired.

Variation: Add 1 or 2 diced, seeded jalapeño chiles.

Serves: 6

Per serving:	Calories	Fat (g)	Cholesterol (mg)	Fiber (g)	Sodium (mg)
	204	4	13	3	395

Couscous Primavera

Couscous, a type of pasta, is a delicious change of pace from rice or potatoes

1 cup couscous
1¹/2 cups low-sodium chicken broth,
  defatted
2 tomatoes, cored and diced
¹/2 cup diced radishes

4 to 6 green onions, thinly sliced
1 carrot, thinly sliced
1 Tbsp. olive oil
1 Tbsp. fresh lemon *or* lime juice
1 tsp. lemon zest

Combine couscous and broth in a medium saucepan. Bring to a boil then reduce heat to low. Cover and cook 10 to 15 minutes or until all liquid is absorbed. Fluff with a fork and let cool slightly.

Add vegetables, oil, lemon juice and zest; mix well. Serve warm.

Serves 4

Per serving:	Calories	Fat (g)	Cholesterol (mg)	Fiber (g)	Sodium (mg)
	110	4	12	1	20

Lemony Barley Pilaf

1 tsp. olive oil
4 green onions, thinly sliced
¹/2 cup chopped red bell pepper
1 cup uncooked barley
2 cups salt-free chicken broth, defatted

2 tsp. lemon zest
1 Tbsp. fresh lemon juice
¹/4 tsp. Lite Salt™
1 cup frozen chopped spinach, thawed

Heat oil in a medium saucepan; saute onion and pepper briefly. Add barley, broth, zest, lemon juice and Lite Salt. Bring to a boil, cover and simmer for 45 to 50 minutes or until done. Stir in thawed spinach, cover and let stand for 5 to 10 minutes. Stir again and serve.

Serves 4 to 6

Per serving:	Calories	Fat (g)	Cholesterol (mg)	Fiber (g)	Sodium (mg)
	47	1	0	3	64

Rich in protein, B Vitamins, iron and
other trace minerals as well as a good source
of cholesterol-lowering fiber, beans deserve to be
promoted from side dish to main entree — a starring
role! Combining vegetable proteins such as beans and
legumes with small amounts of low-fat dairy products,
lean meat, poultry or fish or with other grains, nuts
and seeds provides protein quality comparable
to eating animal protein.

Delitefully HealthMark

Entrees

Bean Enchiladas 144
Black Beans and Brown Rice   141
Cuban Beans 140
Denver Baked Beans 139
Indian Spiced Garbanzos 142
Kidney Beans with Rice 139
Lentil Curry 143
Lentils with Spinach 143
Microwave Lentils 142
Pasta E Fagioli 141
Quick Baked Beans 138
Quick Chili 137
White Chili 138

Salads

Bistro Three Bean 136
Black and White 135
Black Bean 134
Broccoli and Bean 135
Lentil Confetti 134
Lima Bean 133
Marinated Lentil 136
Pickled Blackeye Peas 137
White Bean 133

Soaking Directions

Before cooking, beans need to be soaked. Use whichever method best fits your time schedule:

Quick Soak: Place beans in a large pot and cover with three cups water per cup of beans. Bring to a boil and boil for two minutes. Cover and let stand for one hour. Discard water and add fresh, 3 to 4 cups per cup of beans. Proceed with recipe.

Overnight Soaking: Place beans in a large pot and cover with three cups water per cup of beans. Soak overnight. Discard water and replace with fresh as above. Proceed with recipe.

White Bean Salad

½ cup HealthMark Ranch Dressing (page 282)
2 15-oz. cans white beans,
   rinsed and drained
2 cups steamed broccoli florets
2 tomatoes, cored and diced
½ cup diced red onion

4 green onions, thinly sliced
½ cup diced celery, including tops
½ cup chopped green *or* red bell pepper
⅓ cup chopped fresh parsley
1 Tbsp. chopped fresh oregano *or*
   1 tsp. dried

In a large serving bowl, combine all ingredients mixing well. Cover and let stand 30 to 60 minutes at room temperature to blend flavors.

Variation: Use one can white beans and one can kidney beans.

Serves 8

Per serving:	Calories	Fat (g)	Cholesterol (mg)	Fiber (g)	Sodium (mg)
	126	1	1	10	64

Lima Bean Salad

1 10-oz. pkg. frozen lima beans
1 cup corn kernels (salt-free, if canned)
2 cups thinly sliced zucchini
1/2 cup diced red bell pepper
4 green onions, thinly sliced

1/4 cup sliced black olives
   (rinse and drain before slicing)
2 oz. feta cheese, crumbled
1/2 cup Caesar Dressing (page 51)

Cook lima beans according to package directions (preferably in the microwave). Drain if necessary and cool to room temperature.

Combine with remaining ingredients in a large bowl, tossing gently to mix. Add more dressing as needed.

Serve as a salad or spoon into pita bread for an unusual sandwich.

Serves 4 to 6

Per serving:	Calories	Fat (g)	Cholesterol (mg)	Fiber (g)	Sodium (mg)
	129	4	8	4	161

Black Bean Salad

1 15-oz. can black beans, drained
1 red onion, chopped
1 red *or* green bell pepper,
   seeded and chopped
1 cup fresh corn, cooked (may substitute
   canned, salt-free corn)

1/2 cup cider vinegar
1/3 cup brown sugar
3 Tbsp. water

In a large bowl, combine beans, onion, red or green pepper and corn. Mix vinegar, sugar and water in a small saucepan and bring to a boil, stirring until sugar is dissolved. Cool and pour over salad, mixing until well combined. Cover and chill before serving.

Serves 6 to 8

Per serving:	Calories	Fat (g)	Cholesterol (mg)	Fiber (g)	Sodium (mg)
	146	0	0	2	489

Lentil Confetti Salad

1/2 cup lentils, rinsed and drained
1 1/2 cups water
1/4 tsp. Lite Salt™
1 bay leaf
1 cup cooked brown rice
1/4 cup Italian dressing
1 tomato, cored and diced

1/4 cup each chopped red and green pepper
1/4 cup chopped red *or* green onion
1/4 cup grated carrot
2 stalks celery chopped, including leaves
2 Tbsp. chopped black olives
   (rinse and drain before chopping)

In a saucepan combine lentils, water and salt. Bring to a boil; cover and reduce heat. Simmer 20 minutes or until lentils are tender. Drain.

Combine remaining ingredients in a bowl. Add lentils and toss to combine. Cover and chill before serving.

Variation: Substitute 1 cup cooked (or canned) white beans for brown rice.

Serves 6

Per serving:	Calories	Fat (g)	Cholesterol (mg)	Fiber (g)	Sodium (mg)
	241	7	1	4	294

Broccoli and Bean Salad

This tasty salad adds color to your table at any time of year

3 cups broccoli florets
1/4 cup balsamic *or* red wine vinegar
2 Tbsp. olive oil
2 Tbsp. salt-free chicken broth (defatted) *or*
  2 Tbsp. reserved bean liquid
1 Tbsp. chopped fresh basil *or*
  1 tsp. dried
1 Tbsp. chopped fresh oregano *or*
  1 tsp. dried
1/2 tsp. dried tarragon
1/2 tsp dried savory

Freshly ground black pepper (to taste)
Dash cayenne pepper
1 clove garlic, minced
1 15-oz. can salt-free garbanzo *or*
  kidney beans, drained
1 red *or* green bell pepper, cored,
  seeded and chopped
2 cups cherry tomato halves
1/2 cup chopped red onion *or*
  4 green onions, thinly sliced

Steam broccoli florets for 3 to 4 minutes or until barely tender. Rinse briefly under cold water. Drain well and set aside.

In a small bowl, whisk together vinegar, oil and broth. Mix in herbs, peppers and garlic.

In a large bowl, combine broccoli with beans, chopped bell pepper, tomato and onion. Add dressing and toss to combine well. Cover tightly and chill several hours or overnight before serving.

Serves 6 to 8

Per serving:	Calories	Fat (g)	Cholesterol (mg)	Fiber (g)	Sodium (mg)
	124	5	0	3	16

Black and White Salad

1 15-oz. can white beans,
  rinsed and drained
1/2 cup sliced ripe olives
  (rinse and drain before slicing)

1/4 cup chopped parsley
1/4 cup Tomato Vinaigrette (page 286)

Combine all ingredients in a medium bowl. Serve chilled or at room temperature.

Serves 2 to 4

Per serving:	Calories	Fat (g)	Cholesterol (mg)	Fiber (g)	Sodium (mg)
	219	11	0	12	160

Bistro Three Bean Salad

A new version of an old favorite

1 15-oz. can Great Northern beans	$^1/_3$ cup olive oil
1 15-oz. can salt-free kidney beans	$^1/_4$ cup red wine vinegar
1 15-oz. can salt-free pinto beans	1 Tbsp. fresh lemon juice
6 green onions, thinly sliced	2 Tbsp. minced fresh tarragon *or*
1 cup diced celery	2 tsp. dried tarragon
1 cup sliced radishes	1 *or* 2 cloves garlic, minced
1 cup sliced cucumber (seeded, unpeeled)	2 tsp. orange zest
$^1/_2$ cup minced fresh parsley	Freshly ground black pepper

In a large serving bowl, combine, beans, onions, celery, radishes, cucumber and parsley. In a smaller bowl, whisk remaining ingredients together. Pour dressing over beans and toss gently to coat thoroughly. Chill 2 to 3 hours before serving.

Serves 6 to 8

Per serving:	Calories	Fat (g)	Cholesterol (mg)	Fiber (g)	Sodium (mg)
	189	9	0	9	24

Marinated Lentil Salad

2 cups cooked lentils (see page 142)	4 to 6 green onions, thinly sliced
$^1/_2$ cup thinly sliced celery	$^1/_2$ cup Balsamic Vinaigrette (page 279)
$^1/_2$ cup diced red bell pepper	*or* low-calorie Italian Dressing
$^1/_2$ cup diced green pepper	Chopped fresh parsley
$^1/_2$ cup diced jicama	Cherry tomato halves

Combine all ingredients in a large serving bowl. Cover and marinate 2 to 3 hours in refrigerator before serving.

Serve garnished with chopped parsley and tomato halves.

Yield: 4 cups

Per serving:	Calories	Fat (g)	Cholesterol (mg)	Fiber (g)	Sodium (mg)
	67	2	0	2	132

Pickled Blackeye Peas

1 15-oz. can blackeye peas,
   rinsed and drained
1/4 cup olive oil
1/4 cup red wine *or* cider vinegar
1/4 cup chopped fresh parsley

1/2 onion, thinly sliced
1 clove garlic, minced
1 bay leaf
Pinch cloves

In a large bowl, combine all ingredients. Cover tightly and refrigerate at least 24 hours before serving. Remove garlic clove and bay leaf before serving.

Serve as a salad or side dish. Keeps well in refrigerator for up to two weeks.

Serves 4 to 5

Per serving:	Calories	Fat (g)	Cholesterol (mg)	Fiber (g)	Sodium (mg)
	156	11	0	4	9

Quick Chili

2 16-oz. cans whole tomatoes
2 cups salt-free beef broth, defatted
1 potato, diced (unpeeled)
1 16-oz. can salt-free corn
1 15-oz. can salt-free kidney beans
1 cup lentils (uncooked)

1 onion, chopped
2 carrots, sliced
2 cloves garlic, minced
1 tsp. to 2 Tbsp. chili powder (to taste)
1 tsp. dried basil

Combine all ingredients in a large saucepan. Simmer, covered, 30 to 60 minutes or until lentils are soft.

Serve over hot brown rice, if desired. Sprinkle lightly with grated low-fat cheddar cheese.

Serves 6 to 8

Per serving:	Calories	Fat (g)	Cholesterol (mg)	Fiber (g)	Sodium (mg)
	235	1	0	11	169

White Chili

1 Tbsp. olive oil
1/2 lb. turkey cutlets, cubed
1 onion, chopped
2 carrots, chopped
2 celery stalks, sliced
2 cloves garlic, minced
1 tsp. chili powder (more if desired)
1/4 to 1/2 tsp. cumin

1/2 tsp. dried oregano, crumbled
1/2 tsp. dried sage
2 10 1/2-oz. cans salt-free beef *or* chicken broth, defatted
1 14 1/2-oz. can whole tomatoes, chopped
1 4-oz. can diced green chiles
2 15-oz. cans Great Northern beans, undrained (freshly cooked beans may be substituted)

Heat olive oil in a large saucepan and saute turkey, stirring constantly, until it turns white. Remove to a plate. Add onion, carrots, celery and garlic. Saute over low heat for 5 to 6 minutes, stirring frequently. Add chili powder, cumin, oregano and sage; cook 3 minutes.

Add broth and bring to a boil scraping up browned bits from bottom of pan. Add tomatoes, green chiles and turkey. Reduce heat and simmer for 30 minutes. Add beans and simmer an additional 30 to 45 minutes or until turkey is tender.

Spoon into bowls and serve with warm corn tortillas.

Serves: 4 to 6

Per serving:	Calories	Fat (g)	Cholesterol (mg)	Fiber (g)	Sodium (mg)
	256	5	28	12	153

Quick Baked Beans

2 16-oz. cans vegetarian baked beans
1 onion, diced
2 apples (unpeeled), cored and diced
2 Tbsp. brown sugar
2 Tbsp. molasses

1/2 cup low-sodium barbecue sauce
1 to 2 tsp. liquid smoke
1 tsp. dry mustard
1/8 tsp. cinnamon
1/8 tsp. cloves

Combine beans with remaining ingredients and pour into a 2 quart casserole coated with cooking spray. Bake, covered, at 350° for 15 minutes, then remove lid and continue cooking an additional 15 to 20 minutes or until beans are bubbly. Serve hot or cold.

Serves 6 to 8

Per serving:	Calories	Fat (g)	Cholesterol (mg)	Fiber (g)	Sodium (mg)
	248	6	0	11	492

Denver Baked Beans

1 lb. small white beans
1 onion, chopped
1/3 cup brown sugar
2 Tbsp. molasses
2 Tbsp. pure maple syrup

1 to 2 Tbsp. liquid smoke
1 tsp. dry mustard
1/2 tsp. freshly ground black pepper
Pinch cloves

Prepare beans according to Quick Soak Method (page 132), then simmer until tender, 2 1/2 to 3 hours. Combine beans with remaining ingredients in a large oven-proof casserole coated with cooking spray. Cover and bake at 325° for 2 hours. Remove lid and bake an additional 30 minutes. Add water, orange or tomato juice as needed if beans seem dry.

Serves 4 to 6

Per serving:	Calories	Fat (g)	Cholesterol (mg)	Fiber (g)	Sodium (mg)
	325	1	0	20	38

Kidney Beans with Rice

2 16-oz. cans salt-free kidney beans
2 cups cooked brown rice
4 green onions, thinly sliced

2 Tbsp. low-sodium soy sauce
2 Tbsp. dry sherry (optional)

Combine all ingredients in a medium saucepan. Simmer 15 to 20 minutes or until flavors are blended.

Serves 6 to 8

Per serving:	Calories	Fat (g)	Cholesterol (mg)	Fiber (g)	Sodium (mg)
	165	1	0	10	292

Cuban Beans

8 oz. dry black beans
2 bay leaves
2 cloves garlic, minced
2 whole cloves
1 Tbsp. Worcestershire sauce
Dash nutmeg

Dash cayenne pepper
1 tsp. olive oil
1 onion, chopped
1 red bell pepper, seeded and chopped
2 Tbsp. dry sherry
$^1/_4$ tsp. dried oregano

Rinse beans well and soak in 4 cups water for 1 hour. Drain and place beans in a large pot. Add 4 cups fresh water, bay leaves, garlic, cloves, Worcestershire, nutmeg and cayenne. Simmer until tender, about 2 hours. Drain beans, remove bay leaves and reserve liquid.

Heat olive oil in a large skillet and saute onion and red pepper until soft. Add beans, sherry, oregano and about $^1/_4$ cup of cooking liquid. Simmer 10 to 15 minutes, adding cooking liquid as needed to prevent beans from drying out.

Serve as a side dish or over brown rice. Garnish with fresh lime wedges and squeeze lime juice over beans

Variation: Black Bean Soup — Do not drain beans. Saute onion and red pepper in olive oil and add to beans along with sherry and oregano. Puree beans if desired.

Serve with fresh lime wedges to squeeze into soup. Garnish with chopped cilantro if desired.

Serves 6 to 8

Per serving:	Calories	Fat (g)	Cholesterol (mg)	Fiber (g)	Sodium (mg)
	120	1	0	2	23

Black Beans and Brown Rice

1 Tbsp. olive oil
1/2 cup chopped onion
1/2 cup chopped red *or* green bell pepper
2 cloves garlic, minced
2 cups canned black beans
1 cup salt-free chicken *or* beef broth, defatted

3 Tbsp. strong decaffeinated coffee
2 cups cooked brown rice
2 tsp. Worcestershire sauce
Freshly ground black pepper
Chopped fresh cilantro

Heat oil in a large skillet. Add onion, bell pepper and garlic; saute until onion is soft. Stir in beans, broth and coffee; simmer until slightly thickened, 10 to 15 minutes. Add rice, Worcestershire and pepper to taste. Simmer 10 minutes to blend flavors.

Serve garnished with cilantro.

Serves 6 to 8

Per serving:	Calories	Fat (g)	Cholesterol (mg)	Fiber (g)	Sodium (mg)
	167	2	0	3	156

Pasta E Fagioli

1 lb. small Great Northern beans
1/4 cup olive oil
2 to 3 whole cloves garlic
2 bay leaves

1/2 tsp. Lite Salt™
1 lb. shell *or* spiral macaroni (eggless)
1 tsp. freshly ground black pepper (*or* cayenne)
Chopped fresh parsley

Prepare beans according to Quick Soak method (page 132). Add olive oil, garlic, bay leaves and Lite Salt™. Bring to a boil gradually, skimming foam as necessary. Simmer for 2 to 3 hours or until tender. Remove garlic cloves and bay leaves.

Cook pasta until barely tender, 5 to 6 minutes, omitting salt. Drain well, reserving 1 cup of pasta cooking liquid. Add pasta to the beans along with reserved liquid and pepper. Simmer until pasta is done, about 5 to 6 minutes.

Serve garnished with parsley.

Serves 8

Per serving:	Calories	Fat (g)	Cholesterol (mg)	Fiber (g)	Sodium (mg)
	438	9	0	15	77

Indian Spiced Garbanzos

Exotic seasonings enliven garbanzo beans

1 Tbsp. olive oil
1 onion, chopped
2 stalks celery, sliced
2 cloves garlic, minced
1 1/2 Tbsp. minced fresh ginger
2 tomatoes, cored and chopped
1 tsp. cumin
1 tsp. coriander

1/2 tsp. cayenne
1/2 tsp. turmeric
2 15-oz. cans garbanzo beans,
  rinsed and drained
3/4 cup salt-free chicken broth, defatted
Juice of 1 lime
1/4 cup chopped fresh cilantro

Heat oil in a large skillet and saute onion, celery, garlic and ginger until onion is lightly browned. Add tomatoes and simmer until most of liquid evaporates. Add spices and simmer 5 minutes. Stir in garbanzos and chicken broth.

Cover and simmer, stirring occasionally, until thickened, about 15 to 20 minutes. Stir in lime juice. Spoon garbanzos into a serving bowl and sprinkle with cilantro. Serve with lime wedges.

Serves 4 to 6

Per serving:	Calories	Fat (g)	Cholesterol (mg)	Fiber (g)	Sodium (mg)
	279	6	0	5	26

Microwave Lentils

1/4 cup lentils
1 cup water

1/2 tsp. chicken *or* beef bouillon granules
1/2 tsp. minced dried onion

Rinse lentils and drain. Place in a 1 quart bowl and add remaining ingredients. Cook, uncovered, at full power until mixture boils, about 3 to 4 minutes. Cover with plastic wrap and cook at half power until lentils are tender to the bite, 12 to 15 minutes longer.

Yield: 3/4 cup

Per serving:	Calories	Fat (g)	Cholesterol (mg)	Fiber (g)	Sodium (mg)
	87	0	0	1	243

Lentil Curry

Combining lentils and rice makes a complete protein — that is,
comparable to animal protein

2 tsp. olive oil
1 onion, chopped
2 cloves garlic, minced
4 cups salt-free chicken broth, defatted
1 cup lentils, rinsed and drained
2 carrots, chopped
3 to 4 stalks celery (with leaves), sliced

1 unpeeled green apple, cored and chopped
1 tsp. curry powder
1/2 tsp. Lite Salt™
1/2 tsp. celery seed
1/8 tsp. anise seed, crushed
Cooked brown rice

Heat olive oil in a large pot and saute onion and garlic until tender. Add remaining ingredients (except cooked rice) and simmer about 60 minutes or until lentils are tender.

Serve over hot brown rice.

Serves 4 to 6

Per serving:	Calories	Fat (g)	Cholesterol (mg)	Fiber (g)	Sodium (mg)
	172	2	0	3	121

Lentils with Spinach

1 bunch fresh spinach
2 tsp. olive oil
1 clove garlic, minced
1 1/2 cups cooked lentils (see page 142)
1/4 cup chopped fresh parsley

1/4 tsp. cumin
1/4 tsp. ground coriander
1/4 tsp. Lite Salt™
Freshly ground black pepper

Wash spinach thoroughly and remove stems; chop. Heat olive oil in a large skillet. Add chopped spinach and garlic; stir-fry for 2 to 3 minutes or until spinach is wilted. Add remaining ingredients and continue to stir-fry until heated through. Serve immediately.

Serves 4 to 6

Per serving:	Calories	Fat (g)	Cholesterol (mg)	Fiber (g)	Sodium (mg)
	61	2	0	2	59

Bean Enchiladas

1 15-oz. can salt-free pinto beans,
drained and mashed
1/2 cup 1% cottage cheese
1 cup low-fat Cheddar cheese (divided)
1/2 cup chopped onion
1/4 cup sliced black olives
(rinsed and drained before slicing)
1 15-oz. can salt-free tomato sauce
1 4-oz. can diced green chiles

1 jalapeño chili, seeded and diced (optional)
1 tsp. garlic powder
1/2 tsp. Lite Salt™
12 corn tortillas
1 tsp. chili powder
1/2 tsp. oregano
Dash hot pepper sauce (to taste)
Chopped fresh cilantro
Sliced green onion

Combine mashed beans, cottage cheese, 1/2 cup cheddar cheese, onion, olives, 3/4 cup tomato sauce, green chiles, garlic powder and Lite Salt™. Spoon 1/3 cup bean mixture along center of each tortilla. Roll up and place seam side down into a 9" x 13" baking dish coated with cooking spray.

Combine remaining tomato sauce, chili powder, oregano and hot pepper sauce. Pour sauce over enchiladas and sprinkle with remaining cheese. Bake at 350° for 15 to 20 minutes or until heated through and cheese is melted.

Serve garnished with cilantro, green onion and more black olive slices, if desired.

Serves 4 to 6

Per serving:	Calories	Fat (g)	Cholesterol (mg)	Fiber (g)	Sodium (mg)
	361	6	12	10	409

Removing skin from poultry before cooking minimizes fat — be sure to reduce cooking time slightly to prevent overcooking. Remember: chicken and turkey are lower in fat than red meat, but not lower in cholesterol. Serving three to four ounces per person will keep cholesterol within acceptable limits.

Chicken

Arroz con Pollo 147
Burritos 148
Buttermilk Herb 149
Cinnamon Scented 150
Cranberry Glazed 147
Curried Orange 152
Easy Orange Glazed 155
Fajitas 153
Five Spice 154
Grand Marnier 154
Grilled with Mango Salsa 156
Herbed Chicken Grill 151
Herbed Chicken in Wine 157
Lemony Chicken 151
Mexican 160
in Orange Sauce 159
Pesto Primavera 158
Pineapple 159
Posole 150
Quick Chick 169
Sesame Cashew 161
   Apricot Sweet and Sour Sauce 162
Sesame Honey 158
Spice Islands 162
Spring Roll Ups 163
Stir-Fried with Cashews 164
Stuffed Chicken Marinara 157
Tandoori Chicken 187
with Fresh Tomatoes 156

Turkey

Cutlets Dijon 166
Enchiladas 166
Hawaiian 167
Indienne 168
Italian Turkey Burgers 165
Marinara Sauce 175
Marsala 169
Orange Glazed 169
Oriental Turkey Stir Fry 172
Parmesan 170
Red, White and Green Chili 171
Sausage Patties 176
Scallopini 173
Steaks 167
Van Gogh Turkey-Lentil Salad 174
with Zesty Currant Sauce 165

Arroz con Pollo

Chicken with a Mexican flair

1 tsp. olive oil
1 onion, chopped
1 clove garlic, minced
2 cups raw brown rice
2 tomatoes, cored and diced
1 4-oz. can chopped green chiles

4 cups salt-free chicken broth, defatted
1/2 tsp. Lite Salt™
1/2 tsp. dried oregano
1/4 tsp. cumin
3 skinless, boneless chicken breasts
1/4 cup chopped fresh cilantro (optional)

Heat oil in a large pan. Saute onion, garlic and rice until onion is soft, about 5 minutes. Add diced tomato, chiles, broth, Lite Salt, oregano and cumin. Bring to a boil. Place chicken on top of rice then cover and simmer 10 to 15 minutes or until chicken is done. Remove chicken; replace lid and continue cooking until rice is done, 30 to 40 minutes longer.

Cool chicken, then shred. Stir shredded chicken and cilantro into cooked rice.

Serves 6

Per serving:	Calories	Fat (g)	Cholesterol (mg)	Fiber (g)	Sodium (mg)
	396	6	50	5	148

Cranberry Glazed Chicken

Try this glaze with roast turkey

1 lb. cranberries, rinsed
1/2 cup frozen apple juice concentrate,
   thawed
1/2 cup low-sugar strawberry preserves

1/2 cup low-sugar orange marmalade
1 Tbsp. Dijon mustard
4 chicken breasts, skinned and
   trimmed of excess fat

Combine cranberries and apple juice concentrate in a large saucepan. Add water just to cover berries. Bring to a boil, stirring often, and cook until cranberries begin to pop open. Add preserves, marmalade and mustard. Cook an additional 5 minutes, stirring often. Cool, then process in food processor until pureed but some whole berries remain.

Place chicken breasts in a shallow baking dish coated with cooking spray. Pour cranberry mixture over. Bake, uncovered, at 325° for 30 to 40 minutes or until chicken is done.

Serves 4

Per serving:	Calories	Fat (g)	Cholesterol (mg)	Fiber (g)	Sodium (mg)
	528	5	101	6	158

Chicken Burritos

Filling:
1 Tbsp. olive oil
2 onions, chopped
3 cloves garlic, minced
2 16-oz. cans salt-free tomatoes,
  coarsely chopped
1 4-oz. can green chiles
1 to 3 tsp. chili powder (to taste)
1/2 tsp. cumin
1/2 tsp. dried oregano

1/4 tsp. Lite Salt™
2 cups chopped cooked chicken
  (white meat preferred)
8 flour tortillas (made with soy oil)
Shredded romaine lettuce
Diced tomatoes
Chopped red onion
Mexican Salsa (page 10)

Heat the oil in a large skillet. Saute onions and garlic until onions are soft. Add tomatoes, green chiles, chili powder, cumin, oregano and Lite Salt. Simmer, stirring often, until most of liquid evaporates. Add chicken, mix well and transfer to a serving bowl.

Wrap tortillas in foil and warm in oven at 400° for 5 to 7 minutes. Place about 1/3 cup chicken mixture on a tortilla and roll up. Place on a plate and garnish with remaining ingredients.

Serves 8

Per serving:	Calories	Fat (g)	Cholesterol (mg)	Fiber (g)	Sodium (mg)
	226	4	25	3	336

Buttermilk Herb Chicken

Serve this tender, moist chicken with summer sweet corn and fresh tomatoes

2 cups low-fat buttermilk
1 clove garlic, minced
1/2 tsp. dried basil
1/2 tsp. celery seed
1/4 tsp. onion powder
1/4 tsp. dried oregano
1/4 tsp. white pepper

1 bay leaf
4 chicken breasts,
   skinned and excess fat removed
1/2 cup dry bread crumbs
1/4 cup Parmesan cheese
1/2 tsp. liquid margarine

Combine buttermilk with next 7 ingredients in a 9" x 13" baking dish. Add chicken breasts and turn to coat with marinade. Cover and refrigerate overnight. Drain (discard marinade).

Combine bread crumbs and Parmesan cheese. Dredge chicken in bread crumb mixture coating well all over. Place in a 9" x 13" baking dish coated with cooking spray. Drizzle with margarine. Bake at 350° for 35 to 40 minutes or until chicken is no longer pink when cut in thickest part.

Serves 4

Per serving:	Calories	Fat (g)	Cholesterol (mg)	Fiber (g)	Sodium (mg)
	352	10	109	0	415

Chicken Posole

1 tsp. olive oil
1 onion, chopped
2 cloves garlic, minced
2 tsp. dried oregano
1/2 tsp. cumin
8 cups salt-free chicken broth, defatted
3 skinless, boneless chicken breasts
1 4-oz. can diced green chiles

1 jalapeño chile, seeded and diced
(optional)
1 15-oz. can hominy, undrained
1 15-oz. can salt-free kidney beans,
undrained
1 13-oz. can green tomatillos, chopped
1/2 cup ripe olives, sliced
(rinse and drain before slicing)

Heat olive oil in a large pot and saute onion, garlic, oregano and cumin until onion is soft. Add remaining ingredients, except olives and simmer until chicken is done, about 20 minutes. Remove chicken; let cool, then cut into bite-size pieces. Return to broth; add olives. Bring to a boil to reheat before serving

Serves 6

Per serving:	Calories	Fat (g)	Cholesterol (mg)	Fiber (g)	Sodium (mg)
	286	7	50	4	265

Cinnamon Scented Chicken

Tender chicken bathed in fragrant spices and honey

Marinade:
1/2 cup Marsala *or* dry sherry
1/4 cup honey
1/4 cup raisins *or* currants
2 Tbsp. fresh lemon *or* lime juice
2 cloves garlic, minced

2 tsp. cinnamon
1/2 tsp. cardamom
1/4 tsp. cloves

4 to 6 skinless, boneless chicken breasts

Combine marinade ingredients (easier if honey is warmed) and mix well. Place chicken in a shallow baking dish. Pour marinade over chicken; cover and marinate in the refrigerator 4 to 6 hours or overnight.

Drain chicken well; broil or grill until done, about 4 to 5 minutes per side. Baste occasionally with marinade.

Serves 4 to 6

Per serving:	Calories	Fat (g)	Cholesterol (mg)	Fiber (g)	Sodium (mg)
	291	5	101	0	1005

Lemony Chicken

Fresh herbs and lemon give chicken a gourmet flair

4 skinless, boneless chicken breasts
1/2 cup fresh lemon juice
2 Tbsp. white wine vinegar
1/2 cup sliced fresh lemon peel
6 to 8 green onions, thinly sliced

1 Tbsp. chopped fresh oregano *or*
1 tsp. dried
1/4 tsp. Lite Salt™
1/2 tsp. paprika
1/2 tsp. lemon pepper

Place chicken in a 9" x 13" glass baking dish. Combine lemon juice, vinegar, lemon peel, green onions and oregano. Pour over chicken; turn to coat with marinade. Cover and refrigerate several hours or overnight. Turn occasionally.

Sprinkle chicken with salt, paprika and lemon pepper. Cover and bake at 325° for 15 minutes. Uncover and bake an additional 10 to 15 minutes or until done.

Serves 4

Per serving:	Calories	Fat (g)	Cholesterol (mg)	Fiber (g)	Sodium (mg)
	234	5	101	1	159

Herbed Chicken Grill

Aromatic fresh herbs and lime juice flavor chicken on the grill

4 skinless, boneless chicken breasts
1 Tbsp. olive oil
Juice of one lime
1 Tbsp. chopped fresh basil

1 Tbsp. chopped fresh parsley
1 Tbsp. chopped fresh oregano
1 clove garlic, minced

Pound chicken breasts 1/4" thick. Combine remaining ingredients. Place chicken breasts and marinade into a zip-lock plastic bag and seal tightly. Marinate 3 to 4 hours or overnight. Broil or grill, brushing with marinade while cooking. Cook just until chicken is no longer pink in the center.

Serve with Grilled Peppers (see page 226)

Serves 4

Per serving:	Calories	Fat (g)	Cholesterol (mg)	Fiber (g)	Sodium (mg)
	233	7	101	0	98

Curried Orange Chicken

A great dinner party or buffet dish. Serve with brown
and wild rice pilaf and a bright green vegetable

**¹/₂ cup dry-roasted, unsalted peanuts
  or cashews, finely chopped
1-15 oz. jar low-sugar orange marmalade
2 Tbsp. olive oil
¹/₂ cup fresh orange juice *or*
  2 Tbsp. frozen orange juice concentrate
  plus 4 Tbsp. Marsala *or* dry sherry
¹/₄ cup Dijon mustard**

**2 tsp. dried tarragon
1 clove garlic, minced
1 tsp. curry powder
¹/₂ tsp. cardamom
1 lb. skinless, boneless chicken breasts *or*
  turkey breast slices
4-6 green onions, thinly sliced
¹/₂ cup golden raisins**

In a large bowl, combine nuts, marmalade, oil, juice, mustard, tarragon, garlic, curry and
cardamom. Add chicken pieces and coat well. Place in a 9" x 13" baking dish coated with
cooking spray. Cover and refrigerate, turning occasionally, for 4 to 6 hours.

Bake at 350°, in the marinade, for 30 to 40 minutes or until chicken is done. (If using turkey
slices, decrease cooking time to 20 to 30 minutes.)

Serve garnished with green onions and raisins.

Serves 4 to 6

Per serving:	Calories	Fat (g)	Cholesterol (mg)	Fiber (g)	Sodium (mg)
	455	13	101	4	241

Chicken Fajitas

This zesty marinade can be used for chicken, lean beef or seafood
(try a combination of shrimp and scallops)

4 tsp. lime juice
1/4 cup tequila (optional)
1/4 cup olive oil
1/4 cup chopped fresh cilantro
2 Tbsp. low-sodium soy sauce
1 Tbsp. Worcestershire sauce
2 cloves garlic, minced

1/2 tsp. dried oregano
1/2 tsp. cumin
1 lb. skinless, boneless chicken breasts
1 green pepper, cored and seeded
1 red bell pepper, cored and seeded
1 *or* 2 anaheim chiles, cored and seeded
1 red onion, peeled

In a small bowl, combine lime juice, tequila, oil, cilantro, soy, Worcestershire, garlic, oregano and cumin. Set aside.

Slice chicken into bite-size strips. Pour marinade over chicken strips and marinate, covered, overnight. Drain well, reserving marinade.

Slice peppers, chiles and onion into thin strips. Brush a non-stick pan with 1 to 2 Tbsp. of the marinade. Add vegetables and cook over medium heat until tender-crisp, about 5 to 7 minutes. Remove to platter and keep warm. Again brush skillet (or flat grill) with marinade and add chicken strips. Stir-fry over medium heat for 5 to 7 minutes or until done.

Serve fajitas with warm corn tortillas, vegetarian refried beans, chopped tomatoes, chopped cilantro, salsa and Mary's Guacamole (page 6).

Variation: Marinate chicken breasts, grill then slice before serving

Serves 4

Per serving:	Calories	Fat (g)	Cholesterol (mg)	Fiber (g)	Sodium (mg)
	267	6	101	1	135

Chicken Grand Marnier

Elegant chicken with a sunny orange flavor. Serve with wild rice and a Caesar Salad (page 51)

4 skinless, boneless chicken breasts
2 egg whites
1/2 cup dry breadcrumbs
1 Tbsp. olive oil
1/4 cup Grand Marnier
   ***or* fresh orange juice**

1/4 cup low-sugar orange marmalade
1 tsp. fresh lemon juice
1 tsp. lemon zest
1 tsp. Dijon mustard
1/4 tsp. Worcestershire sauce
1/2 clove garlic, minced

Pound chicken breasts until 1/4" thick. Dip into egg white then coat with breadcrumbs. Heat olive oil in a large non-stick skillet and saute chicken breasts until browned, about 1 1/2 minutes per side. Remove to a plate and keep warm.

Add Grand Marnier to skillet. Bring to a boil then blend in remaining ingredients. Reduce heat to low. Return chicken to skillet. Cover and simmer 10 minutes. Baste then continue cooking until chicken is done. Watch carefully to avoid burning glaze.

Serves: 4

Per serving:	Calories	Fat (g)	Cholesterol (mg)	Fiber (g)	Sodium (mg)
	359	9	101	0	224

Five Spice Chicken

1/4 cup plus 2 Tbsp. low-sodium soy sauce
1/4 cup dry sherry *or* saké
1 clove garlic, minced
1 Tbsp. minced fresh ginger
2 tsp. lemon *or* lime zest

1/4 cup plus 1 Tbsp. brown sugar
1 tsp. five spice powder
2 cups salt-free chicken broth, defatted
4 to 6 skinless, boneless chicken breasts

In a large skillet, combine 1/4 cup soy sauce, sherry, garlic, ginger, zest, 1/4 cup brown sugar and five spice powder. Stir in 1 cup of broth until well blended. Arrange chicken in a single layer and simmer, covered, for 20 to 30 minutes. Add water if necessary.

Turn chicken. Add remaining 1 cup broth, 2 Tbsp. soy sauce and 1 Tbsp. sugar. Continue to simmer for 15 to 20 more minutes or until chicken is done. Add water as necessary to thin sauce.

Serve with brown rice and Stir-Fried Snowpeas (page 230).

Serves 4 to 6

Per serving:	Calories	Fat (g)	Cholesterol (mg)	Fiber (g)	Sodium (mg)
	294	6	101	0	704

Easy Orange Glazed Chicken

4 skinless, boneless chicken breasts
1 cup fresh orange juice
2 Tbsp. brown sugar
3 Tbsp. low-sodium soy sauce
3 cloves garlic, minced

1 Tbsp. minced fresh ginger
1 Tbsp. cornstarch dissolved in
 1 Tbsp. water
2 tsp. orange zest

Place chicken breasts in an 8" square baking dish coated with cooking spray. In a small bowl, combine juice, sugar, soy sauce, garlic and ginger. Pour over chicken, turning to coat evenly. Bake at 325° for 15 minutes.

Drain pan juices into a saucepan. Stir in cornstarch; bring to a boil over high heat stirring constantly. Cook and stir until thickened. Add zest. Pour sauce over chicken in baking pan. Return to oven and bake an additional 5 to 10 minutes or until chicken is done.

Serve over brown and/or wild rice.

Variation: For a stronger orange flavor, replace orange juice with 1/2 cup frozen orange juice concentrate mixed with 1/2 cup water

Serves: 4

Per serving:	Calories	Fat (g)	Cholesterol (mg)	Fiber (g)	Sodium (mg)
	296	5	101	0	552

Grilled Chicken with Mango Salsa

This tangy salsa adds a peppery bite to grilled chicken

Salsa:

2 mangos, peeled, pitted and diced
2 papayas, peeled, pitted and diced
Juice of 2 fresh limes
1 Tbsp. lime zest
1 jalapeño chili, seeded and minced

1/2 tsp. dried red pepper flakes
1/4 cup chopped fresh cilantro

4 skinless boneless chicken breasts
Olive oil

Combine salsa ingredients and refrigerate until chilled.

Using a heavy knife or mallet, pound chicken breasts until 1/2" thick. Brush with olive oil. Grill 2 to 3 minutes per side or until no longer pink in center.

Serve with salsa. Garnish with cilantro sprigs.

Serves 4

Per serving:	Calories	Fat (g)	Cholesterol (mg)	Fiber (g)	Sodium (mg)
	366	9	101	3	141

Chicken with Fresh Tomatoes

4 chicken breast halves,
  skin and excess fat removed
1 Tbsp. olive oil
Freshly ground black pepper
2 Tbsp. minced shallots

1/2 cup Marsala wine
1/2 cup salt-free chicken broth, defatted
2 cups chopped fresh tomatoes
1/2 cup chopped fresh parsley

Heat oil in a large skillet. Add chicken and brown on both sides. Season to taste with pepper. Remove from skillet.

Add shallots, wine, broth and tomatoes. Simmer until juices are reduced, about 10 minutes. Return chicken to skillet, spoon juices over, cover and simmer about 30 minutes or until chicken is done. Serve garnished with parsley.

Serves 4

Per serving:	Calories	Fat (g)	Cholesterol (mg)	Fiber (g)	Sodium (mg)
	314	9	101	1	107

Herbed Chicken in Wine

4 chicken breasts
1/2 tsp. each dried basil, sage and savory
1/4 tsp. dried thyme
1/4 tsp. white pepper
1/2 cup dry white wine
2 Tbsp. unbleached flour
2 Tbsp. water

1 tsp. olive oil
2 carrots, julienne
1 leek, sliced
2 cups sliced mushrooms
1/4 tsp. Lite Salt™
Freshly ground black pepper

Remove skin and excess fat from chicken breasts. Place in a 8" square baking dish coated with cooking spray. Sprinkle with herbs and pour in wine. Cover and bake at 350° for 20 to 30 minutes.

Blend flour and water. Set aside

Heat olive oil in a skillet and saute vegetables over low heat, covered, for 5 to 10 minutes or until tender. Blend pan juices from chicken into flour mixture then pour into skillet. Add salt and pepper to taste. Cook and stir over medium heat until thickened. Serve sauce over chicken breasts.

Serves 4

Per serving:	Calories	Fat (g)	Cholesterol (mg)	Fiber (g)	Sodium (mg)
	291	6	101	3	183

Stuffed Chicken Marinara

3/4 lb. broccoli, chopped
1 tsp. olive oil
1 onion, chopped

3/4 cup grated part-skim mozzarella cheese
6 skinless, boneless chicken breasts
1 1/2 cups Quick Tomato Sauce (page 294)

Steam broccoli until tender-crisp. Set aside. Heat olive oil in a medium skillet and saute onion until soft, about 5 minutes. Add broccoli and 1/2 cup grated cheese; mix well and cool.

Pound chicken breasts until about 1/4" thick. Divide broccoli mixture evenly among chicken breasts. Roll chicken around filling; secure with a toothpick if necessary. Place seam side down in a baking dish coated with cooking spray. Pour sauce over chicken rolls and sprinkle with remaining cheese. Bake at 350° for 20 to 30 minutes or until chicken is done.

Serves 6

Per serving:	Calories	Fat (g)	Cholesterol (mg)	Fiber (g)	Sodium (mg)
	309	9	110	4	277

Chicken Pesto Primavera

¹/2 oz. sun dried tomatoes
Boiling water
1 Tbsp. olive oil
1 to 2 cloves garlic, minced
3 skinless, boneless chicken breasts,
   thinly sliced
1 green *or* red bell pepper, julienne

1 onion, sliced
2 carrots, julienne
2 zucchini, julienne
¹/4 cup Pesto (page 293)
1 lb. eggless fettucini *or* cappelini
Crushed red pepper (optional)

Place tomatoes in a small bowl and cover with boiling water. Let stand for one hour or until softened. Remove stems and slice thinly. Set aside.

Heat olive oil with garlic in a large skillet. Add chicken and vegetables; saute until chicken is done, about 5 to 10 minutes. Add sun-dried tomato and pesto. Cook and stir until chicken and vegetables are coated with pesto. Keep warm.

Cook pasta according to package directions, omitting salt. Drain well and place on a serving platter. Top with chicken mixture. Garnish with crushed red pepper.

Serves 4

Per serving:	Calories	Fat (g)	Cholesterol (mg)	Fiber (g)	Sodium (mg)
	528	13	76	1	180

Sesame-Honey Chicken

2 Tbsp. sesame seeds
3 Tbsp. honey
¹/4 cup Marsala *or* dry sherry
¹/4 cup Dijon mustard

1 Tbsp. lemon *or* orange zest
1 Tbsp. fresh lemon juice
4 skinless, boneless chicken breasts

Toast sesame seeds at 325° for 5 to 10 minutes or until lightly browned. Pour into a small bowl then add honey, Marsala, mustard, zest and lemon juice. Place chicken in a shallow ovenproof baking dish and pour honey mixture over. Turn to coat evenly with sauce.

Bake at 325° for 15 to 20 minutes or until chicken is no longer pink in the thickest part. Baste occasionally.

Serves 4

Per serving:	Calories	Fat (g)	Cholesterol (mg)	Fiber (g)	Sodium (mg)
	325	8	101	0	294

Chicken in Orange Sauce

1/4 cup sliced almonds
6 skinless, boneless chicken breasts
2 Tbsp. liquid margarine
4 Tbsp. unbleached flour
1/2 tsp. cinnamon

1/8 tsp. ginger
2 cups orange juice
1/2 cup golden raisins
11/2 cups orange sections
Orange slices

Toast almonds at 325° for 10 to 12 minutes or until golden brown. Set aside.

In a large skillet, brown chicken breasts lightly in margarine; remove and set aside. Mix flour, cinnamon and ginger into pan drippings. Cook and stir one minute. Gradually blend in orange juice. Cook, stirring constantly, until mixture thickens. Return chicken to skillet along with almonds and raisins.

Cover and simmer for 20 minutes or until chicken is no longer pink. Add orange sections and cook just until warmed.

Serve garnished with orange slices.

Serves 4 to 6

Per serving:	Calories	Fat (g)	Cholesterol (mg)	Fiber (g)	Sodium (mg)
	400	12	101	2	162

Pineapple Chicken

1 cup juice-packed pineapple, drained
1/4 cup low-sodium soy sauce
3 Tbsp. wine vinegar
1 tsp. dry mustard
1 Tbsp. minced fresh ginger

4 chicken breasts, skin and fat removed
2 cups sliced fresh mushrooms
1 green pepper, seeded and cut into 1" chunks
1 red bell pepper, seeded and cut into 1" chunks
4 green onions, sliced into 1" pieces

Combine pineapple, soy sauce, vinegar, mustard and ginger. Arrange chicken breasts and vegetables in a baking dish coated with cooking spray. Pour sauce over. Cover with foil and bake at 325° for 30 to 40 minutes or until chicken is done.

Serves 4

Per serving:	Calories	Fat (g)	Cholesterol (mg)	Fiber (g)	Sodium (mg)
	293	6	101	2	123

Mexican Chicken

This chunky sauce makes chicken a fiesta

4 chicken breasts,
  skin and excess fat removed
1¹/2 cups Mexican Salsa (page 10)
1 15-oz. can salt-free tomato sauce
¹/2 cup chopped red onion

2 Tbsp. chopped fresh cilantro (optional)
1 clove garlic, minced
1 tsp. cumin
1 tsp. dried oregano
8 corn tortillas

Broil chicken until lightly browned, about 4 to 5 minutes per side. Transfer to a shallow baking dish coated with cooking spray.

Combine remaining ingredients (except tortillas) and pour over chicken. Cover tightly with foil and bake at 350° for 20 to 25 minutes. Uncover and continue baking until chicken is done, about 10 to 15 minutes longer. Meanwhile, wrap tortillas in foil and heat while chicken finishes cooking.

To eat: let each person remove chicken from bone with a fork, then add sauce and wrap in a tortilla

Serves 4

Per serving:	Calories	Fat (g)	Cholesterol (mg)	Fiber (g)	Sodium (mg)
	440	7	101	5	200

Quick Chick

¹/2 cup olive oil
¹/3 cup dry sherry
1 Tbsp. fresh lemon juice
1 tsp. lemon zest
¹/3 cup minced onion

1 clove garlic, minced
1 tsp. dried sage
Freshly ground black pepper (to taste)
4 skinless, boneless chicken breasts *or*
  4 6-oz. lean steaks

In a small bowl, whisk together oil, sherry, lemon juice, zest, onion, garlic, sage and pepper. Place chicken in a shallow glass dish and pour marinade over. Cover and marinate, refrigerated, for 2 to 4 hours.

Broil or grill until chicken is done, basting with marinade.

Serves 4

Per serving:	Calories	Fat (g)	Cholesterol (mg)	Fiber (g)	Sodium (mg)
	252	9	101	0	98

Sesame Cashew Chicken

The tangy sauce and crunchy coating makes ordinary chicken extraordinary!

Marinade:
1 1" cube fresh ginger, peeled
1 clove garlic
2 tsp. lemon zest
2 egg whites
1/4 cup dry sherry
2 Tbsp. fresh lemon juice
1 Tbsp. low-sodium soy sauce

4 to 6 skinless, boneless chicken breasts
1/2 cup dry roasted cashews*
1/2 cup sesame seeds
1/2 cup dry bread crumbs

Prepare marinade: With food processor motor running, drop ginger and garlic through feed tube and mince. Add remaining marinade ingredients and process 10 seconds or until well blended. Set aside.

With the back of a heavy knife, pound chicken breasts until about 1/2" thick. Place in a 9" x 13" pan and pour marinade over chicken. Turn to coat evenly. Cover and refrigerate overnight. Drain (discard marinade).

Chop cashews finely in food processor. Combine with sesame seeds and bread crumbs then place in a pie pan or other shallow dish. Dip chicken in cashew mixture, then place on a non-stick baking sheet. Bake at 400° for 8 to 10 minutes or until lightly browned and chicken is no longer pink in thickest part.

Serve with Apricot Sweet and Sour Sauce (page 162)

Variation: Cut chicken into strips. Proceed with recipe reducing baking time to 4 to 5 minutes. Serve as an appetizer

*If nuts are salted, rinse to remove salt. Spread on a baking sheet and toast at 325° for 5 to 10 minutes to dry and crisp.

Serves 4 to 6

Per serving:	Calories	Fat (g)	Cholesterol (mg)	Fiber (g)	Sodium (mg)
	358	13	101	2	289

Apricot Sweet and Sour Sauce

1 8-oz. jar sugar-free apricot conserves
1/4 cup red wine vinegar
3 Tbsp. catsup
1 Tbsp. sherry vinegar (optional)

1 Tbsp. low-sodium soy sauce
1 Tbsp. horseradish *or* Dijon mustard
1/2 clove garlic, minced

Combine all ingredients in a small bowl and mix well. Serve at room temperature.

Yield: about 1 1/2 cups

Per serving:	Calories	Fat (g)	Cholesterol (mg)	Fiber (g)	Sodium (mg)
	45	0	0	0	124

Spice Islands Chicken

This flavorful marinade uses a unique combination of spices.
Serve with brown rice and Grilled Onion Salad (page 57)

1 cup unsweetened pineapple juice
2 cloves garlic, minced
3 Tbsp. brown sugar *or* honey
2 Tbsp. cider *or* red wine vinegar
2 tsp. turmeric
1 tsp. coriander

1 tsp. lemon *or* lime zest
1/2 tsp. cardamom
1/4 to 1/2 tsp. cumin
1/4 tsp. white pepper
2 lbs. chicken breasts, skin and fat removed

Combine all ingredients except chicken and mix well. Pour into a plastic zip-top bag. Add chicken pieces and seal bag. Marinate in refrigerator overnight.

Drain well. Broil or grill about 10 to 15 minutes per side or until chicken is no longer pink in center.

Variation: Substitute skinless boneless chicken breasts; marinate 2 to 3 hours. Remove and drain well. In a large skillet, heat 1/2 Tbsp. olive oil. Saute 1 sliced onion and 2 unpeeled green apples, thinly sliced, until soft. Remove from pan; add chicken and saute 3 to 4 minutes per side or until done. Squeeze lime juice over chicken before serving.

Serves 6 to 8

Per serving:	Calories	Fat (g)	Cholesterol (mg)	Fiber (g)	Sodium (mg)
	254	5	101	0	100

Spring Roll Ups

4 skinless, boneless chicken breasts	1/4 tsp. paprika
1/2 lb. fresh asparagus, trimmed	1/8 tsp. white pepper
1 Tbsp. Dijon mustard *or* Pesto (page 293)	2 tomatoes, cored and sliced
2 Tbsp. unbleached flour	1 red onion, thinly sliced
1/2 tsp. dried thyme, divided	1/4 cup low-sodium chicken broth, defatted
1/4 tsp. garlic powder	1/4 cup dry white wine (optional)

Pound chicken breasts 1/2" thick. Spread with mustard or Pesto. Place 2 or 3 asparagus spears on each chicken breast then roll up and secure with tooth picks. Combine flour with 1/4 tsp. thyme, garlic powder, paprika and pepper. Roll chicken breasts in flour mixture.

Set aside 4 tomato slices. Place remaining tomato and onion slices in a 7" x 11" baking dish coated with cooking spray. Arrange chicken rolls on top, then place reserved tomato slices on top of chicken. Combine chicken broth, wine and remaining 1/4 tsp. thyme. Pour over chicken.

Cover loosely with foil. Bake at 350° for 20 minutes, basting occasionally. Uncover and bake 10 to 15 minutes longer or until chicken is done and vegetables are tender. Drain pan juices into a small saucepan. Boil until reduced by one half. Pour over chicken and serve.

Serves 4

Per serving:	Calories	Fat (g)	Cholesterol (mg)	Fiber (g)	Sodium (mg)
	296	6	101	2	155

Stir-Fried Chicken with Cashews

3 Tbsp. Marsala, cream sherry *or* sake
4 tsp. cornstarch
1 Tbsp. low-sodium soy sauce
1/4 tsp. dried red pepper flakes
2 skinless, boneless chicken breasts,
    cubed
1/2 cup salt-free chicken broth,
    defatted

1 Tbsp. canola *or* safflower oil
1 clove garlic, minced
4 green onions, cut into 1" pieces
3 cups shredded Napa (Chinese) cabbage
1 8-oz. can water chestnuts, sliced
1 Tbsp. oyster sauce (optional)*
1/4 cup dry-roasted, unsalted cashews

In a small bowl, combine Marsala, 2 tsp. cornstarch, 1 tsp. soy sauce and pepper flakes. Add chicken cubes and stir to coat evenly. Set aside to marinate for 15 to 20 minutes. In another small bowl, blend chicken broth into remaining 2 tsp. of cornstarch; stir in remaining 2 tsp. soy sauce.

Heat oil in a wok. Add garlic and green onion; stir-fry 1 minute. Add chicken mixture and stir-fry until chicken loses its pink color, 1 to 2 minutes. Add cabbage and water chestnuts; stir-fry 2 to 3 minutes. Stir broth mixture and add to wok. Stir until sauce boils and thickens, 1 to 2 minutes. Mix in oyster sauce and cashews. Serve with steamed Chinese rice.

* Available in the specialty section in grocery stores.

Serves 4

Per serving:	Calories	Fat (g)	Cholesterol (mg)	Fiber (g)	Sodium (mg)
	315	13	50	4	270

Italian Turkey Burgers

1 lb. ground turkey
1 to 2 cloves garlic, minced
1 tsp. fennel seeds

1/2 tsp. crushed red pepper flakes
1/4 tsp. dried thyme, crushed
1 cup Quick Tomato Sauce (page 294),
  warmed

Combine ground turkey, garlic, fennel, red pepper and thyme. Form mixture into 4 patties and broil or cook in a non-stick skillet coated with cooking spray until done, turning once.

Serve patties topped with Quick Tomato Sauce.

Serves 4

Per serving:	Calories	Fat (g)	Cholesterol (mg)	Fiber (g)	Sodium (mg)
	162	4	74	2	175

Turkey with Zesty Currant Sauce

1 8-oz. turkey tenderloin
1/4 cup plus 1 to 2 Tbsp. fresh
  orange juice
1 tsp. cornstarch

2 Tbsp. low-sugar currant jelly
1/2 tsp. orange zest
1/2 tsp. lemon zest

Place turkey on a broiler pan coated with cooking spray. Brush with 1 to 2 Tbsp. orange juice. Broil 6 to 8 minutes per side or until done; baste occasionally with orange juice. Keep warm.

Blend 2 Tbsp. orange juice into cornstarch. Set aside.

Combine jelly with remaining 2 Tbsp. juice. Cook over low heat until jelly melts, stirring occasionally. Stir in cornstarch mixture and zest. Bring to a boil and cook 1 to 2 minutes, stirring constantly, or until thickened.

Place turkey on a serving platter and spoon sauce over.

Serves 2 to 3

Per serving:	Calories	Fat (g)	Cholesterol (mg)	Fiber (g)	Sodium (mg)
	164	3	57	0	73

Turkey Cutlets Dijon

Have dinner on the table in a jiffy with this tasty dish

8 turkey cutlets
3/4 cup Sweet and Sour Mustard Sauce (page 295)

Coat a 9" x 13" baking dish with cooking spray. Arrange cutlets in dish and spread each with 1 Tbsp. mustard sauce. Bake, uncovered, at 400° for 5 to 10 minutes. Turn, coat with remaining sauce and continue baking until done, about 5 to 10 minutes longer.

Serves 4 to 6

Variation: Substitute 4 skinless boneless chicken breasts for turkey

Per serving:	Calories	Fat (g)	Cholesterol (mg)	Fiber (g)	Sodium (mg)
	194	8	57	0	119

Turkey Enchiladas

This low-fat version of a Mexican favorite is as easy as it is delicious

1 lb. ground turkey
1/2 cup chopped onion
1 clove garlic, minced
1 7-oz. can green chile salsa *or*
 1 7-oz. can chopped green chiles

1 1/2 cups enchilada sauce (canned)
10 to 12 corn tortillas
1 cup grated low-fat cheddar cheese

In a large skillet, saute turkey, onion and garlic until turkey is no longer pink. Crumble turkey into small pieces as it cooks. Add salsa and simmer, uncovered, 10 minutes.

Heat enchilada sauce in a small skillet. Dip each tortilla in sauce to coat both sides. Fill with about 1/4 to 1/3 cup turkey mixture. Roll and place in an 7" by 11" baking dish coated with cooking spray. Pour remaining sauce over. Sprinkle with grated cheese.

Bake, uncovered, at 350° for 10 to 15 minutes or until heated through.

Variation: Decrease turkey to 1/2 lb. Saute turkey, onions and garlic then add 1 cup cooked brown rice and salsa.

Serves 5 to 6

Per serving:	Calories	Fat (g)	Cholesterol (mg)	Fiber (g)	Sodium (mg)
	279	6	60	1	210

Turkey Hawaiian

Loaded with beta-carotene from the sweet potatoes and carrots, this tasty stew
will easily become a family favorite

1¹/2 lbs. turkey tenderloin
¹/4 cup whole wheat flour
1¹/2 tsp. ground ginger
¹/4 tsp. white pepper
1 Tbsp. olive oil
1 onion, cut in 1" dice
1 20-oz. can pineapple chunks, drained
  (reserve juice)

1 cup water
¹/2 cup low-sodium soy sauce
¹/4 cup dry sherry
2 Tbsp. brown sugar
3 Tbsp. lime juice
1 lb. sweet potatoes, cubed
2 carrots, sliced
1 6-oz. can water chestnuts

Cut turkey into cubes. In a plastic bag, combine flour, ginger and white pepper. Add turkey
cubes and shake until evenly coated. Heat oil in a large Dutch oven. Add turkey and onion.
Cook and stir until turkey loses its pink color. Add reserved pineapple juice, water, soy sauce,
sherry, brown sugar and lime juice. Stir well then add cubed sweet potato and sliced carrots.
Bring to a boil over medium heat; reduce heat and simmer, covered, for about 1 hour or until
turkey and potatoes are tender. Stir occasionally.

Add pineapple chunks and water chestnuts. Heat through. Serve over steamed Chinese rice.

Serves 6

Per serving:	Calories	Fat (g)	Cholesterol (mg)	Fiber (g)	Sodium (mg)
	512	8	85	4	655

Turkey Steaks

Serve with brown and wild rice pilaf and baked sweet potatoes

2 lbs. turkey tenderloins (about 4)
¹/2 cup red wine vinegar
¹/4 cup low-sodium soy sauce

2 Tbsp. brown sugar
1 Tbsp. Worcestershire sauce
1 to 2 cloves garlic, minced

Place turkey in a shallow glass dish. In a small bowl, combine remaining ingredients and
pour over turkey. Cover and refrigerate overnight, turning occasionally. Drain well. Broil or
grill turkey until done, basting frequently with marinade.

Serves 4 to 6

Per serving:	Calories	Fat (g)	Cholesterol (mg)	Fiber (g)	Sodium (mg)
	223	5	85	0	413

Turkey Indienne

Depart from the traditional turkey and stuffing with this flavorful holiday dish

1 2 to 3 lb. turkey breast, skinned
1 Tbsp. canola *or* safflower oil
1/4 tsp. white pepper
1 12-oz. can frozen orange juice
   concentrate, thawed
1 cup water *or* white wine
2 Tbsp. brown sugar
1 tsp. cinnamon
1/2 tsp. cloves

1/2 tsp. curry powder
1 8-oz. can pineapple chunks (juice-pack),
   drained
1 2-oz. package slivered almonds
1/4 cup golden raisins *or* currants
3 Tbsp. cornstarch
1/4 cup water
Cooked wild rice

Rub turkey with oil and pepper. Brown in a large Dutch oven.

Combine orange juice concentrate, 1 cup water, brown sugar and spices. Pour over turkey. Add pineapple, almonds and raisins. Bring to a boil, cover and simmer 1 to 1 1/2 hours or until turkey is done. Remove turkey and keep warm.

Combine cornstarch and 1/4 cup water; blend into pan juices. Cook over medium heat, stirring constantly, until thickened. Slice turkey and arrange over wild rice. Spoon sauce over and serve.

Serves 8 to 12

Per serving:	Calories	Fat (g)	Cholesterol (mg)	Fiber (g)	Sodium (mg)
	331	9	85	0	106

Turkey Marsala

1 lb. turkey cutlets	1 Tbsp. olive oil
1/4 cup unbleached flour plus 1 Tbsp.	2 cups sliced fresh mushrooms
1/4 tsp. paprika	1/2 cup Marsala
1/8 tsp. Lite Salt™	Chopped fresh parsley

Place turkey cutlets between 2 sheets of wax paper and pound until thin. Mix flour, paprika and Lite Salt in a plastic bag. Add cutlets, one at a time, and shake until well coated. Heat oil in a large skillet and saute cutlets about 1 to 2 minutes per side. Do not overcook or they will be tough. Remove to a plate and keep warm.

Add mushrooms and Marsala to skillet. Cover and simmer until mushrooms are soft. Sprinkle in remaining flour and mix well. Simmer until sauce thickens. Add cutlets to pan and spoon sauce over. Heat gently until warmed through.

Serves 4

Per serving:	Calories	Fat (g)	Cholesterol (mg)	Fiber (g)	Sodium (mg)
	307	8	85	2	130

Orange Glazed Turkey

2 turkey thighs *or* drumsticks, skinned	2 Tbsp. brown sugar
1 onion, sliced	2 tsp. low-sodium soy sauce
1/2 tsp. paprika	1 tsp. minced fresh ginger
1/2 cup orange juice concentrate	2 Tbsp. chopped fresh parsley
1/3 cup water *or* white wine	

Place turkey in a roasting pan. Arrange onion slices over turkey and sprinkle with paprika.

Combine juice, water, sugar, soy sauce, ginger and parsley. Pour over turkey and onions. Cover and roast at 400° for 50 to 60 minutes or until turkey is tender. Baste 3 to 4 times during cooking. Slice meat and serve with sauce. Garnish with orange twists.

Serves 4

Per serving:	Calories	Fat (g)	Cholesterol (mg)	Fiber (g)	Sodium (mg)
	226	5	43	1	66

Turkey Parmesan

2 Tbsp. unbleached flour
1/2 tsp. paprika
1/4 tsp. pepper
1 egg white
1 Tbsp. water
1/2 cup dry bread crumbs

3 Tbsp. Parmesan cheese
1 1/2 lbs. turkey cutlets
2 Tbsp. olive oil
1 cup Quick Tomato Sauce (page 294)
4 oz. part-skim mozzarella cheese, sliced

In a plastic bag, combine flour, paprika and pepper. Beat together egg white and water in a small bowl. Combine bread crumbs and Parmesan cheese in a shallow dish or pie pan.

Dredge turkey in flour mixture. Dip in egg white, then in bread crumbs. Place on a plate, cover and chill in refrigerator for at least one hour.

Heat oil in a large skillet. Saute cutlets until browned on each side. Remove to a shallow baking dish. Pour Quick Tomato Sauce over turkey and top each cutlet with a slice of cheese. Bake at 350° for 20 to 25 minutes. Serve with eggless pasta.

Serves 6

Per serving:	Calories	Fat (g)	Cholesterol (mg)	Fiber (g)	Sodium (mg)
	359	14	99	1	334

Red, White and Green Chili

Make this low-fat version of green chili as hot or mild as your tastebuds can tolerate

1 tsp. olive oil
1 onion, chopped
2 cloves garlic, minced
1 lb. skinless turkey breast, cubed
1 tsp. to 1 Tbsp. cumin (to taste)
1 tsp. to 1 Tbsp. chili powder (to taste)
2 Tbsp. chopped fresh oregano *or*
  2 tsp. dried

3 10¹/₂-oz. cans salt-free chicken broth, defatted
1 32-oz. can whole tomatoes, crushed
2 Tbsp. salt-free tomato paste
2 Anaheim chiles, seeded and diced
1 8-oz. can chopped green chiles
2 to 5 jalapeño peppers, seeded and diced

Heat oil in a large pot; saute onion, garlic and turkey until turkey is no longer pink. Add remaining ingredients and simmer 2 hours stirring occasionally. If a thicker chili is desired, blend 1 to 2 Tbsp. flour with 1 to 2 Tbsp. water and stir into chili. Simmer, stirring occasionally, for 30 minutes or until thickened.

Serve with warm corn tortillas or over burritos (made with vegetarian refried beans).

Serves 4 to 6

Per serving:	Calories	Fat (g)	Cholesterol (mg)	Fiber (g)	Sodium (mg)
	228	5	57	4	187

Oriental Turkey Stir-Fry

2 tsp. canola *or* safflower oil
2 cups carrots, julienne
1 red bell pepper, julienne
1 onion, thinly sliced
2 cloves garlic, minced
1 Tbsp. minced fresh ginger
2/3 cup low-sodium chicken broth, defatted

2 Tbsp. fresh lemon juice
1 Tbsp. low-sodium soy sauce
1 tsp. cornstarch
1/2 tsp. brown sugar
1 cup cooked turkey, thinly sliced (may substitute cooked chicken)
4 cups cooked brown rice
4 to 5 cups shredded romaine lettuce
1/4 cup chopped fresh cilantro

Heat oil in a wok or large skillet. Stir-fry carrots, red pepper, onion, garlic and ginger for 3 to 5 minutes or until tender-crisp. Combine chicken broth with lemon juice, soy sauce, cornstarch and brown sugar; mix well. Add to wok along with turkey. Cook and stir until sauce boils and thickens.

Serve over hot brown rice topped with shredded lettuce and chopped cilantro.

Serves 4

Per serving:	Calories	Fat (g)	Cholesterol (mg)	Fiber (g)	Sodium (mg)
	417	6	27	8	222

Turkey Scallopini

1 Tbsp. liquid margarine
1/2 lb. sliced mushrooms
1/4 cup unbleached flour
1/2 tsp. dried tarragon
1/8 tsp. pepper

1 lb. turkey breast slices (cutlets)
1/4 cup dry sherry *or* salt-free chicken broth
1 Tbsp. water
Chopped fresh parsley

Heat 2 tsp. margarine in a non-stick skillet. Add mushrooms, cover and cook until mushrooms are tender. Remove from pan, reserving liquid.

Combine flour, tarragon and pepper in a plastic bag. Add turkey slices one at a time and shake to coat well. Remove to a platter. Spray skillet with cooking spray and melt remaining margarine. Add turkey slices a few at a time and cook 1 to 2 minutes per side. Remove from pan and keep warm.

Blend sherry and water. Slowly add to pan, stirring until sauce is thickened and smooth. Return turkey and mushrooms to pan and heat through. Serve garnished with chopped parsley.

Serves 4

Per serving:	Calories	Fat (g)	Cholesterol (mg)	Fiber (g)	Sodium (mg)
	290	8	85	3	140

Van Gogh Turkey-Lentil Salad

The bright colors in the hearty salad will remind you of a brightly hued Van Gogh painting

4 sun-dried tomatoes
1/4 cup boiling water
3 1/2 cups water *or* **salt-free chicken broth, defatted**
1 cup lentils (uncooked)
2 large tomatoes, cored and cut in half
1 shallot *or* **white part of 3 green onions**
2 to 3 garlic cloves

3 Tbsp. sherry wine vinegar
3 Tbsp. fresh orange juice
4 Tbsp. olive oil
1 tsp. dried rosemary
1/2 tsp. dried thyme
1 red bell pepper, diced
1/2 red onion, chopped
1 cup cooked fresh corn kernels *or*
  1 8-oz. can salt-free corn
2 cups cubed turkey breast (skinless)

Cover sun-dried tomatoes with boiling water in a small bowl and let stand one hour or until tomatoes are soft. Drain tomatoes, squeezing out as much water as possible. Reserve soaking water.

Combine water (or broth), soaking water and lentils in a saucepan. Bring to a boil, then simmer for 20 to 30 minutes or until lentils are tender. Drain well then place in a large bowl.

Cut tomatoes in half; cut one half in quarters and reserve for dressing. Dice remainder.

Prepare dressing in food processor or blender: with motor running, drop in shallots, garlic and soaked tomatoes. Add vinegar, juice, olive oil, rosemary, thyme and tomato quarters. Process until well blended, 1 to 2 minutes. Add to lentils along with diced tomato, bell pepper, chopped onion, corn and turkey. Toss to combine well. Cover and chill 2 to 3 hours before serving.

Serve on plates lined with romaine or red leaf lettuce.

Variation: Add 1 cup cooked brown rice (try Citrus Rice, page 128); turkey may be eliminated if desired.

Serves 6 to 8

Per serving:	Calories	Fat (g)	Cholesterol (mg)	Fiber (g)	Sodium (mg)
	380	12	85	3	167

Turkey Marinara Sauce

1 tsp. olive oil
1 onion, chopped
1 green pepper, seeded and chopped
1 red bell pepper, seeded and chopped
2 carrots, grated
1/2 lb. mushrooms, sliced
1/4 cup chopped fresh parsley
2 Tbsp. chopped fresh basil *or*
  2 tsp. dried

1 tsp. dried rosemary
1 tsp. dried oregano
1/4 tsp. dried thyme
1 lb. ground turkey
2 28-oz. cans Italian style tomatoes
1 12-oz. can salt-free tomato paste
1/4 cup dry red wine (optional)
2 bay leaves
Freshly ground black pepper

In a large pot, heat oil and saute onion, peppers, carrots, mushrooms and herbs over low heat for 15 to 20 minutes, stirring often. Remove from pan and set aside.

Add turkey to same pan and cook, stirring frequently, for 10 to 15 minutes or until turkey has lost its pink color and is crumbly. Return vegetables to pan and add remaining ingredients. Break up large tomatoes with a spoon. Cover and simmer for 30 to 45 minutes. Uncover and continue to simmer until sauce thickens, about 15 minutes. Serve over hot pasta.

Yield: about 10 cups

Per serving:	Calories	Fat (g)	Cholesterol (mg)	Fiber (g)	Sodium (mg)
	122	3	25	5	70

Turkey Sausage Patties

Low-fat turkey is a stand-in for pork in this tasty sausage

1 lb. ground turkey
1/4 cup seasoned bread crumbs
1/4 cup minced onion
2 Tbsp. minced parsley
2 Tbsp. salt-free chicken broth, defatted
1 tsp. olive oil

1 clove garlic, minced
1/2 tsp. dried sage, ground
1/4 tsp. dried thyme, ground
1/4 tsp. freshly ground black pepper
1 egg white

In a medium bowl, combine all ingredients blending well with hands. Shape mixture into 12 patties.

Arrange patties on a non-stick baking sheet and broil 3 to 4 inches from heat for 4 to 5 minutes or until lightly browned. Turn and continue to broil an additional 2 to 3 minutes or until done. May also cook in a non-stick skillet.

Serves: 6

Per serving:	Calories	Fat (g)	Cholesterol (mg)	Fiber (g)	Sodium (mg)
	119	3	49	0	90

Low in saturated fat and cholesterol (with a few exceptions) and a good source of Omega-3 fatty acids, fish is perfect for light cuisine. Simple to prepare and endlessly versatile, fish should become part of your meal plan — two to three times a week at least.

Shellfish such as shrimp, crab and lobster contain more cholesterol than other seafood and should be limited to 3 or 4 ounces once or twice a week. Their low fat content, however, makes the cholesterol less of a health problem.

The Canadian Rule for cooking fish applies to all cooking methods (except microwaving): allow 8 to 10 minutes cooking time for each inch of thickness. Oven temperature should be 400° or 425°.

Fish

Apple Baked Butterfish 180
Buttery Baked Fish 182
Chinese Steamed Trout 195
Crispy Coating 179
Creole Catfish 181
Curried Orange Roughy 188
Dijon Sea Bass 179
Fish in Foil 182
Fillets with Basil Sauce 183
Halibut with Chile-Cilantro Salsa 185
Honey Mustard Swordfish 194
Lime Marinated Swordfish 194
Mahi Mahi Hawaiian 188
Monkfish with Creamy Tomato Sauce 189
Mushroom Sherry Glazed Fish 184
Orange Pecan Halibut 186
Salsa Baked Fish 183
San Francisco Cioppino 197
Sesame Crisped Fillets 182
Sesame Halibut 186
Shark with Pesto 187
Snapper Cozumel 191
Snapper with Papaya Salsa 190
Snapper Veracruz 189
Southern Baked Catfish 180
Sole with Almonds 190
Sole Florentine 193
Sole Roulades Poached in Wine 191
Sole with Tomatoes and Mushrooms 193
Sole Veronique 192
Tandoori Halibut 187
Teriyaki Grilled Fish 185
Trout with Orange Vinaigrette 195
Turbot with Avocado Cream 196

Shellfish

Barbequed Seafood with Plum Sauce 196
Beer Boiled Shrimp 202
Pasta with Scallops and Peppers 198
Peppery Shrimp and Scallops 198
Seafood Curry 201
Seafood Oriental 200
Seafood Pesto Saute 199
Seafood Saute with Mushrooms 201
Sesame Scallops 199
Stir-Fried Scallops 200

Crispy Coating

3/4 cup non-fat dry milk
1/4 cup dry bread crumbs *or* cornmeal
1/4 cup wheat germ
2 tsp. dried parsley flakes
1 tsp. paprika
1/2 tsp. dried sage

1/2 tsp. celery salt
1/2 tsp. dry mustard
1/2 tsp. onion powder
1/2 tsp. dried oregano
1/4 tsp. black pepper

Combine all ingredients in a small bowl and mix well. Store in an air-tight container. To use: pour coating mixture into a plastic bag, add fish and shake until well coated.

Bake fish at 400° for 8 to 10 minutes per inch of thickness or until fish flakes easily with a fork.

Variation: May also be used for chicken. Increase sage to 1 tsp. Remove skin and excess fat from chicken before coating. Bake at 325° for 15 to 20 minutes or until chicken is no longer pink in thickest part.

Yield: about 1 1/4 cups

Per serving:	Calories	Fat (g)	Cholesterol (mg)	Fiber (g)	Sodium (mg)
	67	1	2	0	175

Dijon Sea Bass

4 6-oz. sea bass fillets
 (may substitute snapper *or* any other
 thick white fish)
1 Tbsp. lemon juice
1 tsp. lemon zest

1 Tbsp. Dijon mustard
1 clove garlic, minced
1/2 tsp. dried tarragon *or* rosemary
1/8 tsp. paprika
2 Tbsp. capers, rinsed and drained

Arrange fish in a broiler pan coated with cooking spray. Drizzle with lemon juice. Mix together lemon zest, mustard, garlic and tarragon. Spread over fish fillets.

Broil 8–10 minutes per inch of thickness until fish is opaque and flakes easily with a fork. Sprinkle lightly with paprika, then scatter capers over top of fish. Serve hot or chilled.

Serves 4

Per serving:	Calories	Fat (g)	Cholesterol (mg)	Fiber (g)	Sodium (mg)
	170	4	70	0	235

Apple Baked Butterfish

1/2 cup non-fat milk
2 Tbsp. non-fat dry milk
1 Tbsp. soft margarine, divided
2 apples, cored and sliced
1 1/2 lbs. butterfish

1 cup apple juice
2 green onions, thinly sliced
1 Tbsp. unbleached flour
1 tsp. Dijon mustard

Combine liquid and dry milk, blending well. Set aside.

Melt 1/2 Tbsp. margarine in a medium skillet and saute apples until soft. Place fish and apples in a baking dish coated with cooking spray. Pour in juice. Cover with foil and bake at 400° for 10 to 15 minutes or until fish flakes easily with a fork. Drain fish, reserving cooking liquid.

Melt remaining 1/2 Tbsp. margarine in a small saucepan. Saute onion briefly, then stir in flour and cook until bubbly, about 1 minute. Remove from heat and gradually blend in milk mixture, 1/4 cup cooking liquid, and mustard. Return to heat; cook and stir until thickened. Serve over fish

Serves 4 to 6

Per serving:	Calories	Fat (g)	Cholesterol (mg)	Fiber (g)	Sodium (mg)
	120	5	14	1	65

Southern Baked Catfish

1 lb. catfish fillets
1 1/2 cups corn meal
3/4 tsp. baking soda
1/4 tsp. Lite Salt™
1/2 cup grated low-fat cheddar cheese

1 4-oz. can diced green chiles, drained
3 egg whites
1 cup low-fat buttermilk
1/4 cup canola or safflower oil
Dash hot sauce

In a medium bowl, mix together cornmeal, soda, salt, cheese and chiles. In a smaller bowl, beat together egg whites, buttermilk, oil and hot sauce. Combine with cornmeal mixture. Spread half of batter into a baking dish coated with cooking spray. Place fillets on top; spread remaining batter over fish. Bake at 450° for 20 to 25 minutes.

Serves 4 to 6

Per serving:	Calories	Fat (g)	Cholesterol (mg)	Fiber (g)	Sodium (mg)
	340	14	50	0	314

Creole Catfish

Seasonings from the deep South enliven this easy-to-prepare dish

1 Tbsp. olive oil
1 onion, chopped
1/2 cup chopped celery, including tops
1 green *or* red bell pepper, cored,
  seeded and diced
2 cloves garlic, minced
1 28-oz. can salt-free whole tomatoes
  (coarsely chopped)

1 lemon, thinly sliced
1 Tbsp. Worcestershire sauce
1 Tbsp. paprika
2 bay leaves
1/2 tsp. Lite Salt™
1/4 tsp dried thyme
1/4 tsp. liquid hot pepper seasoning
2 lbs. catfish fillets

Heat oil in a large skillet; saute onion, celery, pepper and garlic until soft, about 5 to 7 minutes. Stir often. Add tomatoes and their juice, lemon slices, Worcestershire, paprika, bay leaves, salt, thyme and hot pepper. Simmer 15 to 20 minutes or until sauce is slightly thickened; stir occasionally.

Add fillets to skillet and spoon sauce over fish. Cover and simmer until fish flakes easily with a fork, about 10 to 15 minutes. Serve over hot brown rice.

Serves 6 to 8

Per serving:	Calories	Fat (g)	Cholesterol (mg)	Fiber (g)	Sodium (mg)
	187	7	65	3	182

Buttery Baked Fish

So good you will think it's the real thing

1 lb. fish fillets (e.g. orange roughy,
  bass, salmon)
1 pkg. Butter Buds™
1 Tbsp. fresh lemon juice

1 tsp. lemon zest
1/2 tsp. dried tarragon *or* dried basil *or*
  curry powder

Place fillets in a baking dish coated with cooking spray. Mix Butter Buds according to package directions, substituting lemon juice for 1 Tbsp. of water. Stir in zest and tarragon.

Pour mixture over fillets. Bake at 400° for 8 to 10 minutes or until fish flakes easily with a fork.

Serves: 4

Per serving:	Calories	Fat (g)	Cholesterol (mg)	Fiber (g)	Sodium (mg)
	144	8	23	0	72

Sesame Crisped Fillets

1 egg white
$^1/_3$ cup sesame seed
1$^1/_2$ -2 lbs. firm white fish fillets
   (e.g. orange roughy, flounder, cusk,
   turbot, cod, etc.)

1 Tbsp. canola or safflower oil
Reduced-sodium soy sauce
Lemon wedges

In a shallow dish, beat egg white until frothy. Place sesame seeds in another shallow dish.

Dip one side of fillet into egg white, then into sesame seeds. Coat evenly and heavily with the sesame seeds; set aside. Heat a 9" x 13" baking dish in a 500° oven for 5 minutes. Pour in oil and swirl to coat bottom of dish evenly. Lay fish, sesame seed side down, in dish.

Bake at 500° for 8 to 10 minutes or until fish flakes easily with a fork. Do not turn during cooking. Serve with a splash of reduced-sodium soy sauce and fresh lemon wedges.

Serves 4 to 6

Per serving:	Calories	Fat (g)	Cholesterol (mg)	Fiber (g)	Sodium (mg)
	214	14	23	0	114

Fish in Foil

1 lb. fish, about 1" thick
1 tsp. lemon zest
$^1/_4$ tsp. Lite Salt™
Freshly ground black pepper (to taste)
Garlic powder (to taste)

$^1/_4$ tsp dried savory
$^1/_4$ cup chopped onion
$^1/_2$ cup sliced celery (including tops)
$^1/_2$ cup thinly sliced carrots
$^1/_2$ cup sliced mushrooms

Place fish in the center of a large piece of foil. Sprinkle with zest, Lite Salt™, pepper, garlic powder and savory. Arrange vegetables over fish. Seal foil tightly. Bake at 400° for 10 minutes per inch of thickness or until fish flakes easily with a fork.

Variation: Add diced tomatoes to vegetable mixture.

Serves: 4

Per serving:	Calories	Fat (g)	Cholesterol (mg)	Fiber (g)	Sodium (mg)
	159	8	23	1	160

Fillets with Basil Sauce

1 cup salt-free chicken broth, defatted	1 Tbsp. chopped fresh basil *or*
1 Tbsp. liquid margarine	1/2 tsp. dried
2 Tbsp. unbleached flour	1/4 tsp. dried thyme
2 Tbsp. dry sherry *or* white wine	1 Tbsp. minced fresh chives
1/2 cup non-fat milk	2 lbs. fish fillets (e.g. orange roughy)
1/4 cup Parmesan cheese	3 tomatoes, cored and sliced

Boil chicken broth until reduced by one-half. In a saucepan, melt margarine. Stir in flour and cook over low heat for one minute. Gradually blend in reduced chicken broth, sherry and non-fat milk. Cook and stir until thickened. Stir in Parmesan cheese, basil, thyme and chives; set aside.

Place fish fillets in a baking dish coated with cooking spray. Top with tomato slices. Pour sauce over all. Bake at 350° for 15 to 20 minutes or until fish flakes easily with a fork.

Serves 6 to 8

Per serving:	Calories	Fat (g)	Cholesterol (mg)	Fiber (g)	Sodium (mg)
	199	11	26	1	127

Salsa Baked Fish

1 1/2 lb. firm fish (e.g. swordfish, shark, halibut)	1 avocado, peeled and sliced
1 cup Mexican Salsa (page 10)	Lime wedges
1/2 cup grated low-fat Monterey Jack cheese (optional)	

Place fish in a 9" x 13" baking dish coated with cooking spray. Pour Salsa over fish and sprinkle with cheese. Bake at 400° until fish flakes easily with a fork, about 10 to 15 minutes.

Serve garnished with avocado slices and lime wedges.

Serves 4 to 6

Per serving:	Calories	Fat (g)	Cholesterol (mg)	Fiber (g)	Sodium (mg)
	225	10	41	2	111

Mushroom-Sherry Glazed Fish

Serve with brown rice and a crunchy green salad

1/4 cup salt-free chicken broth, defatted
 or water
1/4 cup dry sherry
1 tsp. cornstarch
1 Tbsp. low-sodium soy sauce
1 clove garlic, minced

1 Tbsp. minced fresh ginger
2 cups sliced mushrooms
2 lbs. white fish fillets (e.g. orange roughy,
 grouper, sea bass, snapper, flounder, etc.)
4 to 6 green onions, thinly sliced

Stir broth (or water) and sherry into cornstarch, mixing until dissolved. Add soy sauce, garlic and ginger. Set aside.

Spray a non-stick skillet with cooking spray. Heat until bubbly then add mushrooms. Cover and cook over low heat for 5 to 10 minutes, or until mushrooms are soft and liquid has accumulated in the pan. Drain juice into cornstarch mixture. Remove mushrooms from pan and set aside.

Spray skillet again and saute fish, turning once, until it flakes easily with a fork, about 3 to 5 minutes per side. Remove from pan and keep warm. Stir sauce and add to pan along with green onions and mushrooms. Cook and stir over low heat until thickened. Serve over fish.

Serves 4 to 6

Per serving:	Calories	Fat (g)	Cholesterol (mg)	Fiber (g)	Sodium (mg)
	218	11	30	1	201

Teriyaki Grilled Fish

1 lb. firm fish (swordfish, halibut, shark,
  mahi-mahi, tuna, marlin, etc.)
1/2 cup low-sodium soy sauce
1/4 cup dry sherry *or* salt-free
  chicken broth, defatted

2 Tbsp. olive oil
1 Tbsp. brown sugar
2 garlic cloves, minced
2 Tbsp. minced fresh ginger
1 Tbsp. orange zest

Place fish in a shallow dish. Whisk together remaining ingredients and pour over fish. Marinate 30 minutes. Drain well. Broil or grill for 10 minutes per inch of thickness, or until fish flakes easily with a fork. Baste frequently with marinade while cooking. If fish is more than 1" thick, turn once during cooking.

Serves 2 to 3

Per serving:	Calories	Fat (g)	Cholesterol (mg)	Fiber (g)	Sodium (mg)
	128	3	36	0	162

Halibut with Chile-Cilantro Salsa

Chile-Cilantro Salsa:
1 4-oz. can diced green chiles
1 fresh anaheim chili,
  seeded and chopped
1/4 cup fresh cilantro
2 cloves garlic
2 Tbsp. chopped onion
2 slices fresh ginger

1/4 cup fresh lime juice *or*
  white wine vinegar
1 tsp. lime zest
1/4 tsp. Lite Salt™

4 halibut (*or* tuna) steaks
Olive oil

Prepare sauce: combine all ingredients in a food processor and process until smooth. Set aside.

Brush fish lightly with oil. Broil or grill 4 to 5 minutes per side or until fish flakes easily with a fork. Serve topped with sauce.

Serves 4

Per serving:	Calories	Fat (g)	Cholesterol (mg)	Fiber (g)	Sodium (mg)
	150	4	36	0	221

Sesame Halibut

This easy dish will soon become a favorite

1/4 cup fresh orange juice
2 Tbsp. low-sodium catsup
1 Tbsp. low-sodium soy sauce
1 Tbsp. fresh lemon juice
1/4 tsp. freshly ground black pepper

1 tsp. sesame oil
1 Tbsp. honey
2 lbs. halibut
1 Tbsp. toasted sesame seeds

Combine orange juice, catsup, soy sauce, lemon juice, pepper, sesame oil and honey; mix well. Place halibut in a shallow baking dish and pour marinade over. Cover and marinate in the refrigerator for no more than 2 hours. Drain well.

Grill or broil, turning once, until fish flakes easily with a fork, 8 to 10 minutes per inch of thickness. Sprinkle with sesame seeds and serve.

Serves 4 to 6

Per serving:	Calories	Fat (g)	Cholesterol (mg)	Fiber (g)	Sodium (mg)
	197	5	48	0	212

Orange Pecan Halibut

1 lb. halibut
1/2 cup unbleached flour
1/2 tsp. paprika
1/4 tsp. black pepper

2 Tbsp. liquid margarine
Juice and zest of 1 orange
2 Tbsp. Dijon mustard
2 Tbsp. chopped toasted pecans

Rinse fish and pat dry. In a plastic bag, combine flour, paprika and pepper. Add fish and shake until well coated.

Melt margarine in a large skillet. Add fish and saute until browned on each side, about 8 to 10 minutes. Remove to a platter lined with paper towels and drain well.

Combine orange juice, zest and mustard. Pour into skillet and boil until slightly thickened. Add fish and baste until well coated with sauce. Serve sprinkled with pecans

Serves 3 to 4

Per serving:	Calories	Fat (g)	Cholesterol (mg)	Fiber (g)	Sodium (mg)
	269	12	36	1	235

Tandoori Halibut

Add an Indian flair to mild halibut

1 cup plain non-fat yogurt
1/4 to 1/2 cup chopped fresh cilantro
1/4 cup fresh lime juice
2 tsp. lime zest
2 cloves garlic, minced
2 Tbsp. minced fresh ginger
1/2 tsp. ground coriander
1/2 tsp. paprika

1/2 tsp. cumin
1/4 tsp. turmeric
1/4 tsp. Lite Salt™
Dash cayenne pepper
1 1/2 lbs. halibut steaks
Lime wedges
Tomato wedges

In a small bowl, whisk together yogurt, cilantro, lime juice, zest, garlic, ginger, paprika, coriander, cumin, turmeric, Lite Salt™ and cayenne. Place halibut in a shallow dish and pour marinade over. Turn fish to coat evenly. Marinate 2 to 4 hours. Drain.

Broil or grill 10 minutes per inch of thickness, basting with marinade, until fish flakes easily with a fork. Serve garnished with lime and tomato wedges.

Variation: Tandoori Chicken — substitute skinless, boneless chicken breasts for halibut.

Serves 4 to 6

Per serving:	Calories	Fat (g)	Cholesterol (mg)	Fiber (g)	Sodium (mg)
	150	3	38	0	133

Shark with Pesto

Fish skeptics often develop a liking for meaty-textured shark

1 lb. shark (*or* tuna, halibut, swordfish or salmon)
1 tsp. olive oil
2 Tbsp. Pesto (page 293)

Brush shark with oil. Grill or broil 8 to 10 minutes per inch of thickness or until fish flakes easily with a fork. Top with Pesto and serve.

Serves 4

Per serving:	Calories	Fat (g)	Cholesterol (mg)	Fiber (g)	Sodium (mg)
	212	11	64	0	0

Mahi-Mahi Hawaiian

3/4 cup fresh orange juice
3 Tbsp. fresh lime juice
1 clove garlic, minced
1 1/2 lbs. mahi-mahi
1 tsp. canola or safflower oil
3 green onions, thinly sliced

1/2 cup chopped green *or* red bell pepper
1 1/2 cups crushed pineapple
(juice-pack), undrained
1 Tbsp. cornstarch
1/8 tsp. five-spice powder*
1 Tbsp. minced fresh ginger

In a small bowl, combine orange juice, lime juice and garlic. Place mahi-mahi in a shallow baking pan and pour marinade over. Cover and marinate in the refrigerator overnight.

Drain well. Place in a baking pan coated with cooking spray. Bake at 400° until fish flakes easily with a fork, about 8 to 10 minutes per inch of thickness. Keep warm.

Heat oil in a small saucepan. Saute onions and peppers until soft. Drain pineapple juice and blend with cornstarch. Add to crushed pineapple, five-spice powder and ginger. Add to onions; cook and stir until thickened. Serve over fish.

Serves 4 to 6

* Found with oriental seasonings.

Per serving:	Calories	Fat (g)	Cholesterol (mg)	Fiber (g)	Sodium (mg)
	250	6	68	0	6

Curried Orange Roughy

1 Tbsp. liquid margarine
2 green onions, thinly sliced
1 1/2 Tbsp. unbleached flour
1/2 tsp. curry powder

1/2 tsp. orange zest
1 cup non-fat milk
1 1/2 lbs. orange roughy (*or* other
firm white fish)

Melt margarine in a small saucepan. Saute green onions briefly then stir in flour, curry powder and orange zest. Cook and stir 1 minute. Gradually blend in non-fat milk. Cook, stirring constantly, until thickened.

Place fish in a 9" x 13" baking pan coated with cooking spray. Pour sauce over fish. Bake, covered, at 350° for 15 to 20 minutes or until fish flakes easily with a fork.

Serves 4 to 6

Per serving:	Calories	Fat (g)	Cholesterol (mg)	Fiber (g)	Sodium (mg)
	183	10	24	0	118

Monkfish with Creamy Tomato Sauce

1/2 cup non-fat milk
2 Tbsp. non-fat dry milk
1 16-oz. can salt-free tomatoes, chopped
2 green onions, thinly sliced
1/2 tsp. sugar
1/2 tsp. Lite Salt™

1 Tbsp. chopped fresh basil *or*
  1/2 tsp. dried
1 Tbsp. cornstarch
1 1/2 lbs. monkfish
2 tsp. olive oil

Combine non-fat milk and dry milk. Stir well to dissolve. In a medium saucepan, combine tomatoes, onion, sugar, Lite Salt™ and basil. Simmer for 15 minutes. Blend cornstarch into milk and add to sauce. Cook and stir until thickened. Keep warm while cooking fish.

Brush fish with oil and broil until it flakes easily with a fork, about 10 minutes. Turn once. Serve with sauce.

Serves 4 to 6

Per serving:	Calories	Fat (g)	Cholesterol (mg)	Fiber (g)	Sodium (mg)
	196	10	24	2	190

Snapper Veracruz

1 lb. snapper fillets
1 lime (3 Tbsp. juice)
1 tsp. olive oil
1/2 onion, chopped *or*
  4-6 green onions, thinly sliced

1 clove garlic, minced
1 red *or* green bell pepper, diced
1/4 cup sliced black *or* green (stuffed) olives
  (rinse and drain before slicing)
Chopped fresh parsley *or* cilantro

Place snapper in a 9" x 13" baking dish coated with cooking spray. Squeeze lime juice over fillets, turning to coat both sides. Set aside while preparing topping.

Heat olive oil in a medium skillet and saute onion, garlic and green pepper until soft, about 5 minutes. Remove from heat and stir in olives.

Spoon topping over fillets. Bake at 400° for 10 to 15 minutes or until fish flakes easily with a fork. Garnish with chopped parsley or cilantro.

Serves 3 to 4

Per serving:	Calories	Fat (g)	Cholesterol (mg)	Fiber (g)	Sodium (mg)
	163	4	76	1	331

Snapper with Papaya Salsa

Papaya Salsa:
1 tsp. canola, safflower *or* olive oil
2 shallots, minced
1 Tbsp. minced fresh ginger
1/2 tsp. curry powder
1 papaya, peeled, seeded and diced
2 Tbsp. fresh lime juice
Zest of 1 lime (1-1 1/2 tsp.)
1 Tbsp. minced fresh cilantro

2 lbs. snapper (*or* other whitefish such as
   grouper, orange roughy, sea bass, etc.)
Fresh cilantro
Lime slices

Heat oil in a non-stick skillet; saute shallots and ginger until softened, about 5 minutes. Mix in curry powder, diced papaya, lime juice, zest and minced cilantro.

Place fish in a baking dish coated with cooking spray. Spread salsa over top. Cover dish with foil and bake at 375° for 20 minutes. Remove foil and continue to bake an additional 10 to 15 minutes or until fish flakes easily with a fork. Garnish with cilantro sprigs and lime slices to serve.

Serves 6 to 8

Per serving:	Calories	Fat (g)	Cholesterol (mg)	Fiber (g)	Sodium (mg)
	165	9	23	1	74

Sole with Almonds

1 lb. sole fillets
1/2 cup bread crumbs
1 Tbsp. liquid margarine
1 Tbsp. chopped fresh parsley

1 tsp. dried savory
1 tsp. lemon zest
1 tsp. fresh lemon juice
2 Tbsp. sliced almonds

Place sole in a 9" x 13" baking dish coated with cooking spray. Combine crumbs, margarine, parsley, savory, zest and juice. Mix well. Sprinkle over fish, then top with almonds. Bake at 400° until fish flakes easily with a fork.

Serves 4

Per serving:	Calories	Fat (g)	Cholesterol (mg)	Fiber (g)	Sodium (mg)
	197	7	55	0	218

Snapper Cozumel

1 cup fresh lemon juice *or* 1/2 cup each
  fresh lemon and lime juice
1/4 cup frozen orange juice concentrate,
  thawed
1 Tbsp. orange zest
1 Tbsp. lemon zest
2 cloves garlic, minced

1/4 cup olive oil
1/2 cup chopped fresh cilantro
1 red onion, thinly sliced
1 jalapeño pepper, seeded and minced
2 lbs. snapper fillets
Fresh cilantro

In a medium bowl, combine lemon juice, orange juice concentrate, zest and garlic. Whisk in oil, then mix in cilantro, onion and jalapeño pepper. Cover and refrigerate overnight. Place snapper in a shallow baking dish and pour marinade over. Cover and marinate in the refrigerator for 1 to 2 hours.

Drain well. Grill or broil, turning once, until fish flakes easily with a fork, 8 to 10 minutes per inch of thickness. Baste frequently. Serve garnished with cilantro sprigs.

Serves 4 to 6

Per serving:	Calories	Fat (g)	Cholesterol (mg)	Fiber (g)	Sodium (mg)
	228	6	101	0	146

Sole Roulades Poached in Wine

1 lb. sole fillets
1/4 cup dry white wine *or* vermouth
1/4 cup water
2 Tbsp. chopped fresh parsley

1 Tbsp. chopped fresh dill *or* 1 tsp. dried
1 tsp. lemon zest
1 tsp. cornstarch
1/8 tsp. Lite Salt™

Place two sole fillets together and roll up; place in a baking dish. Repeat with all fillets. Pour wine and water around fillets; sprinkle parsley, dill and lemon zest over top. Cover and bake at 400° for 10 to 15 minutes or until fish flakes easily with a fork. Remove fillets to a plate and keep warm.

Boil the remaining juices until reduced by half. Dissolve cornstarch in 2 tsp. water then stir into reduced juices. Add Lite Salt™. Cook and stir until thickened.

Pour sauce over fillets and serve.

Serves 2 to 3

Per serving:	Calories	Fat (g)	Cholesterol (mg)	Fiber (g)	Sodium (mg)
	119	1	55	0	125

Sole Veronique

A leaner version of this classic dish

3/4 cup non-fat milk
1/4 cup non-fat dry milk
1 lb. sole *or* other white fish (e.g. flounder,
  orange roughy, turbot)
1/8 tsp. white pepper
1/4 tsp. Lite Salt™
1/4 cup dry white wine

1/4 cup salt-free chicken broth, defatted
1 Tbsp. fresh lemon juice
1 Tbsp. liquid margarine
2 Tbsp. unbleached flour
1/8 tsp. freshly grated nutmeg
1/8 tsp. white pepper
1/2 cup sliced green grapes

Mix together non-fat milk and dry milk, stirring until dissolved; set aside.

Place fish in a baking dish coated with cooking spray. Sprinkle with pepper and Lite Salt™.
Combine wine, broth and lemon juice; pour over fish. Cover and bake at 400° for 8 to 10
minutes or until fish flakes easily with a fork. Drain cooking liquid into a small saucepan and
boil until reduced by half.

Melt margarine in a small suacepan. Add flour and cook until bubbly. Remove from heat and
gradually blend in milk mixture and reduced cooking liquid. Cook over medium heat, stirring
constantly, until thickened. Blend in nutmeg, white pepper, and grapes.

Place fish on a serving platter and pour sauce over. Garnish with whole grapes.

Serves 4

Per serving:	Calories	Fat (g)	Cholesterol (mg)	Fiber (g)	Sodium (mg)
	209	5	57	1	256

Sole with Tomatoes and Mushrooms

1/2 cup white wine, divided
2 Tbsp. chopped shallots *or* onions
1 cup sliced mushrooms
11/2 lbs. sole fillets

White pepper to taste
1 tomato, cored and diced
3 Tbsp. minced fresh parsley
1/4 tsp. Lite Salt™

In a large skillet, simmer 1/2 cup wine, shallots and mushrooms for 5 minutes. Sprinkle sole with pepper, then place over vegetables. Add remaining wine, tomato and parsley. Sprinkle with Lite Salt™. Simmer, covered, 2 to 3 minutes or until fish is just done.

Remove sole; boil sauce for 2 to 3 minutes until thickened. Spoon over fish and serve.

Serves 4 to 6

Per serving:	Calories	Fat (g)	Cholesterol (mg)	Fiber (g)	Sodium (mg)
	129	1	55	1	97

Sole Florentine

1 tsp. liquid margarine
1/2 cup minced onion
1 clove garlic, minced
1 10-oz. package frozen chopped spinach,
  thawed and well drained
1/4 tsp. dried thyme
1/8 tsp. freshly ground black pepper

1/4 cup HealthMark Sour Cream (page 287)
1 Tbsp. toasted sesame seeds
11/2 lbs. sole fillets
1/4 cup dry white wine
1 Tbsp. unbleached flour
1 tsp. lemon zest

Melt margarine in a medium skillet. Saute onion and garlic for 2 to 3 minutes. Add spinach, thyme, pepper, sesame seeds and sour cream. Mix well. Divide filling evenly among fillets. Roll up and place in a 8" by 8" baking dish coated with cooking spray. Pour wine over fish.

Bake at 350° for 20 minutes or until fish flakes easily with a fork. Remove fish to a platter, cover and keep warm. Whisk flour into pan juices. Cook and stir over medium heat until thick. Stir in lemon zest and serve over fish.

Serves 4 to 6

Per serving:	Calories	Fat (g)	Cholesterol (mg)	Fiber (g)	Sodium (mg)
	154	3	55	1	161

Honey Mustard Swordfish

2 Tbsp. Dijon mustard
2 Tbsp. honey
1 Tbsp. lemon juice
1 Tbsp. low-sodium soy sauce

1 clove garlic, minced
1¹/₂ lbs. swordfish (*or* other firm fish
  such as tuna, halibut *or* shark)

In a small bowl, combine mustard, honey, lemon juice, soy sauce and garlic. Pour over swordfish and marinate for one hour. Drain well, reserving marinade. Broil or grill for 10 minutes per inch of thickness, basting often with marinade.

Variation: Substitute skinless, boneless chicken breasts for fish

Serves: 6

Per serving:	Calories	Fat (g)	Cholesterol (mg)	Fiber (g)	Sodium (mg)
	167	5	44	0	267

Lime Marinated Swordfish

This zesty marinade compliments any fish

2 lbs. swordfish (*or* salmon, tuna,
  shark, marlin, etc)
2 tsp. lime zest
¹/₃ cup lime juice

1 clove garlic, minced
¹/₄ cup olive oil
¹/₂ cup chopped fresh cilantro
Fresh cilantro

Place fish in a shallow pan. In a small bowl, combine lime juice, zest, garlic, olive oil and cilantro. Pour over fish and turn to coat thoroughly. Cover and refrigerate for 2 to 3 hours.

Drain fish and broil or grill until fish flakes easily with a fork, about 8 to 10 minutes per inch of thickness. Serve garnished with cilantro.

Serves 6 to 8

Per serving:	Calories	Fat (g)	Cholesterol (mg)	Fiber (g)	Sodium (mg)
	201	11	44	0	104

Chinese Steamed Trout

2 whole trout, dressed*
Freshly ground black pepper
18 thin slices fresh ginger

6 green onions, thinly sliced
1 Tbsp. low-sodium soy sauce
1 tsp. sesame oil

Make several slashes in each side of trout. Rub with pepper inside and out. Insert a slice of ginger into each slash. Place remaining ginger inside trout along with sliced green onion (reserve 1 to 2 Tbsp. for garnish). Fold trout over and place on a steamer rack. Drizzle with soy sauce and sprinkle with remaining green onion.

Steam until fish flakes easily with a fork, 8 to 10 minutes per inch of thickness. Sprinkle with sesame oil and serve

* Dressed: cleaned and head removed.

Serves 2

Per serving:	Calories	Fat (g)	Cholesterol (mg)	Fiber (g)	Sodium (mg)
	236	8	96	0	347

Trout with Orange Vinaigrette

1/2 cup fresh orange juice
1/4 cup white wine vinegar
1 Tbsp. orange zest
1 Tbsp. chopped fresh cilantro (optional)
1 tsp. brown sugar *or* honey

1 tsp. minced jalapeño
1 clove garlic, minced
Freshly ground black pepper
2 Tbsp. olive oil
4 4-oz. trout fillets

Combine orange juice, vinegar, zest, cilantro, brown sugar, jalapeño, garlic and pepper to taste. Whisk in oil. Place trout fillets in a shallow baking dish. Pour marinade over. Cover and marinate in the refrigerator for 30 to 60 minutes. Drain well.

Grill or broil, turning once, until fish flakes easily with a fork, 8 to 10 minutes per inch of thickness.

Serves 2 to 4

Per serving:	Calories	Fat (g)	Cholesterol (mg)	Fiber (g)	Sodium (mg)
	216	11	64	0	43

Turbot with Avocado Cream

A beautiful color and flavor combination

1¹/₂ lbs. turbot, sole, cod *or*
  orange roughy
1 avocado, peeled and pitted
1 cup plain non-fat yogurt

1 clove garlic, minced
1 Thsp. chopped fresh basil *or*
  1 tsp. dried
1 tomato, cored and diced

Place turbot in a baking dish coated with cooking spray. Bake at 400° for 10 to 12 minutes or until fish flakes easily with a fork.

Place avocado, yogurt, garlic and basil in a blender or food processor. Process until smooth. Fold in diced tomato. Serve over fish.

Serves 4 to 6

Per serving:	Calories	Fat (g)	Cholesterol (mg)	Fiber (g)	Sodium (mg)
	235	14	25	1	101

Barbequed Seafood with Plum Sauce

Plum Sauce:
¹/₂ cup plum sauce*
1 Tbsp. dry mustard
2 Tbsp. rice vinegar
1 Tbsp. sesame oil
1 Tbsp. low-sodium soy sauce

1 lb. scallops
¹/₂ lb. shrimp, peeled

For sauce: in a small bowl, combine first five ingredients and mix well. Marinate scallops and shrimp, in refrigerator, in one-half of sauce for 1 to 2 hours. Remove from marinade; thread onto skewers and broil or grill 5 to 10 minutes or until done. Baste frequently. Heat remaining sauce and serve with seafood.

* Available in oriental food section in grocery stores

Serves 4 to 6

Per serving:	Calories	Fat (g)	Cholesterol (mg)	Fiber (g)	Sodium (mg)
	187	5	95	0	410

San Francisco Cioppino

This hearty soup combines low-fat seafood with a robust
tomato broth — delicious with sourdough bread

1/3 cup sun dried tomatoes
1 cup boiling water
1 Tbsp. olive oil
1 onion, chopped
1 leek, chopped
1 green *or* red bell pepper, cored,
  seeded and diced
2 to 3 cloves garlic, minced
1 15-oz. can salt-free tomato sauce
1 28-oz. can Italian style tomatoes
1 cup dry red *or* white wine
1/2 cup chopped parsley
1 bay leaf

1 Tbsp. chopped fresh basil *or*
  1 tsp. dried
1 tsp. dried oregano
1/2 tsp. dried marjoram
1/2 tsp. red chili pepper flakes (optional)
1/4 tsp. dried thyme
1 lb. firm white fish (e.g. sea bass, grouper,
  red snapper, orange roughy, cod)
1 lb. king crab (in the shell), cracked
1/4 lb. bay scallops
1/4 lb. raw shrimp, shelled and deveined
12 clams in the shell, scrubbed
12 mussels in the shell, scrubbed

Place sun-dried tomatoes in a small bowl and cover with boiling water. Let stand 1 to 2 hours. Drain, reserving soaking water; chop tomatoes and set aside.

In a large pot, heat olive oil. Saute onion, leek, peppers and garlic until soft, about 5 minutes. Add tomato sauce, tomatoes (break into smaller pieces with a spoon), soaking water from tomatoes, dried tomato pieces, wine, parsley, bay leaf, basil, oregano, marjoram, red pepper flakes and thyme. Cover and simmer for 30 minutes, stirring occasionally.

Cube fish and add to broth. Simmer 5 minutes. Add scallops, shrimp, clams and mussels. Cover and simmer 4 to 5 minutes or until shellfish opens and shrimp just turns pink. Serve immediately with hot bread to soak up fish broth.

Serves 4 to 6

Per serving:	Calories	Fat (g)	Cholesterol (mg)	Fiber (g)	Sodium (mg)
	320	10	100	3	551

Pasta with Scallops and Peppers

1 Tbsp. olive oil
1 clove garlic, minced
1/2 cup red onion, chopped
4 green onions, thinly sliced
1 red bell pepper, julienne
1 green bell pepper, julienne
8 oz. bay scallops

1 cup fresh corn (cut from 2 ears)
or salt-free canned corn, drained
1 tsp. minced fresh ginger
2 Tbsp fresh lime juice
2 to 4 Tbsp. chopped fresh cilantro
Freshly black ground pepper
8 oz. eggless pasta, cooked and drained

In a large skillet, heat olive oil. Saute garlic, onions and peppers until tender, about 5 minutes. Increase heat to high; add scallops and corn. Stir-fry until scallops are opaque, about 5 minutes. Stir in ginger, lime juice and cilantro; season to taste with pepper.

Toss scallop mixture with pasta and serve garnished with cilantro sprigs and lime wedges.

Serves 4

Per serving:	Calories	Fat (g)	Cholesterol (mg)	Fiber (g)	Sodium (mg)
	347	5	32	3	164

Peppery Shrimp and Scallops

This recipe is not for those with delicate taste buds

1 lb. shrimp
1 lb. scallops
1/2 cup olive oil
1 cup dry white wine

2 to 3 garlic cloves, minced
1 tsp. white wine Worcestershire sauce
2 Tbsp. minced fresh parsley
1/4 cup freshly ground black pepper

Shell and devein shrimp leaving tail intact. Mix shrimp and scallops with remaining ingredients and marinate 2 to 4 hours. Bake at 350° for 15 to 20 minutes or until seafood is done. Serve with hot French or sourdough bread.

Variation: Serve as an appetizer on toothpicks.

Serves 5 to 6

Per serving:	Calories	Fat (g)	Cholesterol (mg)	Fiber (g)	Sodium (mg)
	249	11	95	1	323

Sesame Scallops

Toasted sesame seeds add crunch to these spicy-sweet scallops

¼ **cup sesame seed**	1 **Tbsp. low-sodium soy sauce**
3 **Tbsp. lemon juice**	1 **tsp. minced fresh ginger**
1 **tsp. canola or safflower oil**	1 **clove garlic, minced**
1 **Tbsp. honey**	1 **lb. scallops (cut in half if large)**

In a skillet toast sesame seed over medium heat, stirring occasionally, until golden brown. Set aside.

Combine lemon juice, oil, honey, soy sauce, ginger and garlic in a medium bowl. Mix well, then add scallops. Cover and marinade in the refrigerator for 2 to 4 hours. Stir occasionally.

Drain scallops (reserving the liquid) and thread onto skewers. Broil, basting with marinade, until opaque, about 3 to 5 minutes. Spread sesame seed onto waxed paper or in a shallow dish. Roll scallops, still on skewer, in sesame seed coating evenly. Serve immediately.

Serves 4 to 6

Per serving:	Calories	Fat (g)	Cholesterol (mg)	Fiber (g)	Sodium (mg)
	143	5	42	0	299

Seafood Pesto Saute

1 **Tbsp. olive oil**	1 **cup sliced mushrooms**
1 **onion, chopped**	2 **Tbsp. Pesto (page 293)**
1 **carrot, sliced**	½ **lb. scallops (cut in half if large)**
1 **zucchini, sliced**	¼ **lb. raw shrimp, peeled and deveined**
1 **green *or* red bell pepper, julienne**	

Heat oil in a large skillet. Add onion and carrot; saute for 2 to 3 minutes. Add zucchini, bell pepper and mushrooms; continue cooking until vegetables are just tender-crisp. Remove from pan and keep warm.

Heat pesto in skillet and stir-fry scallops and shrimp until just done (scallops are opaque and shrimp have turned pink). Return vegetables to pan and stir until heated through. Serve over brown rice or noodles (eggless).

Serves 3 to 4

Per serving:	Calories	Fat (g)	Cholesterol (mg)	Fiber (g)	Sodium (mg)
	215	10	71	2	251

Stir-Fried Scallops

2 Tbsp. oyster sauce*
2 tsp. cornstarch
1 tsp. low-sodium soy sauce
1/4 tsp. brown sugar
1/2 lb. scallops (cut in half if large)

1 Tbsp. peanut, canola *or* safflower oil
1 Tbsp. minced fresh ginger
1 1/2 cups snow pea pods
6 green onions, thinly sliced
1/2 cup sliced water chestnuts

In a medium bowl, combine oyster sauce, cornstarch, soy sauce and sugar. Stir in scallops and set aside.

Heat oil in a wok. Add ginger, pea pods, onions and waterchestnuts. Stir-fry until vegetables are tender-crisp, 3 to 4 minutes. Add scallops and stir-fry for 3 to 4 minutes or until scallops are opaque and sauce has thickened slightly. Serve over hot Chinese rice.

Note: Look for oyster sauce in the oriental food section of the grocery store.

Serves 4

Per serving:	Calories	Fat (g)	Cholesterol (mg)	Fiber (g)	Sodium (mg)
	155	5	32	3	270

Seafood Oriental

1/2 lb. halibut
1/2 lb scallops
1/2 lb. shrimp, shelled
2 cloves garlic, minced

4 to 6 green onions, thinly sliced
2 Tbsp. low-sodium soy sauce
2 tsp. sesame oil

Cut halibut into bite-size pieces. Divide seafood, garlic and green onions evenly among 6 squares of foil. Drizzle with soy sauce and sesame oil. Seal tightly. Bake at 400° for about 10 to 15 minutes or until halibut flakes easily with a fork.

Serves 6

Per serving:	Calories	Fat (g)	Cholesterol (mg)	Fiber (g)	Sodium (mg)
	161	4	90	0	437

Seafood Curry

1 cup non-fat milk
2 Tbsp. non-fat dry milk
1 tsp. chicken bouillon granules
1 Tbsp. olive oil
1 onion, chopped
1/2 cup chopped celery
1/2 cup chopped green *or* red bell pepper

1 tsp. curry powder
1/2 tsp. minced fresh ginger
2 Tbsp. unbleached flour
1/4 lb. *each* cooked small shrimp,
   bay scallops and crabmeat
4 green onions, thinly sliced

Mix together non-fat milk, dry milk and bouillon granules. Stir well to dissolve; set aside.

Heat oil in a large saucepan. Saute onion, celery and bell pepper until just tender. Stir in curry powder, ginger and flour; cook until bubbly. Gradually blend in milk mixture. Cook, stirring constantly, until thickened. Stir in shellfish and green onions; cook until heated through, about 2 to 3 minutes.

Serve over hot brown rice.

Serves 2 to 3

Per serving:	Calories	Fat (g)	Cholesterol (mg)	Fiber (g)	Sodium (mg)
	208	5	87	1	731

Seafood Saute with Mushrooms

1 1/2 Tbsp. soft margarine
2 cups sliced mushrooms
2 cloves garlic, minced
1/4 cup minced shallots
3/4 lb. scallops (if large, cut in quarters)

1/2 lb. shrimp, shelled
1/4 cup dry white wine
1/2 tsp. paprika
2 Tbsp. minced fresh chives

Melt margarine in a large skillet. Add mushrooms, garlic and shallots; saute until lightly browned, 8 to 10 minutes. Stir often. Add scallops, shrimp and wine. Cook, stirring often, until shrimp has turned pink and scallops are opaque. Stir in paprika and chives. Serve over hot brown rice.

Serves 4

Per serving:	Calories	Fat (g)	Cholesterol (mg)	Fiber (g)	Sodium (mg)
	169	6	52	2	298

Beer Boiled Shrimp

Especially good on a hot summer day. Serve with lots of napkins

1 lb. raw shrimp, unpeeled
2 cups beer
2 bay leaves

4 peppercorns
1 clove garlic, peeled
3 to 4 lemon slices

Combine all ingredients in a large pot. Cover and bring to a boil over medium heat. Stir, then remove from heat and let stand, covered, until shrimp is pink and firm, about 5 to 10 minutes. Stir occasionally. Drain well. Serve chilled or at room temperature.

Serves 4 to 6

Per serving:	Calories	Fat (g)	Cholesterol (mg)	Fiber (g)	Sodium (mg)
	89	1	106	0	222

*Buy the leanest beef you can find — Select Grade
is a good choice — then trim it well before cooking to
minimize fat. Lean beef and other red meats have a place in
a low-fat, low-cholesterol diet as they are a good source
of protein and important trace minerals. Serve beef
occasionally and in small portions to keep
saturated fat and cholesterol intake low.*

Delitefully HealthMark

All Day Chile Verde 209
Carne Asada Jalisco 210
Cool Beef and Veggie Salad 208
Curried Orange Beef Kabobs 212
Fiesta Salad 205
Gingered Beef and Asparagus Stir-Fry 211
Mustard Marinated Beef 209
Oriental Beef Salad 206
Southwest Grilled Beef 207
Southwestern Stir-Fry 213
Tabbouleh with Beef 207
Thai Sesame Beef 210

Fiesta Salad

A low-fat version of everyone's favorite taco salad

1 lb. *lean* ground beef *or*
  ground turkey
1 jalapeño pepper, seeded and minced
1 clove garlic, minced
1 tsp. to 1 Tbsp. chili powder (to taste)
1/2 tsp. black pepper
1/4 cup tomato juice
2 cups vegetarian refried beans
1/2 cup diced green chiles (canned)

1/2 cup water
1 head romaine lettuce, shredded
1 head red leaf lettuce, shredded
1 tomato, cored and chopped
2 oz. low-fat cheddar cheese, grated
4 to 6 green onions, thinly sliced
4 black olives, rinsed, drained and sliced
1/2 cup chopped fresh cilantro (optional)
Mexican Salsa (page 10)

In a large skillet, cook ground beef, jalapeño, garlic, chili powder and pepper. When beef is no longer pink, add tomato juice and simmer for 5 to 10 minutes. In a saucepan, heat together beans, green chiles and water.

In a large serving bowl (or in individual bowls), layer lettuces, bean and beef mixtures. Garnish with diced tomato, cheese, green onions, sliced olives and cilantro. Serve with Salsa.

Serves 4

Per serving:	Calories	Fat (g)	Cholesterol (mg)	Fiber (g)	Sodium (mg)
	389	15	56	7	405

Oriental Beef Salad

Serve with crusty whole wheat rolls for a luncheon or light dinner

Marinade:
1/2 cup low-sodium soy sauce
3 Tbsp. brown sugar *or* honey
1 Tbsp. minced fresh ginger
2 cloves garlic, minced
1/2 tsp. crushed dried red pepper
 flakes (optional)
1 12-oz. *lean* flank steak, well trimmed

Salad:
8 cups mixed salad greens (romaine,
 spinach, red leaf lettuce, etc.)
1 cup thinly sliced English cucumber
1 cup thinly sliced red onion
1/2 cup diced red bell pepper
1/2 cup thinly sliced carrot
1/2 cup sliced water chestnuts
1/2 cup chopped fresh cilantro

1/4 cup low-sodium soy sauce
2 Tbsp. fresh lemon juice
1/2 to 1 tsp. minced jalapeño chile (to taste)
2 Tbsp. peanut oil
2 Tbsp. olive oil

1 tsp. black sesame seeds
1 tsp. toasted sesame seeds

Combine soy, sugar, ginger, garlic and red pepper flakes in a dish large enough to hold steak. Mix well to dissolve sugar. Add steak, pricking all over with a fork to allow marinade to penetrate. Cover and refrigerate 2 to 3 hours, turning occasionally.

Toss salad ingredients together in a large bowl. Cover and chill. In a small bowl, combine 1/4 cup soy sauce, lemon juice and chile. Gradually whisk in oils.

Remove steak from marinade and grill to desired doneness. Toss salad with dressing and divide among plates. Slice steak thinly across grain and arrange on top of salad. Sprinkle with black and toasted sesame seeds. Serve garnished with cilantro sprigs.

Variation: Substitute boneless, skinless chicken breasts for steak.

Serves 4

Per serving:	Calories	Fat (g)	Cholesterol (mg)	Fiber (g)	Sodium (mg)
	359	14	57	9	454

Tabbouleh with Beef

2 tomatoes, cored and diced
1 cup cucumber slices (seeded)
1/4 cup bulgur, uncooked
1 cup chopped leftover *lean* round steak
1/2 cup diced red bell pepper
1/2 cup diced green pepper
1/3 cup chopped fresh parsley
1/3 cup chopped red onion

2 Tbsp. chopped fresh mint
2 Tbsp. fresh lemon *or* lime juice
1/4 tsp. Lite Salt™
Freshly ground black pepper (to taste)
Romaine lettuce leaves
Cucumber spears
Mint leaves

In a medium bowl, combine tomatoes, cucumber slices and bulgur. Mix well; cover and let stand 1 hour or until bulgur is soft. Add beef, red and green peppers, parsley, onion, mint, lemon juice, Lite Salt and pepper. Cover and refrigerate 2 to 3 hours, stirring occasionally.

Serve on a platter lined with romaine lettuce leaves and garnished with cucumber spears and mint leaves.

Serves 4

Per serving:	Calories	Fat (g)	Cholesterol (mg)	Fiber (g)	Sodium (mg)
	116	2	14	2	85

Southwest Grilled Beef

1 12-oz bottle light beer *or* non alcoholic beer
1/4 cup chopped fresh cilantro
2 cloves garlic, minced
1/4 cup fresh lime juice
3 Tbsp. red wine vinegar

1 Tbsp. lime zest
1 tsp. cumin
1/2 tsp. to 1 Tbsp. chili powder (to taste)
2 lbs. *lean* beef (flank, round *or* sirloin)

Combine all ingredients, except beef, and mix well. Pour into a zip-top plastic bag. Add meat; seal bag and marinate, overnight, in refrigerator.

Drain well and broil or grill until done to your preference.

Serves 6 to 8

Per serving:	Calories	Fat (g)	Cholesterol (mg)	Fiber (g)	Sodium (mg)
	259	8	76	0	82

Cool Beef and Veggie Salad

1 cup plain non-fat yogurt
1/2 cup chopped cucumber
1/4 cup chopped fresh parsley
1 to 2 Tbsp. minced fresh dill *or*
 1 tsp. dried
1 clove garlic, minced
2 cups green beans, trimmed

2 cups cauliflowerets
2 cups thinly sliced cooked *lean* beef
 (e.g. flank, tenderloin)
2 cups cherry tomatoes, halved
1 zucchini, halved and thinly sliced
Baby corn (rinse and drain)
Chopped fresh parsley

In a small bowl, combine yogurt, cucumber, parsley, dill and garlic. Cover and refrigerate for 1 to 2 hours to blend flavors.

Steam green beans and cauliflower for 3 to 4 minutes or until tender crisp. Drain well and cool to room temperature. Combine with beef, tomato halves, zucchini and reserved dressing. Toss gently to coat with dressing. Garnish with baby corn, additional tomato halves and sprinkle with chopped parsley.

Serve at room temperature or cover and chill 2 to 3 hours before serving.

Serves 4 to 6

Per serving:	Calories	Fat (g)	Cholesterol (mg)	Fiber (g)	Sodium (mg)
	146	4	28	3	60

All Day Chile Verde

1/2 Tbsp. olive oil
1 onion, chopped
2 cloves garlic, minced
1 lb. *lean* round steak *or* skinless turkey
   cut into 1" cubes
1/4 tsp. freshly ground black pepper
3 16-oz. cans salt-free stewed tomatoes
2 13-oz. cans green tomatoes, chopped*

1 4-oz. can chopped green chiles
1/3 cup chopped fresh cilantro
2 Tbsp. lemon juice
11/2 tsp. dried oregano, crushed
1 tsp. ground cumin
1 tsp. ground coriander
1/8 tsp. allspice

Heat olive oil in a large skillet. Saute onion and garlic until soft. Add meat and saute until browned. Place in a crock pot with remaining ingredients. Mix well. Cover and cook on low heat for 6 to 8 hours, or simmer in a large pot for 3 to 4 hours, adding water if needed.

Serve over brown rice or with corn tortillas.

Serves 6 to 8

* Look for canned green tomatoes in the Mexican food section of the grocery store

Per serving:	Calories	Fat (g)	Cholesterol (mg)	Fiber (g)	Sodium (mg)
	199	5	38	6	187

Mustard Marinated Beef

1/2 cup Dijon mustard
2 Tbsp. low-sodium soy sauce
3 Tbsp. dry sherry *or* salt-free
   chicken broth, defatted
1 Tbsp. brown sugar *or* honey
1 Tbsp. olive oil

2 cloves garlic, minced
1 tsp. dried tarragon
1/4 to 1/2 tsp. red pepper sauce
11/2 lbs. *lean* flank *or* sirloin steak,
   well trimmed

In a small bowl, whisk together all ingredients except meat. Place steak in a shallow dish or plastic zip-lock bag. Pour marinade over steak and coat thoroughly. Cover and refrigerate 4 to 6 hours, turning occasionally. Grill or broil, brushing with marinade, until desired doneness.

Variation: substitute turkey breast slices or skinless chicken breasts for beef.

Serves 6

Per serving:	Calories	Fat (g)	Cholesterol (mg)	Fiber (g)	Sodium (mg)
	301	11	76	0	552

Carne Asada Jalisco

Serve with Ensalada Escabeche and warm corn tortillas for a special south-of-the-border meal

Juice of one lime
Zest of one lime
1 clove garlic, minced
1/4 cup chopped fresh cilantro
1 tsp. low-sodium soy sauce

1/4 tsp. dried oregano
1/4 tsp. cumin
Freshly ground black pepper
1 *lean* eye of round *or* flank steak,
   well trimmed

In a zip-top plastic bag, combine lime juice, zest, garlic, cilantro, soy sauce, oregano, cumin and pepper to taste. Pierce steak all over with fork then place in bag. Seal top and turn bag to coat meat thoroughly with marinade. Marinate, refrigerated, 1 to 2 hours. Drain well.

Broil or grill steak until desired doneness. Slice into thin strips and serve.

Serves 2 to 4

Per serving:	Calories	Fat (g)	Cholesterol (mg)	Fiber (g)	Sodium (mg)
	246	8	76	0	125

Thai Sesame Beef

1 cup thinly sliced green onions
1 cup low-sodium soy sauce
1/2 cup water
1/2 cup dry sherry (optional)
1/4 cup brown sugar

1/4 cup sesame seeds
5 cloves garlic, minced
1 tsp. freshly ground black pepper
1 lb. *lean* beef (e.g. sirloin *or* round),
   well trimmed

Combine onions, soy sauce, water, sherry, sugar, sesame seeds, garlic and pepper in a bowl; mix well to dissolve sugar. Place meat in a shallow glass dish and pour marinade over. Prick all over with a fork to allow marinade to penetrate. Cover and marinate in the refrigerator overnight; turn occasionally.

Drain meat; broil or grill to desired doneness, basing occasionally with marinade.

Serve with hot brown rice; garnish with green onions.

Serves 4

Per serving:	Calories	Fat (g)	Cholesterol (mg)	Fiber (g)	Sodium (mg)
	291	9	76	0	673

Gingered Beef and Asparagus Stir-Fry

A variety of stir-fry recipes appear in this book as it is the perfect dish
for a high-carbohydrate, low-fat, low-cholesterol meal — lean meat is used
sparingly just to provide flavor and texture

3/4 lb. *lean* sirloin *or* tenderloin steak,
  well trimmed
1/2 cup dry sherry
2 Tbsp. low-sodium soy sauce
1 Tbsp. minced fresh ginger
2 cloves garlic, minced
1 tsp. lemon zest
1 Tbsp. sesame oil
1 lb. fresh asparagus,
  trimmed and cut into 2" pieces

1 cup julienne carrots
1 cup celery, sliced on the diagonal
1 red bell pepper, julienne
1 onion, thinly sliced
2 tsp. cornstarch
Cooked brown rice
1 Tbsp. toasted sesame seeds

Trim all fat from steak. Partially freeze, then slice diagonally across the grain into thin strips. Combine with sherry, soy sauce, ginger, garlic and zest in a medium bowl; mix well. Cover and refrigerate for 2 to 3 hours; stir occasionally.

Heat a wok or a large skillet. Add sesame oil. Stir-fry asparagus, carrots, celery, pepper and onion until tender-crisp, 3 to 5 minutes. Add small amounts of water to wok as necessary to prevent vegetables from sticking. Remove and keep warm.

Remove steak from marinade and drain well. Add steak to skillet and stir-fry for 2 to 3 minutes. Add cornstarch to reserved marinade and mix well. Add marinade and vegetables to wok; stir-fry until vegetables are heated through and sauce thickens slightly.

Serve over hot rice garnished with toasted sesame seeds.

Serves 6 to 8

Per serving:	Calories	Fat (g)	Cholesterol (mg)	Fiber (g)	Sodium (mg)
	185	6	38	1	120

Curried Orange Beef Kabobs

1 lb. *lean* sirloin *or* tenderloin steak,
  well trimmed
2 oranges, unpeeled
1/3 cup low-sugar orange marmalade
1/4 cup fresh orange juice

2 Tbsp. dry sherry (optional)
1 clove garlic, minced
1/2 tsp. curry powder
1/4 tsp. crushed red pepper flakes
1 lb. mushrooms

Partially freeze steak; cut into 1" cubes.

Cut oranges into 1/2" slices, then cut each slice into 8 wedges.

Combine marmalade, juice, sherry, garlic, curry and red pepper in a small saucepan. Heat until marmalade melts, stirring occasionally.

Thread steak, orange wedges and whole mushrooms onto skewers. Place on pre-heated grill coated with cooking spray and cook for 10 minutes or until done. Baste frequently with marmalade mixture.

Serves 4

Per serving:	Calories	Fat (g)	Cholesterol (mg)	Fiber (g)	Sodium (mg)
	389	8	76	7	92

Southwestern Stir-Fry

A small amount of meat adds flavor and texture to this unique stir-fry

1/2 cup fresh orange juice
Juice of one lime
1 tsp. to 1 Tbsp. chili powder (to taste)
1/2 tsp. dried oregano
1 clove garlic, minced
1 tsp. cornstarch
1/4 lb. *lean* round steak, well trimmed
  and thinly sliced

1 Tbsp. olive oil
1 onion, sliced
1 red bell pepper, cored, seeded and julienne
1 green pepper, cored, seeded and julienne
1 15-oz. can salt-free kidney beans, drained
1 cup salt-free corn, drained
2 tomatoes, cored and sliced into wedges
Chopped fresh cilantro

In a medium bowl, combine juices, chili powder, oregano, garlic and cornstarch. Add sliced round steak. Mix well and marinate, refrigerated, for 1 to 2 hours. Drain, reserving liquid

Heat half of oil in a wok or large skillet. Add onion and peppers. Stir-fry until vegetables are tender-crisp. Remove and keep warm. Add remaining oil then stir-fry beef mixture until just browned. Stir in kidney beans, corn, tomato wedges, reserved vegetables and reserved marinade. Stir gently until warmed through and sauce is slightly thickened. Serve garnished with chopped cilantro.

Variation: Substitute skinless, boneless chicken breasts for round steak.

Serves 4 to 6

Per serving:	Calories	Fat (g)	Cholesterol (mg)	Fiber (g)	Sodium (mg)
	168	6	13	5	28

Rich in carotene, Vitamin C, potassium
and fiber, vegetables supply loads of nutritional value
for few very calories. Eat a variety of vegetables
daily to fill you up, but not out.

Delitefully HealthMark

Apple Filled Acorn Squash 231
Brussels Sprouts with Chestnuts 218
Chilled Asparagus in Dijon Mustard Sauce 217
Cinnamon Sticks 229
Cranberry Walnut Sauce 236
Creamed Spinach 229
Crispy Breaded Eggplant 222
Eggplant Crepes 223
Eggplant Parmesan 224
Glazed Vegetables 234
Golden Mashed Potatoes 227
Green Beans Itailan 223
Grilled Peppers 226
Herbed Summer Vegetables 235
Herbed Eggplant 222
Jalapeño Corn Cassrole 221
Mushrooms Provencal 225
Mustard Glazed Carrots 219
Olive Salsa 228
Orange Glazed Sweet Potatoes 228
Oriental Sesame Beans 224

Parmesan Tomatoes 232
Raspberry Carrots 220
Roasted Potato Packets 225
Spicy Orange Broccoli 218
Stir-Fried Asparagus with Cashews 217
Stir-Fried Broccoli 219
Stir-Fried Snow Peas 230
Stuffed Onions 226
Stuffed Red Peppers 227
Sweet and Sour Red Cabbage 221
Sweet and Sour Zucchini 233
Sweet Potato and Apple Casserole 231
Szechwan Spinach 230
Tart Cranberry Relish 236
Three Cabbage Stir-Fry 220
Tomatoes with Pesto 232
Tomatoes Provencal 233
Vegetable Medley Saute 235
Zucchini Pizza 234

Chilled Asparagus in Dijon Mustard Sauce

1 lb. fresh asparagus, trimmed
1 cup Dijon Mustard Sauce (page 290)
2 Tbsp. chopped fresh dill

2 Tbsp. chopped fresh chives
Freshly ground black pepper

Steam asparagus until tender-crisp. Chill one hour. Arrange on a platter or on individual plates lined with romaine or red leaf lettuce.

Combine Mustard Sauce, dill, chives and pepper to taste. Spoon sauce over asparagus and serve chilled.

Serves 4

Per serving:	Calories	Fat (g)	Cholesterol (mg)	Fiber (g)	Sodium (mg)
	45	1	2	1	71

Stir-Fried Asparagus with Cashews

Simple and simply delicious

1 1/2 lbs. asparagus
2 tsp. olive oil
2 tsp. sesame oil
1 Tbsp. minced fresh ginger

1/4 cup chopped dry-roasted,
unsalted cashews *or* almonds
1 Tbsp. low-sodium soy sauce

Trim tough ends of asparagus and slice diagonally into bite-size pieces. Heat a wok and add oils. Swirl to coat entire surface. Add ginger and stir-fry for 1 minute. Add asparagus and stir-fry until bright green and tender-crisp, about 4 to 5 minutes. Stir in cashews and soy sauce and mix well. Serve immediately.

Serves 4 to 6

Per serving:	Calories	Fat (g)	Cholesterol (mg)	Fiber (g)	Sodium (mg)
	54	3	0	1	101

Spicy Orange Broccoli

1 lb. broccoli, trimmed
1 cup fresh orange juice
1 Tbsp. cornstarch
1 tsp. orange zest

$^1/_2$ tsp. dried tarragon
$^1/_2$ tsp. dry mustard
2 or 3 drops hot pepper sauce
Chopped fresh parsley *or* chives

Cut broccoli into spears and steam until tender-crisp. Keep warm while preparing sauce.

In a small saucepan, blend orange juice gradually into cornstarch. Add zest, tarragon, mustard and hot pepper sauce. Cook over low heat, stirring constantly, until thickened.

Serve sauce over broccoli garnished with chopped parsley or chives and additional orange zest.

Note: This sauce is also good served over grilled chicken or fish

Serves 4

Per serving:	Calories	Fat (g)	Cholesterol (mg)	Fiber (g)	Sodium (mg)
	70	1	0	4	34

Brussels Sprouts with Chestnuts

2 cups fresh chestnuts
2 cups brussels sprouts
1 cup salt-free chicken broth, defatted
1 Tbsp. caraway seeds

1 Tbsp. kummel (caraway flavored
  liqueur) (optional)
$^1/_4$ tsp. white pepper

Cut an "X" in the bottom of each chestnut. Place in a saucepan, cover with water and simmer for 5 minutes. Remove from water a few at a time and peel, removing shell and skin. Set aside.

Steam brussels sprouts until tender crisp and set aside.

Combine chestnuts and broth in a skillet. Simmer until chestnuts are tender, about 10 minutes. Add caraway seeds and simmer until broth is reduced by half, about 5 minutes. Add brussels sprouts, kummel and pepper. Stir until heated through.

Serves 6 to 8

Per serving:	Calories	Fat (g)	Cholesterol (mg)	Fiber (g)	Sodium (mg)
	40	0	0	1	10

Stir-Fried Broccoli

Good as a side dish or served over brown rice

2 tsp. oriental sesame oil
1 clove garlic, minced
1 Tbsp. minced fresh ginger
4 green onions, thinly sliced
1/2 lb. mushrooms, sliced
1 lb. broccoli, cut into flowerets

1 8-oz. can water chestnuts, sliced
1 Tbsp. cornstarch
1 tsp. brown sugar
3/4 cup salt-free chicken broth, defatted
2 tsp. low-sodium soy sauce

Heat a wok and add oil. Swirl to coat entire surface. Add garlic, ginger, green onions and mushrooms. Stir-fry for 2 to 3 minutes. Do not let garlic burn. Add broccoli and water chestnuts; stir-fry 3 to 4 minutes.

Combine cornstarch and brown sugar. Gradually add chicken broth, then stir in soy sauce. Pour into wok. Cook and stir until thickened. Reduce heat and simmer, covered, until broccoli is tender crisp, about 5 minutes. Serve immediately.

Variation: Add 1/3 cup almonds, peanuts or cashews along with broccoli.

Serves 6 to 8

Per serving:	Calories	Fat (g)	Cholesterol (mg)	Fiber (g)	Sodium (mg)
	68	2	0	4	76

Mustard Glazed Carrots

1 lb. carrots, peeled and sliced
1 Tbsp. liquid margarine
1 Tbsp. Dijon mustard
2 Tbsp. honey

1 tsp. lemon zest
1/4 tsp. white pepper
1/4 tsp. ginger

Steam carrots until tender-crisp. In a small pan, combine remaining ingredients over low heat, stirring until just combined. Pour sauce over carrots and toss gently to coat.

Serves 4

Per serving:	Calories	Fat (g)	Cholesterol (mg)	Fiber (g)	Sodium (mg)
	105	3	0	2	136

Raspberry Carrots

4 carrots, peeled and sliced
2 Tbsp. raspberry vinegar

1 tsp. orange zest
1 tsp. lemon zest

Steam carrots until tender-crisp. Toss with vinegar and zest before serving.

Serves 4

Per serving:	Calories	Fat (g)	Cholesterol (mg)	Fiber (g)	Sodium (mg)
	31	0	0	1	35

Three Cabbage Stir-Fry

2 Tbsp. rice vinegar
2 Tbsp. low-sodium soy sauce
2 tsp. oriental sesame oil
2 tsp. cornstarch
1 tsp. brown sugar
2 cups shredded red cabbage
2 cups shredded green cabbage
3 cups shredded Chinese cabbage

1 cup thinly sliced carrots
1 Tbsp. peanut *or* olive oil
3 cloves garlic, minced
1 Tbsp. minced fresh ginger
2 Tbsp. sesame seeds *or* chopped
   unsalted peanuts
2 to 3 drops hot chili oil (optional)

In a small bowl, combine vinegar, soy sauce, oil, cornstarch and sugar. Set aside. In a large bowl, combine cabbages and carrots; mix well.

Heat a wok. Add peanut oil and swirl to coat entire surface. Add garlic, ginger and sesame seeds. Stir-fry 1 minute. Add cabbage mixture and stir-fry until wilted, 5 to 6 minutes. Pour in soy mixture and stir-fry 1 minute more. Add chili oil if desired. Serve immediately.

Serves 6 to 8

Per serving:	Calories	Fat (g)	Cholesterol (mg)	Fiber (g)	Sodium (mg)
	64	3	0	3	178

Sweet and Sour Red Cabbage

2 Tbsp. (or less) olive oil
1 head red cabbage, cored and shredded
1 onion, chopped
2 Golden Delicious apples,
   cored and diced (unpeeled)

1/2 cup dry red wine *or* red wine vinegar
2 bay leaves
1/3 cup red currant jelly
Water

Heat olive oil in a large skillet; saute cabbage, onion and apple, stirring often, for 5 to 10 minutes or until wilted. Add remaining ingredients. Cover pan and simmer for 15 to 20 minutes. Add water as needed to prevent cabbage from sticking.

Serves 6 to 8

Per serving:	Calories	Fat (g)	Cholesterol (mg)	Fiber (g)	Sodium (mg)
	124	4	0	4	20

Jalapeño Corn Casserole

Add a tossed green salad, rolls and fresh fruit for a complete meal.

1 Tbsp. olive oil
2 to 3 jalapeño chilies,
   seeded and chopped
1 onion, chopped
1 red bell pepper, seeded and chopped
4 cups fresh *or* frozen (thawed) corn

1 cup 1% cottage cheese
1 egg
2 egg whites
1 Tbsp. cornstarch
1/2 tsp. celery seed
1/2 cup grated low-fat cheddar cheese

Heat olive oil in a medium skillet; saute chilies, onion and bell pepper until tender. Mix in 2 cups corn.

Combine remaining 2 cups corn, cottage cheese, egg, egg whites, cornstarch and celery seed in blender or food processor; process until smooth, 1 to 2 minutes.

Combine corn mixture with sauteed vegetables. Pour into a 9" by 13" baking dish coated with cooking spray. Sprinkle with cheese. Bake at 375° for about 30 minutes, or until mixture puffs in the center.

Variation: Substitute 1-4 oz. can chopped green chiles for jalapeños.

Serves 6 to 8

Per serving:	Calories	Fat (g)	Cholesterol (mg)	Fiber (g)	Sodium (mg)
	166	5	41	4	251

Crispy Breaded Eggplant

3 egg whites
1/2 cup seasoned bread crumbs
2 Tbsp. Parmesan cheese
1/2 tsp. dried basil

1/2 tsp. dried oregano
1/4 tsp. dried thyme
1 large eggplant
1 Tbsp. olive oil

Place egg whites into a small shallow dish and beat lightly. In another shallow bowl, combine bread crumbs, cheese and herbs.

Remove stem from eggplant and slice 1/2" thick. Brush oil onto a non-stick baking sheet. Dip eggplant into egg whites, then into bread crumb mixture. Place slices onto baking sheet and bake at 425° for 15 to 20 minutes or until browned and soft.

Serves 4 to 6

Per serving:	Calories	Fat (g)	Cholesterol (mg)	Fiber (g)	Sodium (mg)
	93	3	2	4	98

Herbed Eggplant

2 Tbsp. Herbed Oil (page 292) *or*
  low-calorie Italian dressing
1 eggplant

Remove stems from eggplant. Cut into 1/2" slices. Brush lightly with Herbed Oil. Place eggplant slices onto a non-stick baking sheet in a single layer. Bake, uncovered, at 425' for 20 to 30 minutes or until browned and soft. Turn, if necessary, to brown evenly.

May be served hot or cold.

Serves 3 to 4

Per serving:	Calories	Fat (g)	Cholesterol (mg)	Fiber (g)	Sodium (mg)
	80	7	0	3	1

Eggplant Crepes

1 eggplant
2 Tbsp. olive oil
1 cup low-fat ricotta cheese
2 to 3 Tbsp. Pesto (page 293)
2 egg whites

1/4 tsp. nutmeg
1/4 tsp. white pepper
1 cup Quick Tomato Sauce (page 294)
1/3 cup grated low-fat Monterey Jack cheese

Trim stem from eggplant. Cut lengthwise into 1/4" thick slices. Place on a non-stick baking sheet. Brush lightly with olive oil. Bake at 400° for 10 to 15 minutes or until soft and lightly browned. Let cool.

In a food processor or blender, combine ricotta cheese, Pesto, egg whites, nutmeg and pepper. Divide filling evenly among eggplant slices, spooning filling down center of each slice. Fold sides over filling. Place in a 9" x 13" baking dish coated with cooking spray. Pour Quick Sauce over crepes, then sprinkle cheese on top.

Bake at 350° for 15 to 20 minutes or until heated through.

Serves 3 to 4

Per serving:	Calories	Fat (g)	Cholesterol (mg)	Fiber (g)	Sodium (mg)
	283	17	30	8	286

Green Beans Italian

1 lb. fresh green beans,
  trimmed and sliced
  into bite-sized pieces
1 red *or* green bell pepper, julienne
1/2 cup chopped red onion

1 clove garlic, minced
1 16-oz. can plum tomatoes, chopped
1 Tbsp. chopped fresh basil
Freshly ground black pepper

Combine all ingredients in a medium saucepan and simmer 15 to 20 minutes or until beans are tender crisp.

Serves 6 to 8

Per serving:	Calories	Fat (g)	Cholesterol (mg)	Fiber (g)	Sodium (mg)
	32	0	0	2	246

Eggplant Parmesan

Delicious served with a green salad and crunchy sourdough bread

1 large eggplant	**3 cups Quick Tomato Sauce (see page 294)**
1-2 Tbsp. olive oil	**1/2 cup Parmesan cheese**

Remove stem from eggplant and slice into 1/2" thick slices. Brush lightly with olive oil and broil 3 minutes per side. Place in a baking dish coated with cooking spray. Cover with Quick Tomato Sauce and sprinkle with Parmesan cheese. Bake at 350° for 20 to 30 minutes or until cheese is bubbly.

Variation: Saute 1/2 lb. ground turkey with 1/2 cup chopped onion and 1 clove minced garlic in a large non-stick skillet until no longer pink. Add Quick Tomato Sauce and simmer 15 minutes. Place one layer of eggplant sliced in baking dish, cover with sauce, add another layer of eggplant slices then sprinkle with cheese. Bake as above.

Serves 4 to 6

Per serving:	Calories	Fat (g)	Cholesterol (mg)	Fiber (g)	Sodium (mg)
	152	8	9	8	260

Oriental Sesame Beans

1 tsp. canola *or* safflower oil	**Freshly ground black pepper**
1 tsp. oriental sesame oil	**3/4 cup fresh bean sprouts**
3 to 4 green onions, thinly sliced	**1 Tbsp. toasted sesame seeds**
1 clove garlic, minced	**2 tsp. low-sodium soy sauce**
1 tsp. grated fresh ginger	
2 cups fresh green beans,	
cut in bite-size pieces	

Heat oils in a large skillet or wok. Saute onions, garlic and ginger for 1 to 2 minutes. Add green beans and pepper to taste. Stir-fry 5 to 6 minutes. Add remaining ingredients. Stir-fry 1 to 2 minutes longer or until bean sprouts are just wilted.

Serves 4

Per serving:	Calories	Fat (g)	Cholesterol (mg)	Fiber (g)	Sodium (mg)
	61	4	0	2	103

Mushrooms Provencal

2 Tbsp. olive oil
1 lb. button mushrooms
2 cloves garlic, minced
1/2 cup minced fresh parsley

1 Tbsp. chopped fresh thyme *or*
  1/4 to 1/2 tsp. dried
Freshly ground black pepper
Juice of 1/2 lemon

Heat olive oil in a large skillet and saute mushrooms with garlic until mushrooms begin to soften. Sprinkle in parsley and thyme. Saute 2 to 3 minutes longer. Season to taste with freshly ground pepper.

Transfer to a serving bowl and squeeze fresh lemon juice over mushrooms. Serve warm or at room temperature on a salad plate lined with lettuce. Garnish with lemon wedges and halved cherry tomatoes.

Serves 4 to 6

Per serving:	Calories	Fat (g)	Cholesterol (mg)	Fiber (g)	Sodium (mg)
	68	5	0	4	14

Roasted Potato Packets

A delicious combination of flavors to enhance the simple potato

3 new potatoes, unpeeled
1 green *or* red bell pepper,
  cored, seeded and diced
4 shallots, peeled and halved *or*
  1 onion, peeled and sliced

2 tsp. olive oil
1 1/2 tsp. minced fresh sage *or*
  1/2 tsp. dried sage
Freshly ground black pepper

Slice potatoes in 1/4" slices. Combine with remaining ingredients and mix well. Coat a sheet of heavy-duty foil with cooking spray. Place potato mixture in center and seal packets tightly. Place on barbecue grill and cook until potatoes are tender, about 30 minutes (or bake at 400° for 40 to 45 minutes).

Serves: 2 to 3

Per serving:	Calories	Fat (g)	Cholesterol (mg)	Fiber (g)	Sodium (mg)
	132	3	0	2	8

Stuffed Onions

2 large red onions
1 lb. fresh spinach *or*
  1 10-oz. pkg. frozen spinach, thawed
1/2 cup chopped red bell pepper

1/4 cup Parmesan cheese
2 Tbsp. seasoned bread crumbs
Freshly ground pepper to taste

Peel onions and slice in half crosswise. Boil for 4 to 5 minutes; drain well. Remove centers leaving a 1/2" thick shell. Chop onion centers.

Steam fresh spinach then drain well and chop. (Or squeeze frozen spinach dry.) Combine spinach, chopped onion, red pepper, cheese and bread crumbs. Season to taste with pepper. Divide mixture equally between onions. Place in an 8" by 8" baking dish coated with cooking spray. Bake at 350° for 20 to 30 minutes or until onions are soft.

Serves 4

Per serving:	Calories	Fat (g)	Cholesterol (mg)	Fiber (g)	Sodium (mg)
	103	2	6	5	162

Grilled Peppers

2 green *or* red bell peppers
Italian dressing *or* olive oil

Slice bell peppers in half; core and seed. Brush with Italian dressing or olive oil. Broil or grill until soft, about 20 to 25 minutes. Turn once.

Serves 2 to 4

Per serving:	Calories	Fat (g)	Cholesterol (mg)	Fiber (g)	Sodium (mg)
	27	2	0	0	78

Stuffed Red Peppers

Combining rice with beans makes a complete
protein — and a complete meal without meat!

2 large red bell peppers
1 1/2 cups Citrus Rice (page 128)
3/4 cup kidney beans, rinsed and drained
1/4 cup chopped green pepper
1/4 cup chopped celery, including tops
1 carrot, grated
3 to 4 green onions, thinly sliced

1 Tbsp. olive oil
2 Tbsp. balsamic *or* red wine vinegar
1 Tbsp. chopped fresh basil *or*
 1/2 tsp. dried
Freshly ground pepper
1/4 cup grated part-skim mozzarella *or*
 part-skim Monterey Jack cheese

Cut peppers in half; remove stems and seeds. Arrange in a baking dish; cover with plastic wrap. Microwave on full power for 5 to 6 minutes or until softened. Turn pan halfway after cooking for 3 to 4 minutes.

Combine remaining ingredients except cheese. Divide mixture evenly among peppers. Microwave, uncovered, for 4 to 5 minutes or until heated through. Sprinkle with cheese during last 30 seconds of cooking. Serve hot.

Serves 4

Per serving:	Calories	Fat (g)	Cholesterol (mg)	Fiber (g)	Sodium (mg)
	219	7	8	6	96

Golden Mashed Potatoes

2 sweet potatoes
3 to 4 carrots
1 Tbsp. soft margarine

4 Tbsp. evaporated non-fat milk
1/4 tsp. white pepper
1/4 tsp. nutmeg

Peel and slice potatoes and carrots. Steam 10 to 15 minutes or until very soft. Puree in food processor with remaining ingredients. Add additional non-fat milk or cooking liquid if puree is too thick. Serve hot.

Serves 4

Per serving:	Calories	Fat (g)	Cholesterol (mg)	Fiber (g)	Sodium (mg)
	150	3	1	3	98

Olive Salsa

Great on baked potatoes — also good on grilled fish
or chicken or as a filling for an omelette

1/3 cup chopped fresh parsley
4 green onions, cut in 2" pieces
1/2 cup pimiento-stuffed olives,
    rinsed and drained
1/4 cup capers, rinsed and drained

4 tomatoes, cored and quartered
2 Tbsp. fresh lime juice
1 Tbsp. olive oil
Baked potatoes
Plain non-fat yogurt

In a food processor, chop parsley and green onions. Add olives, capers and tomatoes, lime juice and olive oil; pulse 8 to 10 times or until coarsely chopped. Do not puree.

Serve as a topping for baked potatoes: split a baked potato and spoon in plain, non-fat yogurt. Top with Olive Salsa.

Yield: about 2 cups

Per serving:	Calories	Fat (g)	Cholesterol (mg)	Fiber (g)	Sodium (mg)
	25	1	0	1	305

Orange Glazed Sweet Potatoes

3 lbs. sweet potatoes, peeled
1/3 cup frozen orange juice
    concentrate, thawed
1/3 cup water
2 Tbsp. orange liqueur (optional)

1 Tbsp. Butter Buds™
1 tsp. cinnamon
1/2 tsp. allspice *or* nutmeg
1/2 tsp. ground ginger

Slice potatoes crosswise into 1/2" thick slices. Arrange in a single layer in two 9" by 13" baking dishes coated with cooking spray. In a small bowl, combine remaining ingredients and mix well . Pour over potato slices.

Cover dishes with foil and bake at 350° for 25 to 30 minutes or until potatoes are tender. Baste often.

Variation: Add 2 cored, peeled and sliced apples.

Serves 6 to 8

Per serving:	Calories	Fat (g)	Cholesterol (mg)	Fiber (g)	Sodium (mg)
	105	0	0	2	8

Cinnamon Sticks

Kids love these

2 sweet potatoes
1 Tbsp. canola *or* safflower oil
Ground cinnamon

Scrub and peel potatoes. Cut into strips as for french fries. Toss with oil and sprinkle with cinnamon to taste. Spread onto a non-stick baking sheet. Bake at 350° for 10 to 15 minutes or until soft.

Serves 4 to 6

Per serving:	Calories	Fat (g)	Cholesterol (mg)	Fiber (g)	Sodium (mg)
	74	2	0	2	5

Creamed Spinach

Delicious as a baked potato topping

1 cup Bechamel Sauce (page 288)　　　　**¹/4 tsp. nutmeg *or* tarragon**
1 10-oz. pkg. frozen chopped spinach,　　**¹/4 tsp. Lite Salt™**
**　thawed and drained *or***
**　2 cups chopped fresh spinach, steamed**

In a medium saucepan, combine all ingredients. Simmer until warm.

Variation: Substitute chopped cooked broccoli for spinach.

Yield: about 2 cups

Per serving:	Calories	Fat (g)	Cholesterol (mg)	Fiber (g)	Sodium (mg)
	59	2	1	1	114

Szechwan Spinach

*Quick cooking is the key to flavorful spinach — overcooking produces
a bitter flavor and dull color. Cook just until bright green*

2 Tbsp. low-sodium soy sauce
1 Tbsp. rice *or* cider vinegar
2 tsp. oriental sesame oil
1 tsp. orange zest
1/2 tsp. brown sugar

1/2 tsp. chili oil
2 lbs. fresh spinach, washed and stemmed
1/2 cup sliced water chestnuts
1 Tbsp. toasted sesame seeds

In a small bowl, whisk together soy sauce, vinegar, sesame oil, zest, sugar and chili oil. Set aside.

Place spinach in a large pan, cover and steam until just wilted — about 2 minutes. Drain off
excess liquid. Stir in soy mixture and water chestnuts. Cook and stir for 1 to 2 minutes or
until heated through. Serve garnished with sesame seeds.

Serves 6

Per serving:	Calories	Fat (g)	Cholesterol (mg)	Fiber (g)	Sodium (mg)
	78	3	0	5	308

Stir-Fried Snowpeas

1 tsp. canola *or* safflower oil
1 tsp. oriental sesame oil
1 clove garlic, minced
1 tsp. minced fresh ginger
1 1/2 cups fresh snowpeas

1/2 cup sliced water chestnuts
1/2 red bell pepper, julienne
1 tsp. low-sodium soy sauce
Freshly ground black pepper

Heat oils in a large skillet or wok. Saute garlic and ginger about 1 minute. Add snowpeas,
water chestnuts, red pepper and soy sauce. Stir-fry 4 to 5 minutes or until snowpeas are just
tender-crisp. Season to taste with pepper.

Serves 4

Per serving:	Calories	Fat (g)	Cholesterol (mg)	Fiber (g)	Sodium (mg)
	77	3	0	2	122

Apple Filled Acorn Squash

2 acorn squash, halved and seeded
1 to 2 tsp. soft margarine

1 cup Summer Fresh Applesauce (page 249)
Cinnamon

Place squash, cut side down, into a baking dish. Fill about 1" full with water. Bake at 350° for 30 to 40 minutes or until partially soft. Drain off water and brush cut side of each squash lightly with margarine. Fill each with 1/2 cup Applesauce. Sprinkle lightly with cinnamon. Return to baking dish and bake 30 minutes longer or until done.

Serves 4

Per serving:	Calories	Fat (g)	Cholesterol (mg)	Fiber (g)	Sodium (mg)
	103	2	0	3	20

Sweet Potato and Apple Casserole

2 sweet potatoes, peeled and sliced
4 carrots, peeled and sliced on the diagonal
1 cup orange juice
1 Tbsp. brown sugar

2 tsp. orange zest
1 1/2 tsp. cinnamon, divided
1 tsp. nutmeg
2 apples, cored and sliced

In a large skillet, combine sweet potatoes and carrots. Pour in orange juice then sprinkle with sugar, zest, 1 tsp. cinnamon and nutmeg. Bring to a boil, cover and simmer for 20 minutes. Add apple slices and sprinkle with remaining cinnamon. Cover and continue cooking for 10 to 15 minutes or until potatoes and carrots are tender.

Add orange juice as needed during cooking to keep vegetables moist. If too much liquid remains after cooking, remove lid and simmer until most of liquid evaporates.

Serves: 4 to 6

Per serving:	Calories	Fat (g)	Cholesterol (mg)	Fiber (g)	Sodium (mg)
	131	1	0	4	30

Parmesan Tomatoes

2 ripe tomatoes
2 Tbsp. Parmesan cheese
1/2 tsp. dried basil

Cut tomatoes in half. Place on a broiler pan face down and broil 2 to 3 minutes. Turn over; sprinkle each with 1/2 Tbsp. Parmesan cheese and 1/8 tsp. basil. Broil an additional 2 to 3 minutes or until cheese is golden brown.

Serves 4

Per serving:	Calories	Fat (g)	Cholesterol (mg)	Fiber (g)	Sodium (mg)
	26	1	3	1	28

Tomatoes with Pesto

4 large ripe tomatoes   **1/4 cup Pesto (page 293)**
2 cups cooked brown rice   **Parmesan cheese**

Slice tops from tomatoes. Hollow out tomatoes and invert on a rack to drain. Toss rice with pesto and spoon into tomatoes. Serve at room temperature or to serve hot: sprinkle lightly with Parmesan cheese and broil until cheese melts and rice is hot.

Serves 4

Per serving:	Calories	Fat (g)	Cholesterol (mg)	Fiber (g)	Sodium (mg)
	254	12	3	4	308

Tomatoes Provencal

2 tsp. olive oil
1 onion, sliced
1 clove garlic, minced
3 tomatoes, cored and diced
1 zucchini, diced
1/2 cup chopped green *or*
   red bell pepper
1 Tbsp. chopped fresh basil *or*
   1/2 tsp. dried

1 tsp. chopped fresh oregano *or*
   1/4 tsp. dried
1/4 cup chopped fresh parsley
Freshly ground black pepper
2 Tbsp. black olives, rinsed,
   drained and sliced

Heat olive oil in a saucepan; saute onion and garlic until soft, about 5 minutes. Stir in tomatoes and simmer, covered, 3 to 5 minutes.

Add remaining ingredients, except olives. Cook, stirring occasionally, until zucchini is tender, about 5 minutes. Serve garnished with olives.

Variation: May also be served cold.

Serves 4

Per serving:	Calories	Fat (g)	Cholesterol (mg)	Fiber (g)	Sodium (mg)
	80	3	0	2	50

Sweet and Sour Zucchini

1/3 to 1/2 cup honey
1 cup white wine vinegar
6 medium zucchini, thinly sliced
1/2 cup chopped red onion

1 green *or* red bell pepper, diced
1 cup diced celery, including tops
2 Tbsp. olive *or* canola *or* safflower oil
1 tsp. white pepper

Warm honey over low heat or in microwave oven. Pour into a large bowl and blend in vinegar; stir until well mixed. Stir in remaining ingredients. Cover and refrigerate overnight. Drain and serve as a salad or as a vegetable.

Yield: about 6 cups

Per serving:	Calories	Fat (g)	Cholesterol (mg)	Fiber (g)	Sodium (mg)
	76	2	0	1	14

Zucchini Pizza

4 to 5 medium zucchini, grated	1/2 tsp. dried oregano
4 egg whites	Freshly ground black pepper
1/3 cup unbleached flour	2 tsp. olive oil *or* 1 Tbsp. Pesto (page 293)
1/4 cup Parmesan cheese	4 ripe tomatoes, sliced
1 cup grated part-skim mozzarella cheese	Oregano to taste
1 Tbsp. chopped fresh basil *or*	
1 tsp. dried	

Let zucchini stand for 15 minutes, then squeeze out excess moisture. Combine zucchini with egg whites, flour, Parmesan cheese, 1/2 cup mozzarella, basil, 1/2 tsp. oregano and pepper to taste. Spread mixture into a 9" x 13" pan coated with cooking spray or spread onto a round pizza pan. Bake at 350° for 20 to 25 minutes or until surface is firm and dry.

Spread oil or pesto over surface, then broil for 4 to 5 minutes. Arrange tomato slices over crust, sprinkle with remaining mozzarella and oregano. Bake at 350° for an additional 15 to 20 minutes.

Serves 6 to 8

Per serving:	Calories	Fat (g)	Cholesterol (mg)	Fiber (g)	Sodium (mg)
	157	7	19	2	187

Glazed Vegetables

1/2 cup salt-free chicken broth, defatted	2 cups cooked fresh vegetables
1/8 tsp. garlic *or* onion powder	Chopped fresh parsley

Place chicken broth and garlic powder in a small saucepan; boil until reduced by half. Pour over cooked vegetables; stir well. Garnish with chopped parsley.

Serves 2 to 4

Per serving:	Calories	Fat (g)	Cholesterol (mg)	Fiber (g)	Sodium (mg)
	33	0	0	4	34

Herbed Summer Vegetables

Fresh summer vegetables make a tasty and colorful addition to your dinner plate

3 ears fresh corn, shucked	1 to 2 Tbsp. fresh basil, chopped
2 cups fresh green beans,	1 Tbsp. fresh parsley, chopped
trimmed and cut into bite-size pieces	1 tsp. olive oil
2 tomatoes, cored and chopped	1 to 2 Tbsp. Parmesan cheese

Steam corn and green beans until tender-crisp, about 10 minutes. Let corn cool and remove from cob. Combine in a large saucepan with green beans and remaining ingredients, except cheese. Heat gently over low heat until warmed through. Sprinkle with cheese.

Serves 4 to 6

Per serving:	Calories	Fat (g)	Cholesterol (mg)	Fiber (g)	Sodium (mg)
	112	1	1	5	12

Vegetable Medley Saute

1 red bell pepper	1 Tbsp. olive oil
1 yellow bell pepper	1 clove garlic, minced (optional)
1 small eggplant	2 Tbsp. chopped fresh basil *or* parsley
1 zucchini	

Slice vegetables into thin strips (julienne). Heat olive oil in a large skillet and saute garlic briefly. Add vegetables and stir-fry until tender-crisp and soft. Stir in chopped basil and serve.

Serves 6

Per serving:	Calories	Fat (g)	Cholesterol (mg)	Fiber (g)	Sodium (mg)
	46	2	0	3	5

Cranberry Walnut Sauce

A delicious alternative to canned cranberry sauce; makes a nice hostess gift

1 lb. fresh cranberries, rinsed
1 cup golden raisins
1 cup red wine *or* port (*or* water)
1 10-oz. jar red currant jelly

2 tsp. orange zest
1/2 tsp. allspice
1/3 cup chopped walnuts

In a medium saucepan, combine cranberries, raisins, wine, jelly, zest and allspice. Bring to a boil, stirring often. Cook over medium heat for 10 to 15 minutes or until cranberries have popped open. Cool then stir in walnuts.

Best when made one or two days ahead of serving.

Serve with turkey or chicken.

Yield: about 4 cups

Per serving:	Calories	Fat (g)	Cholesterol (mg)	Fiber (g)	Sodium (mg)
	134	2	0	2	6

Tart Cranberry Relish

Dried fruit and fresh orange juice add sweetness naturally

3 cups fresh cranberries, rinsed
  (about 1 lb.)
1 1/2 cups fresh orange juice
1/4 cup honey
1 cup dried apple slices, coarsely chopped
1/2 cup golden raisins

1/2 cup dark raisins
2 tsp. orange zest
1 3-inch cinnamon stick, broken in half
8 whole cloves
2 to 3 Tbsp. red wine vinegar

Combine all ingredients, except vinegar, in a large non-aluminum pan. Bring to a boil, stirring frequently. Reduce heat, cover and simmer until cranberries burst and mixture thickens slightly, about 10 minutes. Stir occasionally. Remove from heat. Stir in vinegar to taste. Cool.

Spoon relish into containers. Cover and refrigerate at least overnight or up to 1 week. Remove from refrigerator 20 minutes before serving.

Yield: 4 cups

Per serving:	Calories	Fat (g)	Cholesterol (mg)	Fiber (g)	Sodium (mg)
	71	0	0	2	3

Desserts and Cookies

When your sweet tooth cries out, these desserts satisfy it without an overload of fat and cholesterol. Keep the portions just big enough to make you feel decadent, but not so large that you overdo the calories.

Delitefully HealthMark

Cakes

Amaretto Fruit Loaf 267
Applesauce 258
Chocolate Pound 260
Date Nut Torte 267
Fudge Nut 259
Mocha Pound 260
Orange Pound 260
Pineapple Oatmeal 261
Poppy Seed 262
Pumpkin Apple Bundt 262
Pumpklin Fruit 266
Spiced (Bean) 263
Sherried Fruit 265
Triple Ginger 264

Cheesecake

Chocolate Amaretto 268
Coffee 268
Mocha 268
Piña Colada 268
Pittsfield 268
Pumpkin Maple 268

Cookies

Almond Macaroons 273
Applesauce Date Bars 273
Apricot Squares 274
Carrot Raisin Cookies 275
Chocolate Almond Macaroons 273
Oatmeal Cookie Squares 274
Peanut Butter Crunchers 276
Peanut Butter Oatmeal Cookies 275
Raspberry Squares 276

Fruit

Apple Pie 257
Apricot Orange Souffle 250
  Marmalade Sauce 250
Baked Pears with Apricot Glaze 243
Berries 'n' Cream 240
Brandied Baked Apples 239
Cranberry Crunch 241
Flummery 242
Gala Grapefruit 241
Grilled Banana and Papaya 239
Oriental Melon Compote 242
Peach Mousse 251
Poached Pears
    with Raspberry Orange Sauce 244
Raspberry Mousse 253
Sherried Oranges 243
Sherry Baked Bananas 240
Summer Fresh Applesauce 249

Sorbets and Frozen Desserts

Blueberry Mint Sorbet 247
Chocolate Frozen Yogurt 246
Chocolate Mint Parfait 254
Cran-Raspberry Sorbet 247
Frozen Raspberry Mousse 252
Frozen Yogurt 246
Fruit 'n' Yogurt Pops 245
Instant Sorbet 248
Mocha Cheesecake Parfait 254
Pineapple Freeze 244
Pumpkin Frozen Yogurt 245
Rhubarb-Raspberry Sherbet 249
Strawberry Margarita Mousse 252

Miscellaneous

Bittersweet Chocolate Sauce 272
Butterscotch Pudding 255
Brandied Pumpkin Pudding 256
Chocolate Pudding 255
Creamy Caramel Dip 269
Meringue Shells 269
Oat Crust 256
Pavlova 270
Pie Crust 257
Raspberry Orange Sauce 272
Vanilla Pudding 255
Whipped Topping One 271
Whipped Topping Two 271

Brandied Baked Apples

These also make a nice addition to a Sunday brunch

6 pitted dates, chopped
1/4 cup raisins *or* currants
1/4 cup chopped walnuts *or* pecans
2 Tbsp. brown sugar
1 tsp. cinnamon

1/8 tsp. cloves
8 Golden Delicious apples, cored
1/4 cup brandy (*or* apple juice)
1/4 cup water

In a small bowl combine first six ingredients. Place apples in a 9" x 13" baking dish coated with cooking spray. Fill apples with date mixture. Combine brandy and water; pour over apples. Cover and bake at 400° until tender, about 1 hour. Baste occasionally with cooking liquid.

To serve, place apples in a dish or on a serving plate and top with cooking liquid.

Serves 8

Per serving:	Calories	Fat (g)	Cholesterol (mg)	Fiber (g)	Sodium (mg)
	166	3	1	4	4

Grilled Banana and Papaya

1 papaya, peeled and sliced
1 banana, peeled and sliced
2 Tbsp. Grand Marnier *or* orange juice

2 Tbsp. fresh lime juice
1 tsp. lime zest
1 tsp. orange zest

Arrange papaya and banana slices on heavy duty foil. Pour juices over fruit and sprinkle with zest. Wrap foil tightly. Place over medium heat on barbecue grill and cook for 10 minutes. Turn and grill 10 minutes longer.

Serves 2–3

Per serving:	Calories	Fat (g)	Cholesterol (mg)	Fiber (g)	Sodium (mg)
	99	0	0	2	4

Sherry Baked Bananas

2 Tbsp. brown sugar
4 bananas

1/4 cup cream sherry, brandy *or* Amaretto
Freshly grated nutmeg

Generously coat a baking dish with cooking spray. Sprinkle with brown sugar. Peel bananas and slice in half crosswise, then lengthwise. Arrange in baking dish. Sprinkle with nutmeg and pour sherry over. Bake, uncovered, at 350° for 10 to 15 minutes or until bananas are soft.

Variation: Substitute orange or apple juice for sherry.

Serves 4

Per serving:	Calories	Fat (g)	Cholesterol (mg)	Fiber (g)	Sodium (mg)
	166	0	0	2	4

Berries 'n' Cream

1 1/2 cups 1% cottage cheese
1/3 cup sugar *or* honey
1 tsp. vanilla

1 tsp. orange *or* lemon zest
2 cups fresh berries

Combine all ingredients, except berries, in blender or food processor and puree for 3 to 4 minutes or until very smooth.

Divide berries among 6 dishes and top with cheese mixture.

Serves 6

Per serving:	Calories	Fat (g)	Cholesterol (mg)	Fiber (g)	Sodium (mg)
	115	1	3	1	231

Cranberry Crunch

2 cups fresh cranberries, rinsed
1/2 cup honey
1/3 cup soft margarine
1/2 cup brown sugar

1 cup rolled oats
2/3 cup whole wheat flour
1 tsp. cinnamon
1 tsp. lemon zest

In a medium saucepan, combine cranberries and honey. Bring to a boil and cook over low heat until berries pop, 10 to 15 minutes. Remove from heat and cool slightly.

In a food processor or a large bowl, combine margarine, brown sugar, oats, flour, cinnamon and zest until crumbly. Press one-half of mixture into an 8" by 8" square pan coated with cooking spray. Pour in the cranberry mixture. Sprinkle remaining oatmeal mixture over the top. Bake at 350° for 45 minutes or until top is browned and bubbly.

Serves 8

Per serving:	Calories	Fat (g)	Cholesterol (mg)	Fiber (g)	Sodium (mg)
	264	9	0	3	105

Gala Grapefruit

1 grapefruit
2 tsp. honey *or* brown sugar
2 tsp. Amaretto, cream sherry, brandy
  or Cointreau (optional)
Cinnamon *or* freshly grated nutmeg

Halve grapefruit and cut around sections. Drizzle with honey (or sprinkle with brown sugar) and liqueur. Sprinkle with cinnamon or nutmeg. Broil for 2 to 3 minutes or until top is lightly browned.

Serves 2

Per serving:	Calories	Fat (g)	Cholesterol (mg)	Fiber (g)	Sodium (mg)
	62	0	0	1	1

Flummery

Flummery refers to a soft, light pudding. It also means "utter nonsense".
This cloud-soft pudding is easy to make and fun to eat

2 lbs. apricots *or* peaches
1 cup unsweetened pineapple juice
1/4 cup honey
1/3 cup tapioca

1/2 tsp. orange zest
1 tsp. vanilla
2 Tbsp. Grand Marnier (optional)

Wash fruit thoroughly; remove skin from peaches if necessary. Cut fruit in half and remove pits. Process in food processor or blender until smooth. There should be about 3 cups of puree.

Pour puree into a medium saucepan. Add juice, honey and tapioca. Let stand 5 minutes to soften tapioca then bring to a boil over medium heat, stirring constantly. Remove from heat and stir in zest, vanilla and Grand Marnier. Cover and refrigerate for about 2 hours or until softly set.

To serve, spoon into clear serving dishes and garnish with fruit and mint leaves.

Variation: Other fruit may be substituted: mango, papaya, melon, pear.

Serves 4 to 6

Per serving:	Calories	Fat (g)	Cholesterol (mg)	Fiber (g)	Sodium (mg)
	104	0	0	2	2

Oriental Melon Compote

4 cups assorted melon balls: cantaloupe,
  honeydew, crenshaw, casaba,
  watermelon, etc.

1/2 cup Midori liqueur
2 Tbsp. chopped crystallized ginger
Mint leaves

Combine melon balls and liqueur in a glass serving bowl. Cover and refrigerate overnight. Sprinkle with crystallized ginger and garnish with mint leaves.

Serves 4 to 6

Per serving:	Calories	Fat (g)	Cholesterol (mg)	Fiber (g)	Sodium (mg)
	89	0	0	1	13

Sherried Oranges

4 oranges
1/2 cup Marsala, cream sherry *or*
   Grand Marnier
2 Tbsp. brown sugar *or* **honey**

6 cloves
2 cinnamon sticks
1 tsp. vanilla
1/4 cup currants *or* **golden raisins**

Peel and slice oranges. Place in a glass serving bowl.

In a small saucepan, combine Marsala, sugar, cloves, cinnamon and vanilla. Bring to a boil, then simmer until sugar dissolves. Stir occasionally. Increase heat and boil until reduced by half, 10 to 12 minutes. Watch carefully. Stir in currants.

Pour over orange slices. Cover and chill 2 to 3 hours or overnight, stirring occasionally. Discard cloves and cinnamon sticks before serving.

Serves 4 to 6

Per serving:	Calories	Fat (g)	Cholesterol (mg)	Fiber (g)	Sodium (mg)
	121	0	0	2	3

Baked Pears with Apricot Glaze

4 pears
1/2 cup low-sugar apricot preserves

1/3 cup brandy *or* **Grand Marnier**
  (*or* fresh orange juice)

Peel pears; cut in half lengthwise and remove core, stem and blossom end. Place cut side down in a 9" x 13" baking dish.

In a small bowl, combine apricot preserves and brandy. Add water as necessary to thin. Pour over pears. Cover and bake at 350° for 10 to 15 minutes, basting occasionally. Turn pears over, baste and continue baking for 5 to 10 minutes or until tender when pierced with a fork. Baste occasionally.

Pears may be served hot or cold. If desired, garnish with chopped toasted almonds or pistachios.

Serves 8

Per serving:	Calories	Fat (g)	Cholesterol (mg)	Fiber (g)	Sodium (mg)
	103	0	0	2	18

Poached Pears with Raspberry-Orange Sauce

2 pears, unpeeled
1¹/2 cups water *or* 1 cup water
  and ¹/2 cup white wine (e.g. Riesling)
2 Tbsp. frozen orange juice concentrate,
  thawed

2 strips orange zest
1 cinnamon stick
1 cup Raspberry-Orange Sauce (see page 272)
Mint leaves

Cut pears in half and remove core. Place cut side down in a large skillet. Combine water (and wine), orange juice concentrate, zest and cinnamon stick. Pour over pears. Bring to a boil; cover and simmer 10 to 15 minutes or until pears are tender but still firm. Remove from heat and cool in cooking liquid.

Drain pears and slice into 1/4" strips leaving stem end intact. Spoon 1/4 cup Raspberry-Orange Sauce onto each of 4 dessert plates. Place pear halves onto sauce fanning out slices. Garnish with mint.

Serves 4

Per serving:	Calories	Fat (g)	Cholesterol (mg)	Fiber (g)	Sodium (mg)
	186	1	0	7	4

Pineapple Freeze

Nothing could be simpler than this refreshing, nutritious sherbet

1 20-oz. can crushed pineapple
  (juice pack), undrained
1 cup orange-pineapple juice

1 cup low-fat buttermilk
¹/4 cup honey (less if desired)

Combine all ingredients in a food processor or blender and process until smooth. Pour into a 8" x 8" pan and freeze until slushy. Return to processor and process until smooth. Pour into pan, cover with foil and freeze solid.

To serve, let sherbet stand at room temperature until slightly softened.

Variation: Add 4 ripe kiwi fruit, peeled and diced.

Yield: about 4 cups

Per serving:	Calories	Fat (g)	Cholesterol (mg)	Fiber (g)	Sodium (mg)
	185	0	1	0	84

Fruit 'n' Yogurt Pops

Kids love these — and so will you

2 8-oz. cartons plain *or*
  vanilla non-fat yogurt
1 6-oz. can frozen juice concentrate

1 cup chopped fruit
1 tsp. vanilla

Combine all ingredients in a blender or food processor. Process until well mixed but fruit is still chunky. Pour into popsicle molds and freeze until firm.

Suggested combinations:

• orange juice and strawberries or bananas.

• raspberry or cranberry juice and raspberries.

• apple juice and peaches or nectarines.

• grape juice and blueberries.

Yield: 12–16 pops

Per serving:	Calories	Fat (g)	Cholesterol (mg)	Fiber (g)	Sodium (mg)
	77	1	3	1	41

Pumpkin Frozen Yogurt

2 cups plain non-fat yogurt
1 cup canned pumpkin
1/2 cup brown sugar *or*
  1/2 cup maple syrup

1 tsp. cinnamon
1 tsp. nutmeg
1 tsp. vanilla

In a medium bowl, blend all ingredients together. Pour into an 8" by 8" pan; cover and freeze. Let soften slightly. Beat with an electric mixer or puree in a food processor until smooth. Return to pan and refreeze. Let stand at room temperature 5 to 10 minutes before serving.

Yield: 3 cups

Per serving:	Calories	Fat (g)	Cholesterol (mg)	Fiber (g)	Sodium (mg)
	133	1	5	1	59

Frozen Yogurt

1 envelope unflavored gelatin
1/4 cup cold water
4 cups plain non-fat yogurt
3 to 4 cups fresh *or* frozen (unsweetened)
   fruit of your choice

1/4 to 1/2 cup sugar *or* honey
   (amount depends on sweetness of fruit)
1 Tbsp. vanilla

Sprinkle gelatin over water in a small saucepan. Let stand for a few minutes to soften. Place over medium heat and stir until dissolved.

In a food processor or blender, combine remaining ingredients. Process until smooth. Stir about 1/2 cup yogurt mixture into dissolved gelatin. Then add gelatin to yogurt mixture and process until well blended.

Pour into a 9" x 13" pan. Freeze about 1 hour or until frozen nearly solid. Break into chunks; puree in food processor until smooth. Return mixture to pan. Freeze then puree again until smooth and airy. Spoon into a freezer container. Cover tightly and freeze until solid. Let stand at room temperature for 5 to 10 minutes before serving.

(May also be frozen in an ice cream freezer.)

Yield: 4 to 5 cups

Per serving:	Calories	Fat (g)	Cholesterol (mg)	Fiber (g)	Sodium (mg)
	138	2	7	1	81

Chocolate Frozen Yogurt

2 cups vanilla non-fat yogurt
1/4 cup unsweetened cocoa
1/4 cup sugar

2 Tbsp. honey
1 tsp. vanilla

Combine all ingredients in a food processor or blender. Process until well blended. Pour into a shallow pan and freeze until firm, several hours or overnight. Break into chunks and process until smooth, but not melted. Serve immediately or pour into a storage container, cover tightly and freeze. Let stand at room temperature for 5 to 10 minutes to soften slightly before serving.

Serves 4

Per serving:	Calories	Fat (g)	Cholesterol (mg)	Fiber (g)	Sodium (mg)
	171	2	7	0	105

Blueberry Mint Sorbet

1¹/2 cups fresh *or* canned (juice-pack)
  pineapple, frozen
1 pint fresh blueberries,
  rinsed and drained, then frozen

¹/4 cup fresh mint leaves
1 Tbsp. creme de menthe (optional)
Honey *or* Equal™ to taste (if necessary)

Combine all ingredients in a food processor and process until smooth. Taste and add honey or Equal to taste if necessary. Serve immediately or freeze in a covered container. Let thaw slightly and process again before serving.

Tip: Freeze pineapple and blueberries in a zip-top plastic bag

Serves 4 to 6

Per serving:	Calories	Fat (g)	Cholesterol (mg)	Fiber (g)	Sodium (mg)
	89	0	0	1	3

Cran-Raspberry Sorbet

This unique sorbet is a grand finale to any holiday meal

1 cup fresh cranberries
1 12-oz. package frozen raspberries
  (unsweetened)

¹/4 cup Grenadine syrup (*or* honey)
2 Tbsp. honey
2 Tbsp. orange-flavored liqueur (optional)

Freeze cranberries solid then thaw 5 to 10 minutes. With motor of food processor running, drop in cranberries a few at a time. Repeat with raspberries. Scrape down sides of bowl occasionally. With motor still running, pour in Grenadine, honey and liqueur. Continue to process until smooth.

Serve immediately in chilled dessert glasses. Or spoon into a shallow pan, cover and freeze solid. Thaw slightly, process again until smooth then refreeze. Let stand at room temperature 5 to 10 minutes before serving.

Serves 6

Per serving:	Calories	Fat (g)	Cholesterol (mg)	Fiber (g)	Sodium (mg)
	117	1	0	3	2

Instant Sorbet

Quick and easy, this delicious dessert is low in calories and retains
all of the nutrients and fiber of fresh fruit

**1 20-oz. can crushed pineapple
(juice-pack), frozen
1 banana, sliced**

**3 nectarines *or* peaches, seeded
1 cup berries, fresh *or* frozen
(strawberries *or* raspberries are good)**

Thaw pineapple just enough to cut into chunks . Place all fruit into food processor and process until pureed. Scrape down sides of bowl occasionally.

Serve immediately or spread mixture into an 8" by 8" pan and freeze. Thaw enough to break into chunks. Process again in food processor. May be served immediately or frozen in a tightly covered container.

Variations:

• Use seasonal fruit of your choice.

• Add 1 8-oz. container non-fat yogurt to processor along with fruit.

• Add 2 to 3 Tbsp. orange or other fruit-flavored liqueur.

Serves 6

Per serving:	Calories	Fat (g)	Cholesterol (mg)	Fiber (g)	Sodium (mg)
	106	0	0	3	5

Rhubarb-Raspberry Sherbet

1 lb. fresh rhubarb
1/2 cup sugar
2 Tbsp. water

1 1/2 cups fresh *or* frozen raspberries
1 cup plain non-fat yogurt
1 cup non-fat milk

Clean rhubarb and cut into 1" pieces. Place in a 2 quart baking dish and sprinkle with sugar; add water. Bake, covered, at 325° until tender, 20 to 30 minutes. Cool to room temperature.

Place rhubarb and raspberries in food processor and puree. Add yogurt and milk and mix well. Taste and add sugar or honey (sparingly) as necessary. Pour into a 9" x 13" pan and freeze. Soften slightly to remove from pan. Break into chunks and place half into food processor. Process until smooth and creamy. Repeat with remaining sherbet.

Serve immediately or scoop into a freezer container, cover tightly and freeze.

Variation: Substitute 1/4 cup low-sugar raspberry jam for raspberries.

Serves 10 to 12

Per serving:	Calories	Fat (g)	Cholesterol (mg)	Fiber (g)	Sodium (mg)
	83	1	2	1	24

Summer Fresh Applesauce

Enjoy the fresh flavor of apples in this crunchy sauce

4 apples, cored and chopped
1/4 to 1/3 cup apple, orange or cranberry juice
2 to 4 Tbsp. honey or brown sugar
1/2 tsp. cinnamon
1/4 tsp. nutmeg

Combine all ingredients in a food processor and puree to desired smoothness.

Yield: about 2 cups

Per serving:	Calories	Fat (g)	Cholesterol (mg)	Fiber (g)	Sodium (mg)
	61	0	0	2	1

Apricot-Orange Souffle

3/4 cup dried apricots, chopped
1/2 cup fresh orange juice
2 Tbsp. honey
1 Tbsp. Grand Marnier *or* Cointreau
1/4 tsp. ground ginger

1 Tbsp. orange zest
6 egg whites
1/8 tsp. cream of tartar
1 tsp. vanilla
Marmalade Sauce (below)

In a small saucepan, combine apricots and orange juice. Simmer until juice is syrupy, about 20 minutes. Cool to room temperature.

Pour apricot mixture into a food processor and add honey, Grand Marnier and ginger. Process until smooth, about 1 minute. Add zest and pulse just to blend.

Beat egg whites and cream of tartar and vanilla until firm but not dry. Spoon 1/4 of egg whites into apricot mixture and pulse until just blended, 4 or 5 times. Fold apricot mixture into remaining egg whites until just blended. Spoon mixture into an 8" square baking dish coated with cooking spray (or use individual ovenproof dishes). Bake at 350° for about 15 minutes, until top is lightly browned.

Serve warm or at room temperature. Garnish with an orange twist and serve with Marmalade Sauce.

Serves 4 to 6

Per serving:	Calories	Fat (g)	Cholesterol (mg)	Fiber (g)	Sodium (mg)
	95	0	0	2	238

Marmalade Sauce

1 cup low-sugar orange marmalade
2 1/2 cups fresh (*or* frozen unsweetened)
  raspberries *or* sliced strawberries

1 Tbsp. lemon zest
1/4 cup Grand Marnier *or* Cointreau

Combine all ingredients in a medium saucepan. Simmer for 10 to 15 minutes. Serve as a topping for angel food cake, frozen yogurt or fresh fruit.

Yield: about 3 1/2 cups

Per serving:	Calories	Fat (g)	Cholesterol (mg)	Fiber (g)	Sodium (mg)
	58	0	0	1	19

Peach Mousse

Sweet summer peaches, on the verge of being overripe, are perfect for this airy dessert

6 peaches
2 to 4 Tbsp. honey
  (depending on sweetness of fruit)
2 tsp. fresh lemon juice
2 Tbsp. Amaretto *or*
  1 tsp. almond extract

1/2 tsp. nutmeg
1 Tbsp. gelatin
5 egg whites
1/8 tsp. cream of tartar
1/4 cup sugar
1 tsp. vanilla

Dip peaches into boiling water for one minute. Remove; cool and peel. Slice and place in food processor with honey and lemon juice. Process until very smooth. Pour into a medium saucepan; stir in Amaretto and nutmeg. Sprinkle gelatin over top of mixture and stir over low heat until gelatin dissolves. Cool to room temperature.

Beat egg whites with cream of tartar until soft peaks form. Gradually beat in sugar and continue beating until whites are stiff but not dry. Beat in vanilla. Gently fold peach mixture into egg whites. Pour into a 6 cup souffle dish. Chill until firm, 2 to 3 hours.

Serves 6 to 8

Per serving:	Calories	Fat (g)	Cholesterol (mg)	Fiber (g)	Sodium (mg)
	93	0	0	1	33

Frozen Raspberry Mousse

1 12-oz. can evaporated skim milk
1 12-oz. bag frozen raspberries

3 Tbsp. honey (less if desired)
2 tsp. vanilla *or* almond flavoring

Pour milk into an 8" square dish and chill in freezer for 2 to 2^1/$_2$ hours or until frozen solid. Thaw slightly and break into chunks. Turn on food processor or blender. Drop in frozen milk and berries. Drizzle in honey and vanilla. Process until smooth and creamy.

Spoon into dessert glasses and serve immediately. Garnish with fresh raspberries and mint leaves. May also be frozen; thaw in refrigerator for 1 hour before serving to soften.

Per serving:	Calories	Fat (g)	Cholesterol (mg)	Fiber (g)	Sodium (mg)
	109	0	2	2	55

Variation: Strawberry Margarita Mousse — Substitute strawberries for raspberries; eliminate vanilla; add 3 Tbsp. each tequila and Cointreau (or other orange-flavored liqueur; add zest from one lime.

Serves 6 to 8

Per serving:	Calories	Fat (g)	Cholesterol (mg)	Fiber (g)	Sodium (mg)
	103	0	2	3	56

Raspberry Mousse

2 cups fresh *or* frozen (unsweetened)
  raspberries
1 apple, peeled,
  cored and cut into eighths
2 tsp. lemon zest
1 tsp. fresh lemon juice

2 Tbsp. Chambord *or* Cointreau
2 Tbsp. sugar plus 1/4 cup
Scant 1/8 tsp. cloves
1 Tbsp. unflavored gelatin
6 egg whites
1/8 tsp. cream of tartar

Puree raspberries and apple chunks in a food processor until smooth. Place a sieve over a medium saucepan. Press raspberry mixture through the sieve and discard the seeds. Stir in zest, lemon juice, Chambord, 2 Tbsp. sugar and cloves. Place saucepan over low heat; sprinkle gelatin over mixture. Stir until gelatin dissolves. Cool to room temperature.

Beat egg whites and cream of tartar until soft peaks form. Gradually beat in remaining 1/4 cup sugar. Continue beating until whites are firm but not dry. Gently fold raspberry mixture into whites. Spoon into a 6 cup souffle dish and refrigerate until firm, 2 to 3 hours.

Variation: Substitute sliced fresh strawberries for raspberries or use a combination of raspberries and strawberries.

Serves 6 to 8

Per serving:	Calories	Fat (g)	Cholesterol (mg)	Fiber (g)	Sodium (mg)
	87	0	0	2	39

Mocha Cheesecake Parfait

1 pkg. unflavored gelatin
1 cup strong brewed decaffeinated coffee
1/4 cup brown sugar
1 1/2 cups 1% cottage cheese

1/2 cup cocoa powder
1 tsp. vanilla
1 1/2 cups vanilla frozen yogurt (non-fat)
2 Tbsp. Kahlua (optional)

Combine gelatin and coffee in a small pan; let stand one minute. Heat mixture over medium heat and add sugar. Reduce heat to low and cook until gelatin and sugar dissolve. Remove from heat and cool.

Process cottage cheese, cocoa powder and vanilla in blender or food processor until very smooth. Add coffee mixture and process until well blended. Pour into an 8" square pan and freeze.

Place in refrigerator to soften one hour before serving. Spoon mixture into blender or food processor. Add yogurt and Kahlua; process until smooth, but not runny. Serve immediately in parfait glasses.

Variation: Chocolate Mint Parfait — Substitute water for coffee and use 1 to 2 tsp. mint extract in place of Kahlua.

Serves 12

Per serving:	Calories	Fat (g)	Cholesterol (mg)	Fiber (g)	Sodium (mg)
	86	1	1	0	134

Vanilla Pudding

3 Tbsp. cornstarch
1/3 cup sugar
1/3 cup non-fat dry milk

2 cups non-fat milk
2 tsp. vanilla

Mix cornstarch, sugar and dry milk. Blend in 1/2 cup liquid milk. Add remaining milk and bring to a boil over medium heat, stirring constantly. Reduce heat and cook, stirring, until thickened. Pour into serving dishes and chill.

Serves 4

Per serving:	Calories	Fat (g)	Cholesterol (mg)	Fiber (g)	Sodium (mg)
	175	0	4	0	116

Variations:

• Butterscotch: Substitute brown sugar for white. Blend 1 Tbsp. liquid margarine into cooked mixture.

Per serving:	Calories	Fat (g)	Cholesterol (mg)	Fiber (g)	Sodium (mg)
	183	0	4	0	121

• Chocolate: Add 1/3 cup unsweetened cocoa to cornstarch mixture.

Per serving:	Calories	Fat (g)	Cholesterol (mg)	Fiber (g)	Sodium (mg)
	198	1	4	0	149

Brandied Pumpkin Pudding

A delicious change from pumpkin pie

6 to 8 slices crystallized ginger
1 16-oz. can pumpkin
1/2 cup brown sugar
1 1/2 tsp. cinnamon
1 tsp. nutmeg
1 tsp. orange zest

1/4 tsp. ground ginger
1 egg
3 egg whites
1 12-oz. can evaporated non-fat milk
1/4 cup brandy *or* Grand Marnier (optional)

With food processor motor running, drop in ginger slices and process until finely chopped. Add pumpkin, sugar, cinnamon, nutmeg, zest, ginger, egg and egg whites; process until well blended. Gradually blend in evaporated milk and brandy.

Pour into a 1 1/2 quart mold or baking dish coated with cooking spray. Bake at 350° for about 1 hour or until a cake tester inserted into the center comes out clean. Serve warm or at room temperature with Whipped Topping (page 271)

Serves 6 to 8

Per serving:	Calories	Fat (g)	Cholesterol (mg)	Fiber (g)	Sodium (mg)
	130	1	33	0	86

Oat Crust

Use this for a crunchy pie crust or as a topping for a fruit crisp

1 cup rolled oats
1/4 cup whole wheat flour

1/4 cup brown sugar
1/4 cup liquid margarine

Combine all ingredients in a food processor and pulse until well mixed. Press onto bottom and sides of a pie pan then add filling and bake.

For an unbaked pie, bake crust at 350° for 10 to 15 minutes. Cool slightly before adding filling.

For cheesecake: press onto bottom of a springform pan; bake at 325° for 5 minutes, cool slightly then add filling.

Yield: One bottom crust

Per serving:	Calories	Fat (g)	Cholesterol (mg)	Fiber (g)	Sodium (mg)
	122	7	0	1	77

Pie Crust

2 cups unbleached *or*
  whole wheat pastry flour
Pinch Lite Salt™ (optional)

¹/₂ cup canola *or* safflower oil
¹/₄ cup non-fat milk *or* cold water

In a medium bowl or in a food processor, combine flour and salt. Pour in oil and milk then until crumbly. Gather together in a ball. Divide in half and roll out each half between two sheets of wax paper. Handle carefully.

Yield: One top and bottom crust (8 servings)

Per serving:	Calories	Fat (g)	Cholesterol (mg)	Fiber (g)	Sodium (mg)
	228	14	0	1	42

Apple Pie

4 large Golden Delicious apples
¹/₃ to ¹/₂ cup brown *or* white sugar
1 tsp. cinnamon
¹/₂ tsp. nutmeg

1 recipe Pie Crust (above)
Non-fat milk
Sugar
Cinnamon

Peel, core and slice apples. In a large bowl, combine apple slices with sugar, cinnamon and nutmeg. Roll out crust and place in a pie pan. Fill with apples and cover with top crust. Cut several slits in top to allow steam to escape.

Brush crust with non-fat milk and sprinkle with a mixture of sugar and cinnamon. Bake at 400° for about 40 minutes or until pastry is lightly browned.

Yield: One pie (8 slices)

Per serving:	Calories	Fat (g)	Cholesterol (mg)	Fiber (g)	Sodium (mg)
	309	14	0	3	43

Applesauce Cake

1 cup whole wheat flour
1 cup unbleached flour
1/2 cup rolled oats
1 cup brown sugar
1 tsp. cinnamon
1 tsp. allspice
1 tsp. baking powder
1/2 tsp. baking soda
1/2 cup canola *or* safflower oil

4 egg whites
1 cup unsweetened applesauce
2 tsp. vanilla
1/3 cup chopped walnuts (optional)

Topping:
1/3 cup chopped walnuts
1/4 cup brown sugar
1/2 tsp. cinnamon

In a large bowl, combine flours, oats, brown sugar, cinnamon, allspice, baking powder, and baking soda. Add oil, egg whites, applesauce and vanilla. With an electric mixer, beat at medium speed until well mixed, about 2 minutes. Stir in nuts.

Pour batter into a 9" x 13" baking pan coated with cooking spray. Combine topping ingredients and sprinkle evenly over cake. Bake at 375° for 30 to 35 minutes or until a cake tester inserted in center comes out clean. Cool cake in pan on a rack.

Yield: One 9" x 13" cake (12 pieces)

Per serving:	Calories	Fat (g)	Cholesterol (mg)	Fiber (g)	Sodium (mg)
	284	12	0	2	93

Fudge Nut Cake

2¹/₂ cups unbleached flour
1 cup sugar
1 cup unsweetened cocoa powder
1 tsp. baking powder
1 tsp. baking soda
¹/₂ cup chopped walnuts

1 cup low-fat buttermilk
¹/₂ cup 1% cottage cheese
4 egg whites
¹/₂ cup canola *or* safflower oil
2 tsp. vanilla

In a large bowl, combine flour, sugar, cocoa, baking powder, baking soda and nuts; mix well. In another bowl or in a food processor, combine remaining ingredients and beat until well combined and cottage cheese is very smooth. Combine liquid with dry ingredients and mix until thoroughly blended. Spoon batter into a bundt pan coated with cooking spray. Bake at 350° for 40 to 45 minutes or until a cake tester inserted into center comes out clean. Cool 10 minutes in pan then turn out onto rack to cool completely.

To serve, sprinkle with powdered sugar or drizzle with Bittersweet Chocolate Sauce (page 272).

Variation: Add ¹/₄ cup orange juice concentrate and 2 tsp. orange zest to batter.

Yield: One bundt cake (12 pieces)

Per serving:	Calories	Fat (g)	Cholesterol (mg)	Fiber (g)	Sodium (mg)
	307	13	1	1	218

Orange Pound Cake

1 1/2 cups unbleached flour
2 tsp. baking powder
3/4 cup sugar
1/2 cup canola *or* safflower oil

1/2 cup unsweetened orange juice *or*
   orange-pineapple juice
1 tsp. orange zest
4 egg whites, stiffly beaten

Coat the bottom of a 9" x 5" loaf pan with cooking spray; dust with flour and set aside.

Combine flour, baking powder and sugar in a large bowl. Add oil and orange juice. Beat with an electric mixer until well blended (batter will be thick). Add orange rind and about 1/3 of egg whites; stir gently. Fold in remaining whites.

Spoon batter into prepared pan. Bake at 350° for 45 minutes or until cake tester inserted into center of cake comes out clean. Cool in pan for 10 minutes then remove from pan and cool on wire rack.

Variations:

• Chocolate Pound Cake: eliminate orange juice and zest; add 1/3 cup cocoa to flour mixture; add 1/2 cup non-fat milk, 1 Tbsp. vanilla and 1 tsp. chocolate flavoring to oil.

• Mocha Pound Cake: as for chocolate pound cake but substitute 1/2 cup strong brewed decaffeinated coffee for non-fat milk.

Yield: One 9" x 5" loaf (16 slices)

Per serving:	Calories	Fat (g)	Cholesterol (mg)	Fiber (g)	Sodium (mg)
	141	7	0	0	63

Pineapple-Oatmeal Cake

3/4 cup brown sugar
1/2 cup liquid margarine,
   canola *or* safflower oil
1/2 cup plain non-fat yogurt
4 egg whites
1 tsp. vanilla
1 cup whole wheat flour
1 cup unbleached flour
1 tsp. baking soda

1 tsp. baking powder
1 tsp. orange zest
1 tsp. cinnamon
1/2 tsp. nutmeg
1/2 tsp. ginger
1 1/2 cups rolled oats
1 cup crushed pineapple (juice-pack),
   undrained

In a large bowl, combine sugar and margarine; beat well. Add egg whites, yogurt and vanilla; mix well. Combine flours, baking soda, baking powder, zest and spices. Add half the flour mixture and all of the oats to the sugar mixture. Mix well. Alternately add remaining flour mixture and pineapple, mixing well after each addition.

Pour batter into a 9" x 13" baking pan coated with cooking spray. Bake at 350° for 25 to 30 minutes or until a cake tester inserted in center comes out clean.

Variation: Add 1/2 cup golden raisins.

Yield: One 9"x13" cake (12 pieces)

Per serving:	Calories	Fat (g)	Cholesterol (mg)	Fiber (g)	Sodium (mg)
	211	10	1	2	127

Poppy Seed Cake

This elegant dessert easily doubles as a luscious coffeecake

1/2 cup poppy seeds
1 cup non-fat milk
1/2 cup liquid margarine
1 cup sugar
1 tsp. vanilla

1 tsp. almond extract
2 cups unbleached flour
2 tsp. baking powder
4 egg whites, beaten stiff

Soak poppy seeds in milk for 1 hour. Cream margarine, sugar, vanilla and almond extract. Mix in flour and baking powder until well blended. Fold in stiffly beaten egg whites.

Pour batter into a non-stick bundt pan coated with cooking spray. Bake at 375° for 30 to 35 minutes or until a cake tester inserted into the center comes out clean. Cool in pan then remove to a wire rack. Sprinkle with powdered sugar, if desired.

Variation: Fold in 1 cup fresh blueberries or raspberries along with egg whites.

Yield: One bundt cake (12 pieces)

Per serving:	Calories	Fat (g)	Cholesterol (mg)	Fiber (g)	Sodium (mg)
	246	11	0	1	197

Pumpkin Apple Bundt Cake

1 cup whole wheat flour
1 cup unbleached flour
1 Tbsp. baking powder
1/2 tsp. baking soda
1/2 tsp. each cinnamon and nutmeg
1/4 tsp. each ginger and cloves

1 cup brown sugar
4 egg whites
1/2 cup canola *or* safflower oil
1 cup canned pumpkin
2 cups chopped apple (unpeeled)

In a large bowl combine dry ingredients. Make a well and add remaining ingredients in order given. Mix well.

Pour batter into a bundt pan coated with cooking spray. Bake at 350° for 50–55 minutes or until a cake tester comes our clean. Cool in pan

Yield: One bundt cake (12 pieces)

Per serving:	Calories	Fat (g)	Cholesterol (mg)	Fiber (g)	Sodium (mg)
	244	10	0	2	159

Spiced (Bean) Cake

If you don't tell, no one will know the secret ingredient — pinto beans!

¹/₄ cup liquid margarine
³/₄ cup brown sugar
2 tsp. vanilla
1 egg
2 egg whites
2 cups pinto beans, mashed
1 cup whole wheat flour

2 tsp. cinnamon
1 tsp. baking soda
¹/₂ tsp. nutmeg
¹/₂ tsp. cloves
2 cups diced (unpeeled) apples
¹/₂ cup raisins
¹/₄ cup chopped walnuts (optional)

In a large bowl, cream together margarine, brown sugar and vanilla. Add egg and egg whites, mixing well. Stir in mashed beans. Mix together dry ingredients and add to creamed mixture, blending well. Fold in apples, raisins and nuts.

Pour batter into a 9" x 13" baking pan coated with cooking spray. Bake at 375° for 45 to 50 minutes or until a cake tester inserted into center comes out clean.

Yield: One 9" x 13" cake (12 pieces)

Per serving:	Calories	Fat (g)	Cholesterol (mg)	Fiber (g)	Sodium (mg)
	244	7	21	6	138

Triple Ginger Cake

A delicious cake made quickly in a food processor

1/4 cup crystallized ginger slices
1 1" cube fresh ginger, peeled
11/4 cups whole wheat flour *or*
   whole wheat pastry flour
1 tsp. baking soda
1 tsp. ground ginger
1/2 tsp. cinnamon
1/2 tsp. nutmeg

1/8 tsp. freshly ground black pepper
1 Tbsp. lemon *or* orange zest
1/2 cup brown sugar
1/3 cup liquid margarine
2 egg whites
1/2 cup strong brewed decaffeinated coffee
1/4 cup molasses

With food processor motor running, drop in crystallized and fresh ginger; mince. Add flour, baking soda, ground ginger, cinnamon, nutmeg, pepper, zest and brown sugar. Pulse 4 or 5 times to blend. Add margarine, egg whites, coffee and molasses. Blend for 30 seconds, scraping down sides of bowl once.

Pour batter into an 8" square pan coated with cooking spray. Bake at 350° for 30 minutes or until a cake tester inserted into center comes out clean.

Yield: One 8" square cake (9 pieces)

Per serving:	Calories	Fat (g)	Cholesterol (mg)	Fiber (g)	Sodium (mg)
	199	7	0	2	196

Sherried Fruit Cake

1 cup chopped dried apricots
1 cup chopped pitted dates
1 cup golden raisins
1/2 cup dark raisins
1 cup chopped dried figs
2 Tbsp. minced fresh ginger
3/4 cup dry *or* Marsala sherry
3/4 cup unbleached flour

1/2 cup brown sugar
1/2 tsp. ground ginger
1/2 tsp. baking powder
1/2 cup chopped crystallized ginger
1/2 cup slivered almonds *or* chopped pecans
1 egg
2 egg whites
1 tsp. vanilla

In a large bowl, combine apricots, dates, raisins, figs, fresh ginger and 1/2 cup sherry. Let stand 1 to 2 hours.

In a medium bowl, combine flour, brown sugar, ground ginger, baking powder, crystallized ginger, and nuts. Beat together egg, egg whites and vanilla. Add flour and egg mixtures to fruit mixture. Stir well to blend. Spoon batter into a 9" x 5" loaf pan coated with cooking spray; spread evenly.

Bake at 300° for about 11/2 hours or until top is golden brown. Cool in pan for 10 minutes then turn out on a rack to cool completely. Wrap cake in cheesecloth or a clean dish towel. Drizzle remaining 1/4 cup sherry over cake. Wrap in foil. Let age 2 days to 2 months before serving. Additional sherry may be drizzled over cloth-wrapped cake as cake dries out.

Cut into thin slices to serve

Yield: One 9" x 5" loaf (16 slices)

Per serving:	Calories	Fat (g)	Cholesterol (mg)	Fiber (g)	Sodium (mg)
	215	3	16	4	42

Pumpkin Fruit Cake

A welcome holiday gift

3/4 cup apple juice *or* cider
1/2 cup dark raisins
1/2 cup chopped dried figs *or* dates
1 cup pumpkin
1/4 cup brown sugar
2 Tbsp. canola *or* safflower oil
1 1/2 cups whole wheat flour

1 tsp. baking soda
1 tsp. cinnamon
1 tsp. orange zest
1/2 tsp. allspice
1/2 tsp. nutmeg
1/4 tsp. cloves
1/4 cup chopped walnuts

Heat apple juice to a boil then pour over dried fruit; let cool. In a large bowl, beat together the pumpkin, brown sugar and oil. In a smaller bowl, mix together flour, baking soda, spices and walnuts. Alternately add the fruit mixture and the dry ingredients to the pumpkin mixture. Stir until just blended.

Spoon the batter into an ungreased 9" x 5" loaf pan. Bake at 300° for about 1 hour and 15 minutes or until a cake tester inserted in the center comes out clean. Remove from pan and cool on a rack. Wrap tightly to store. May be frozen.

Yield: One 9" x 5" loaf (16 slices)

Per serving:	Calories	Fat (g)	Cholesterol (mg)	Fiber (g)	Sodium (mg)
	115	3	0	3	30

Amaretto Fruit Loaf

8 oz. dried apricots	1 egg
8 oz. pitted prunes *or* dried figs	4 egg whites
1 cup coarsely chopped almonds	1/4 cup canola *or* safflower oil
1 cup unbleached flour	1/4 cup Amaretto
3/4 cup brown sugar, divided	1 Tbsp. vanilla
2 1/4 tsp. baking powder	1 tsp. almond extract

In a large bowl, combine apricots, prunes, almonds, flour, 1/2 cup of the sugar and baking powder. Beat egg, egg whites and remaining 1/4 cup sugar until light and frothy. Mix in oil, Amaretto, vanilla and almond extract. Pour over fruit mixture and blend well.

Spoon batter into a 9" x 5" loaf pan coated with cooking spray. Bake at 300° for 1 3/4 to 2 hours or until lightly browned. Let cool in pan for 10 to 15 minutes then remove to a rack to cool completely. Wrap tightly to store. Freezes well.

Yield: One 9" x 5" loaf (16 slices)

Per serving:	Calories	Fat (g)	Cholesterol (mg)	Fiber (g)	Sodium (mg)
	236	8	16	5	96

Date Nut Torte

3/4 cup brown sugar	2 tsp. baking powder
4 egg whites	2 tsp. vanilla
1/2 cup unbleached flour	1 lb. pitted dates
1/2 cup whole wheat pastry flour	1 cup chopped walnuts *or* pecans

In a medium bowl, beat together sugar and egg whites. Stir in flours, baking powder and vanilla; mix well. Stir in dates and nuts.

Pour batter into a 8" x 8" baking dish coated with cooking spray. Bake at 350° for 30 to 40 minutes or until a cake tester inserted in center comes out clean.

Cool for 10 minutes in pan, then turn out onto a wire rack to finish cooling.

Yield: One 8" x 8" torte (9 pieces)

Per serving:	Calories	Fat (g)	Cholesterol (mg)	Fiber (g)	Sodium (mg)
	352	9	0	4	119

Pittsfield Cheesecake

This delicious cheesecake is a reduced fat version of a sinfully rich family favorite recipe

1 Oat Crust (page 256)	Zest of one lemon
2 15-oz. cartons low-fat ricotta cheese	1 tsp. vanilla
4 oz. light cream cheese, softened	1/2 tsp. lemon extract
1 egg	1 cup low-fat sour cream
2 egg whites	2 Tbsp. sugar
1/2 cup sugar	1 tsp. vanilla
1/3 cup honey	

Press crust into bottom of a springform pan. Bake at 325° for 5 minutes. Remove from oven and let cool briefly.

In a food processor or with a mixer, blend ricotta, cream cheese, egg, egg whites, sugar, honey, zest, vanilla and lemon extract until very smooth. Pour into crust and bake at 300° for 1-1 1/2 hours, or until set. Let cool 15 to 20 minutes.

Combine sour cream, 2 Tbsp. sugar and 1 tsp. vanilla. Spread over cooled cheesecake and bake at 425° an additional 10 minutes.

Cool to room temperature then chill 6 hours or overnight before serving.

Variations:

• Piña-Colada: Substitute 2 tsp. coconut extract for vanilla. Fold in 1 cup crushed pineapple (juice pack), well-drained.

• Chocolate Amaretto: Eliminate lemon zest and lemon extract. Substitute brown sugar for white. Add 1 tsp. almond extract, 2 Tbsp. Amaretto, and 1/2 cup unsweetened cocoa powder.

• Pumpkin-Maple: Substitute brown sugar for white and replace honey with maple syrup. Eliminate lemon zest and extract. Add 1 1/2 cups canned pumpkin, 1 tsp. cinnamon, 1 tsp. nutmeg and 2 to 4 Tbsp. praline liqueur, Amaretto or rum. Bake about 1 1/2 hours.

• Coffee: Eliminate lemon extract. Add 2 Tbsp. instant decaffeinated coffee dissolved in 1/4 cup coffee-flavored liqueur (optional) or 2 Tbsp. water.

• Mocha: Eliminate lemon extract. Substitute brown sugar for white. Add 1/2 cup unsweetened cocoa powder, 2 Tbsp. instant decaffeinated coffee dissolved in 1/4 cup coffee-flavored liqueur (optional) or 2 Tbsp. water.

Serves 12 to 16

Per serving:	Calories	Fat (g)	Cholesterol (mg)	Fiber (g)	Sodium (mg)
	231	11	40	1	164

Meringue Shells

3 egg whites, at room temperature
1/8 tsp. cream of tartar
2 tsp. vanilla
1 tsp. vinegar

1 tsp. water
2/3 cup granulated sugar
  (do not use brown sugar)

In a medium bowl, beat egg whites until frothy. Add cream of tartar and continue beating until stiff but not dry. Combine vanilla, vinegar and water. Gradually beat sugar into egg whites (1 to 2 Tbsp. at a time), alternately adding vanilla mixture a few drops at a time. Beat to stiff, glossy peaks.

Spread meringue into a pie pan coated with cooking spray and bake at 275° for 1 hour or

Shape meringue into 6 nests on a cookie sheet lined with wax paper. Bake at 275° for 45 minutes. Remove carefully from wax paper and cool on wire racks.

Fill with frozen yogurt, fresh fruit or Instant Sorbet (page 248). Drizzle with Raspberry Orange Sauce (page 272) or Bittersweet Chocolate Sauce (page 272).

Variation: After beating egg whites stiff, fold in 1/2 cup cocoa powder.

Yield: One 9" pie crust or six individual shells

Per serving:	Calories	Fat (g)	Cholesterol (mg)	Fiber (g)	Sodium (mg)
	92	0	0	0	25

Creamy Caramel Dip

1 8-oz. Neufchatel cheese
  (light cream cheese)
1 1/2 cups 1% cottage cheese

1/2 cup dark brown sugar
2 tsp. vanilla
Fresh fruit

Combine all ingredients (except fruit) in a food processor and process 2 to 3 minutes or until very smooth. Serve chilled as a dip or a topping for fresh fruit.

Yield: about 2 cups
Serving size: 2 tablespoons

Note: Entire recipe contains 1285 calories (2 Tbsp. = 80 calories), 57 grams of fat and 42% of calories as fat! Eat sparingly!!

Per serving:	Calories	Fat (g)	Cholesterol (mg)	Fiber (g)	Sodium (mg)
	80	4	12	0	145

Pavlova

This lovely dessert makes an elegant finale to your special meal

3 egg whites
2/3 cup sugar
1 tsp. cornstarch
1 tsp. vinegar

2 tsp. vanilla
Sliced kiwi
Fresh raspberries

In a large bowl, beat egg whites until stiff. Mix together sugar and cornstarch. Beat into egg whites along with vinegar and vanilla.

Line a baking sheet with brown paper; draw a 9" circle in the center. Spoon meringue into circle mounding about 2" high. Bake at 300° for 50 to 60 minutes. Turn off heat and allow to cool in oven.

Invert onto a plate and carefully remove paper. Arrange kiwi and raspberries decoratively over the top. Serve with Whipped Topping (page 271).

Variation: Use fresh fruit of your choice.

Serves 8

Per serving:	Calories	Fat (g)	Cholesterol (mg)	Fiber (g)	Sodium (mg)
	98	0	0	1	21

Whipped Topping One

1/2 cup ice water *or* fruit juice*
1 tsp. fresh lemon juice
2 tsp. vanilla

1/2 cup non-fat dry milk
2 to 3 Tbsp. sugar

Chill a small bowl and beaters for mixer. Mix water (or juice), lemon juice and vanilla. Stir in dry milk and beat until thick, 5 to 7 minutes. Gradually beat in sugar.

Serve over fresh fruit or other desserts in place of whipped cream. Serve immediately; does not keep well

• Use orange juice and Grand Marnier (optional) or apple juice and Calvados (optional) — delicious on a baked apple — or cranberry juice and Chambord (optional)

Yield: about 2 cups
Serving size: 1/4 cup

Per serving:	Calories	Fat (g)	Cholesterol (mg)	Fiber (g)	Sodium (mg)
	35	0	2	0	4

Whipped Topping Two

1 cup evaporated non-fat milk
1/4 cup sugar
11/2 tsp. vanilla

Pour milk into a medium bowl and chill until ice crystals form around the edges and mixture is slushy. Chill beaters. Beat milk on high speed until fluffy. Add remaining ingredients and beat until stiff. Serve immediately; does not keep well.

Variation: Sprinkle 1 tsp. gelatin over 2 Tbsp. water in a small saucepan. Stir over low heat until dissolved. Do not chill milk. Add dissolved gelatin to milk and beat until stiff. Beat in remaining ingredients.

This topping may be kept in refrigerator until ready to serve.

Yield: about 4 cups
Serving size: 1/4 cup

Per serving:	Calories	Fat (g)	Cholesterol (mg)	Fiber (g)	Sodium (mg)
	25	0	0	0	19

Bittersweet Chocolate Sauce

Even though this rich sauce is lower in fat than fudge sauce, it still contains about 80 calories per tablespoon — use sparingly!

3/4 cup unsweetened cocoa
1/2 cup brown sugar
2 to 3 Tbsp. honey
3/4 cup non-fat milk

2 tsp. vanilla
2 Tbsp. brandy, Grand Marnier,
    Amaretto *or* liqueur of your choice (optional)

In a small saucepan, combine cocoa and brown sugar. Stir in skim milk and honey. Cook over medium heat, stirring frequently, until sugar dissolves. Remove from heat; stir in vanilla and liqueur. Serve hot, or cool and store in a tightly covered container in the refrigerator.

Serve over frozen yogurt, angel food cake or use as a dip for fresh strawberries or bananas.

Variation: Add 1 to 2 tsp. orange or tangerine zest.

Yield: about 1 1/2 cups
Serving size: 2 Tablespoons

Per serving:	Calories	Fat (g)	Cholesterol (mg)	Fiber (g)	Sodium (mg)
	77	0	0	0	36

Raspberry Orange Sauce

1 12-oz. bag frozen raspberries, thawed
1 Tbsp. orange juice concentrate, thawed
1 Tbsp. Grand Marnier *or* Chambord
  (optional)

2 tsp. cornstarch
1 tsp. orange zest
1 tsp. lemon zest

Puree berries in blender or food processor. Strain puree and discard seeds.

Combine puree with remaining ingredients in a small saucepan. Bring to a boil over medium heat, then cook 1 minute, stirring constantly. Remove from heat and serve, or chill before using.

Serve over pancakes, waffles, angel food cake, frozen yogurt or fresh fruit.

Yield: about 1 cup
Serving size: 2 Tablespoons

Per serving:	Calories	Fat (g)	Cholesterol (mg)	Fiber (g)	Sodium (mg)
	54	0	0	2	0

Almond Macaroons

1 8-oz. can almond paste
3/4 cup sugar
3 egg whites
Few drops lemon juice
2 Tbsp. flour

Combine almond paste and sugar in food processor; process until well combined. Add egg whites, lemon juice and flour; pulse 5 to 6 times or until well blended.

Drop by teaspoonfuls onto non-stick cookie sheets. Bake at 325° for 18 to 20 minutes or until lightly browned.

Variation: Chocolate Almond Macaroons — add 1/4 cup cocoa powder to almond mixture.

Yield: about 4 dozen

Per serving:	Calories	Fat (g)	Cholesterol (mg)	Fiber (g)	Sodium (mg)
	57	3	0	0	16

Applesauce Date Bars

1 8-oz. package pitted dates, chopped
3/4 cup apple juice or water
1/2 cup unsweetened applesauce
1/2 cup brown sugar, divided
1 tsp. cinnamon
1/2 tsp. nutmeg
1/4 cup chopped walnuts
1 cup whole wheat flour
1 cup rolled oats
1/3 cup soft margarine

In a medium saucepan, combine dates, juice, applesauce, 1/4 cup brown sugar, cinnamon and nutmeg. Cook over medium heat, stirring occasionally, until thickened about 10 to 15 minutes. Stir in nuts and set aside to cool slightly.

In a large bowl or in a food processor, combine flour and remaining 1/4 cup brown sugar. Add margarine and cut in (or process) until mixture resembles coarse crumbs. Stir in oats.

Coat an 11" by 7" baking pan with cooking spray. Press one-half of the crumb mixture firmly into the pan. Spread with applesauce mixture. Sprinkle remaining crumb mixture evenly over the top and press firmly. Bake at 350° for 30 to 35 minutes.

Yield: about 20 bars

Per serving:	Calories	Fat (g)	Cholesterol (mg)	Fiber (g)	Sodium (mg)
	124	4	0	2	42

Apricot Squares

Rich in carotene, these cookies are elegant enough for tea

1 cup dried apricots
1/4 cup soft margarine
1/4 cup brown sugar
1/2 cup whole wheat flour
1/2 cup rolled oats
1/2 tsp. cardamom
1/3 cup brown sugar

1 egg
2 egg whites
1/3 cup whole wheat flour
1/2 tsp. baking powder
1 1/2 tsp. vanilla
1/3 cup chopped pecans

Cover apricots with water and let stand several hours to soften. Drain well and set aside.

In a food processor, mix margarine, 1/4 cup brown sugar, 1/2 cup flour, rolled oats and car-damom until crumbly. Press onto bottom of an 8" by 8" baking pan. Bake at 325' for 10 to 12 minutes.

Meanwhile, beat together 1/3 cup brown sugar, egg, egg whites, 1/3 cup flour, baking powder and vanilla. Add nuts and apricots. Spread over crust. Return to oven and bake an additional 30 minutes. Cool in pan, then cut into squares.

Yield: 12 squares

Per serving:	Calories	Fat (g)	Cholesterol (mg)	Fiber (g)	Sodium (mg)
	165	7	22	3	92

Oatmeal Cookie Squares

1/2 cup soft margarine
1/3 cup honey
2 egg whites
2 tsp. vanilla
1 1/4 cups rolled oats

1/2 cup whole wheat flour
1 tsp. baking powder
1/2 cup raisins
1/4 cup chopped walnuts (optional)

In a medium bowl, cream margarine, honey, egg whites and vanilla. In a separate bowl, com-bine oats, flour and baking powder. Mix into creamed mixture along with raisins and nuts.

Spread batter into an 8" by 8" baking pan coated with cooking spray. Bake at 350° for 25 minutes.

Yield: 18 bars

Per serving:	Calories	Fat (g)	Cholesterol (mg)	Fiber (g)	Sodium (mg)
	120	7	0	1	74

Carrot-Raisin Cookies

1 cup whole wheat flour
1/2 cup unbleached flour
1 tsp. baking soda
1 tsp. *each* cinnamon and nutmeg
1 1/2 cups rolled oats
1/2 cup soft margarine *or* safflower oil

4 egg whites
3/4 cup honey
2 cups grated carrots
1 cup raisins
1/4 cup chopped nuts

In a medium bowl mix together dry ingredients. In a large bowl beat together margarine, egg whites and honey. Mix in carrots. Stir in flour mixture then add raisins and nuts.

Drop by tablespoonfuls 2" apart on a non-stick cookie sheet. Bake at 350° for 12-15 minutes. Cool on racks.

Yield: about 4 dozen

Per serving:	Calories	Fat (g)	Cholesterol (mg)	Fiber (g)	Sodium (mg)
	71	3	0	1	50

Peanut Butter Oatmeal Cookies

1/3 cup liquid margarine
1/2 cup natural style peanut butter
1/2 cup brown sugar
1/4 cup granulated sugar
1 tsp. vanilla

2 egg whites
3/4 tsp. baking soda
1/2 cup *each* whole wheat flour,
   unbleached flour and rolled oats

With a beater or in a food processor, cream together margarine, peanut butter, sugars and vanilla. Mix in egg whites, baking soda, flours and rolled oats.

Shape into balls and place 2" apart on a non-stick cookie sheet. Flatten with a fork. Bake at 375° for 8 to 10 minutes.

Variation: Roll cookies in sugar before baking.

Yield: about 24 cookies

Per serving:	Calories	Fat (g)	Cholesterol (mg)	Fiber (g)	Sodium (mg)
	103	6	0	1	66

Peanut Butter Crunchers

2/3 cup natural-style peanut butter
1/4 cup frozen apple juice concentrate,
   thawed
1 tsp. cinnamon
1 tsp. orange zest

3 cups bran flakes, crushed
1/2 cup wheat germ
1/4 cup non-fat dry milk
1/2 cup raisins

In a large bowl, stir together peanut butter and apple juice concentrate. Mix in cinnamon and zest. Gradually mix in remaining ingredients using hands if necessary. Form into 1" balls. Store in refrigerator.

Yield: about 24 balls

Per serving:	Calories	Fat (g)	Cholesterol (mg)	Fiber (g)	Sodium (mg)
	166	8	1	2	110

Raspberry Squares

1 1/4 cups whole wheat pastry flour
1 1/4 cups rolled oats
1/3 cup brown sugar
2/3 cup liquid margarine
3/4 cup sugar-free rapsberry preserves

In a food processor, combine flour, oats, brown sugar and margarine. Process until well combined. Press one-half of mixture into an 8" by 8" baking pan coated with cooking spray. Spread with preserves. Press remaining mixture evenly over preserves. Bake at 350° for 30 minute. Cool then cut into squares.

Yield: about 16 cookies

Per serving:	Calories	Fat (g)	Cholesterol (mg)	Fiber (g)	Sodium (mg)
	159	8	0	2	113

Add interest and flair to your meals with sauces that are delicious even without butter and salt. Learn to cook creatively with herbs and spices as you gradually decrease salt.

Olive oil is currently thought to be a healthier choice than other fats and oils as it is rich in monounsaturated fat which lowers dangerous LDL cholesterol. Use it sparingly as it is no less caloric than other oils. Use its distinctive rich flavor to enhance, rather than overpower, foods.

*Delite*fully HealthMark

Dressings

Balsamic Vinaigrette 279
Celery Seed 279
Creamy Herbed 281
Creamy Orange 280
Cucumber 281
Fabulous French 282
HealthMark Ranch 282
Herbed Dijon Vinaigrette 283
Lemony Mustard 283
Mustard Vinaigrette 284
Orange Vinaigrette 284
Poppy Seed 280
Sesame Cilantro 285
Sesame Orange Vinaigrette 285
Thousand Island 286
Tomato Vinaigrette 286

Salsas

Grilled Red Pepper 291
Pineapple 294

Sauces

Bechamel 288
Bombay Lime 289
Cheese 288
Citrus Dijon 289
Curry 288
Dijon Mustard 290
Fresh Tomato 290
Green 291
HealthMark Mayonnaise 287
HealthMark Sour Cream 287
Herbed Oil 292
Mignonette 292
Orange Curry 293
Parmesan 288
Pesto 293
Quick Tomato 294
Sherry Mushroom 288
Slim Gravy 295
Sweet and Sour Mustard
Veloute 288
White (Bechamel) 288

Balsamic Vinaigrette

1/2 cup Balsamic vinegar
1/4 cup water
2 Tbsp. minced fresh parsley
2 cloves garlic, minced
1 tsp. dried basil
1 tsp. dried oregano

1 tsp. minced fresh chives
1 tsp. dry mustard
1/2 tsp. freshly ground black pepper
1/2 tsp. paprika
3/4 cup olive oil

In a small bowl, whisk together all ingredients, except oil. Gradually whisk in oil.

Yield: 1 1/2 cups

Per serving:	Serving size	Calories	Fat (g)	Cholesterol (mg)	Fiber (g)	Sodium (mg)
	1 Tbsp	62	7	0	0	0

Celery Seed Dressing

1 Tbsp. celery seed
1 tsp. dry mustard
1/4 cup brown sugar *or* honey
1 Tbsp. minced onion

1/3 cup cider vinegar
2 Tbsp. water
1 cup olive *or* canola *or* safflower oil

In a small bowl, combine celery seed, dry mustard, sugar, onion, vinegar and water. Whisk in oil until well combined. Serve with tossed salad or fresh fruit.

Yield: about 1 1/2 cups

Per serving:	Serving size	Calories	Fat (g)	Cholesterol (mg)	Fiber (g)	Sodium (mg)
	1 Tbsp	90	9	0	0	1

Creamy Orange Dressing

Serve this light dressing over fresh fruit salad

1 cup plain non-fat yogurt
3 Tbsp. frozen orange juice concentrate
1 to 2 Tbsp. honey
1 Tbsp. orange zest *or*
  1 tsp. each orange and lemon zest

2 tsp. raspberry vinegar (optional)
1 tsp. minced fresh ginger

Blend all ingredients thoroughly. Refrigerate before serving.

Yield: 1 1/2 cups

Per serving:	Serving size	Calories	Fat (g)	Cholesterol (mg)	Fiber (g)	Sodium (mg)
	2Tbsp	27	0	1	0	16

Poppy Seed Dressing

Nice on fresh fruit salad

1/3 cup honey
1/3 cup raspberry *or* white wine vinegar
1 tsp. orange *or* lemon zest

1/2 tsp. dry mustard
1 cup canola *or* safflower oil
2 Tbsp. poppy seeds

In a small bowl, whisk together honey, vinegar, zest and mustard. Gradually whisk in oil until all is incorporated. Stir in poppy seeds. (May also be prepared in blender or food processor.)

Yield: about 1 3/4 cups

Per serving:	Serving size	Calories	Fat (g)	Cholesterol (mg)	Fiber (g)	Sodium (mg)
	1 Tbsp	123	8	0	0	1

Creamy Herbed Dressing

1 cup plain non-fat yogurt
2 Tbsp. light, cholesterol-free mayonnaise
1 Tbsp. chopped fresh parsley
1 Tbsp. minced red onion
1 tsp. fresh lemon juice
1 tsp. lemon zest

1 tsp. dry mustard *or*
  2 tsp. Dijon mustard
1 tsp. low-sodium soy sauce
1/2 tsp. red wine *or* rice vinegar
1/2 tsp. Worcestershire sauce
1/8 tsp. white pepper

Combine all ingredients in a food processor or whisk together in a small bowl. Chill before serving. Store in a tightly covered container.

Yield: about 1 1/4 cups

Per serving:	Serving size	Calories	Fat (g)	Cholesterol (mg)	Fiber (g)	Sodium (mg)
	2 Tbsp	22	1	1	0	49

Cucumber Dressing

1 English cucumber, chopped
1/2 cup 1% cottage cheese
1 1/4 cups low-fat buttermilk
1 clove garlic, minced
1/4 cup fresh lemon juice *or*
  white wine vinegar

1 tsp. horseradish *or* Dijon mustard
1 Tbsp. chopped fresh dill *or* 1 tsp. dried
1/4 tsp. dried tarragon

Combine all ingredients in a food processor or blender. Puree until smooth.

Yield: about 2 cups

Per serving:	Serving size	Calories	Fat (g)	Cholesterol (mg)	Fiber (g)	Sodium (mg)
	2 Tbsp	32	0	1	0	116

Fabulous French Dressing

2 cloves garlic
1 shallot *or* white part of 3 green onions
3 Tbsp. red *or* sherry wine vinegar
3 Tbsp. fresh orange juice
4 Tbsp. olive oil

1 tsp. dried rosemary
1/2 tsp. dried thyme
1 small tomato, cored and quartered
1/4 cup chopped fresh parsley

Drop garlic and shallot into a food processor or blender with motor running. Add remaining ingredients and process until well blended, 1 to 2 minutes.

Yield: about 3/4 cup

Per serving:	Serving size	Calories	Fat (g)	Cholesterol (mg)	Fiber (g)	Sodium (mg)
	1 Tbsp	46	5	0	0	1

HealthMark Ranch Dressing

A low-calorie, low-sodium version of everyone's favorite salad dressing.
Equally good on baked potatoes

1/2 cup 1% cottage cheese
1/3 cup low-fat buttermilk
2 Tbsp. Parmesan cheese
1 Tbsp. fresh lemon juice
1 tsp. lemon zest
1 green onion *or* 1 shallot
1 clove garlic

1 Tbsp. minced fresh parsley
1 Tbsp. minced fresh dill *or* 1 tsp. dried
1/2 tsp. onion powder
1/2 tsp. dried oregano
1/2 tsp. dried basil
1/4 tsp. dried thyme
1/8 tsp. white pepper

Combine all ingredients in a blender or food processor and puree until smooth. Chill before using. Store in tightly covered container in the refrigerator.

Yield: about 1 cup

Per serving:	Serving size	Calories	Fat (g)	Cholesterol (mg)	Fiber (g)	Sodium (mg)
	2 Tbsp	24	1	2	0	85

Herbed Dijon Vinaigrette

2 Tbsp. Dijon mustard
4 Tbsp. red wine *or* balsamic vinegar
1/4 tsp. Lite Salt™
2 cloves garlic, minced
1 Tbsp. chopped fresh basil *or*
  1 tsp. dried basil

1 tsp. dried savory
1/2 tsp. dried oregano
1/8 tsp. pepper
2 drops hot sauce (optional)
1 Tbsp. minced onion
1/2 cup olive oil

Combine all ingredients, except oil, in a blender or food processor. Blend briefly. With motor running, add oil in a thin stream. Transfer to a small container and store in refrigerator.

Yield: about 3/4 cup

Per serving:	Serving size	Calories	Fat (g)	Cholesterol (mg)	Fiber (g)	Sodium (mg)
	1 Tbsp	84	9	0	0	53

Lemony Mustard Dressing

Virtually no calories, but lots of flavor

1/4 cup fresh lemon juice
1/2 tsp. dry mustard *or*
  2 tsp. Dijon mustard

1 clove garlic, minced
1/4 tsp. white pepper
1 Tbsp. chopped fresh parsley

Combine ingredients in a small bowl and blend well. Serve as a salad dressing or as a topping for steamed vegetables

Yield: about 1/4 cup

Per serving:	Serving size	Calories	Fat (g)	Cholesterol (mg)	Fiber (g)	Sodium (mg)
	2 Tbsp	17	0	0	0	2

Orange Vinaigrette

1/2 cup fresh orange juice
2 Tbsp. red wine *or* raspberry vinegar
1 Tbsp. Dijon mustard

1/2 tsp. ground coriander
3/4 cup olive oil
Freshly ground pepper

In a small bowl whisk together juice, vinegar, mustard and coriander. Whisk in olive oil until blended and slightly thickened. Season to taste with freshly ground pepper.

Yield: about 1 1/4 cups

Per serving:	Serving size	Calories	Fat (g)	Cholesterol (mg)	Fiber (g)	Sodium (mg)
	1 Tbsp	75	8	0	0	10

Mustard Vinaigrette

1 clove garlic
1 Tbsp. Dijon mustard
2 Tbsp. fresh lemon juice
1 tsp. lemon zest
1/4 cup water

1/2 tsp. honey
1/4 cup olive oil
1 tsp. Parmesan cheese
Freshly ground black pepper

Mince garlic in food processor. Add mustard, lemon juice, zest, water and honey. Pulse until well blended. With motor running, add oil in a thin stream mixing until well blended. Add Parmesan and pepper to taste.

Yield: about 2/3 cup

Per serving:	Serving size	Calories	Fat (g)	Cholesterol (mg)	Fiber (g)	Sodium (mg)
	1 Tbsp	87	9	0	0	36

Sesame Cilantro Dressing

Adds an oriental touch to ordinary salads

3 Tbsp. rice vinegar
2 1/2 Tbsp. fresh lemon juice
1 Tbsp. sake *or* dry sherry (optional)
1 Tbsp. low-sodium soy sauce
1/4 cup sesame seeds, toasted

1 clove garlic, minced
1/4 to 1/2 cup chopped fresh cilantro
1 Tbsp. oriental sesame oil
1/2 cup peanut oil

In a small bowl, combine vinegar, lemon juice, sake and soy sauce. Add sesame seeds, garlic and cilantro. Combine oils and whisk into soy mixture. Serve as a salad dressing for lettuce or pasta salads.

Yield: about 1 1/2 cups

Per serving:	Serving size	Calories	Fat (g)	Cholesterol (mg)	Fiber (g)	Sodium (mg)
	1 Tbsp	58	6	0	0	26

Sesame-Orange Vinaigrette

1 cup fresh orange juice
1/4 cup red wine vinegar
1 Tbsp. low-sodium soy sauce
1 Tbsp. toasted sesame seeds
1 clove garlic, minced

1 tsp. Dijon mustard
1/2 cup olive *or* canola *or* safflower oil
1 *or* 2 Tbsp. oriental sesame oil
1 Tbsp. chopped fresh dill *or*
  1 Tbsp. chopped fresh cilantro

In a small bowl, combine juice, vinegar, soy sauce, sesame seeds, garlic and mustard. Gradually add olive and sesame oil, whisking until well blended. Stir in dill or cilantro.

Yield: about 2 cups

Per serving:	Serving size	Calories	Fat (g)	Cholesterol (mg)	Fiber (g)	Sodium (mg)
	1 Tbsp	40	4	0	0	21

Thousand Island Dressing

A light version of the classic

1 cup 1% cottage cheese
1/4 cup plain non-fat yogurt
1/4 cup low-sodium ketchup
2 Tbsp. light, cholesterol-free mayonnaise

Dash cayenne pepper
2 Tbsp. minced red onion
1 Tbsp. minced dill pickle
   (rinse and drain before mincing)

Puree cottage cheese in food processor or blender until very smooth. Mix in remaining ingredients. Thin, as needed, with non-fat milk or red wine vinegar.

Yield: about 1 1/2 cups

Per serving:	Serving size	Calories	Fat (g)	Cholesterol (mg)	Fiber (g)	Sodium (mg)
	2 Tbsp	24	1	1	0	127

Tomato Vinaigrette

1 tomato, cored and chopped
1/4 cup chopped red bell pepper
1/4 cup chopped green pepper
1/4 cup finely chopped carrot
1 shallot, chopped *or* white part of
   1 green onion, chopped
1 clove garlic

1 Tbsp. chopped fresh parsley
1 Tbsp. chopped fresh basil *or* 1 tsp. dried
1 tsp. dried oregano
1 tsp. freshly ground black pepper
1 Tbsp. brown sugar
1 cup olive oil
1/2 cup red wine vinegar

Combine all ingredients in food processor and process until well combined, but still slightly chunky. Store in a tightly covered container.

Yield: about 2 cups

Per serving:	Serving size	Calories	Fat (g)	Cholesterol (mg)	Fiber (g)	Sodium (mg)
	1 Tbsp.	64	7	0	0	2

HealthMark Mayonnaise

1 cup plain non-fat yogurt
1/2 cup light, cholesterol-free mayonnaise

Combine yogurt and mayonnaise in a small bowl and mix well. Cover and store in refrigerator. Use for a sandwich spread or mix with tuna, turkey or chicken salad.

Variation: Add 1 to 2 tsp. Dijon mustard.

Yield: 1 1/2 cups

Per serving:	Serving size	Calories	Fat (g)	Cholesterol (mg)	Fiber (g)	Sodium (mg)
	1 Tbsp	23	2	1	0	40

HealthMark Sour Cream

1 cup 1% cottage cheese
1/4 cup plain non-fat yogurt *or*
**   2 Tbsp. lemon juice**

Combine cottage cheese and yogurt or lemon juice in a blender or food processor. Puree until very smooth, about 2 to 4 minutes.

May be used as a substitute for sour cream on baked potatoes or as a base for dips or salad dressings.

Variations:

• Add white part only from 2 green onions.

• Add 2 to 4 Tbsp. chopped fresh cilantro and 2 Tbsp. chopped red onion. Use as a dip, salad dressing or topping for Mexican food in place of sour cream

Yield: about 1 cup

Per serving:	Serving size	Calories	Fat (g)	Cholesterol (mg)	Fiber (g)	Sodium (mg)
	1 Tbsp	13	0	1	0	60

White (Bechamel) Sauce

This low fat version of a classic white sauce can be the start of many interesting sauces and soups

1 cup non-fat milk
1/4 cup non-fat dry milk
1 1/2 Tbsp. liquid margarine

2 Tbsp. unbleached flour
1/4 tsp. white pepper

Combine liquid and dry milk; mix well to dissolve powdered milk. Set aside.

In a small saucepan, melt margarine. Stir in flour and cook for 1 minute. Do not brown. Remove from heat and gradually whisk in milk mixture. Add pepper. Cook and stir over medium heat until thickened.

Tip: for a subtle herb flavor, combine 1 bay leaf, 2 peppercorns, 1 slice onion and 2 sprigs parsley with milk mixture; cover and refrigerate overnight to infuse flavors. Strain before using.

Per serving:	Serving size	Calories	Fat (g)	Cholesterol (mg)	Fiber (g)	Sodium (mg)
	2 Tbsp	82	4	2	0	102

Variations:

• Cheese Sauce:
3/4 cup grated part-skim mozzarella
  (*or* other low-fat) cheese

1/4 tsp. dry mustard *or* nutmeg
1/4 tsp. paprika

Add above to cooked sauce and stir until cheese melts

• Curry Sauce:
1/2 to 1 tsp. curry powder
1/4 tsp. dry mustard
1/4 tsp. paprika

Stir into sauce along with milk.

• Parmesan Sauce:
1/3 cup Parmesan cheese
1 clove garlic, finely minced
1/4 tsp. nutmeg
1/4 tsp. white pepper

Add above to cooked sauce and stir until cheese melts.

• Sherry Mushroom Sauce — Add 1/2 cup finely diced mushrooms along with milk. Stir 1 to 2 Tbsp. dry sherry into sauce along with milk

• Veloute Sauce — Substitute 1 cup salt-free chicken broth (defatted) for 1 cup skim milk

Yield: 1 1/4 cups

Bombay Lime Sauce

Hot, cool and refreshing all in the same bite

1 cup plain non-fat yogurt
3 to 4 sprigs fresh mint, chopped
1/4 cup chopped fresh cilantro
1 Tbsp. fresh lime juice

Zest of 1 lime
1 jalapeño chile, seeded and minced
1 tsp. grated fresh ginger
1/4 tsp. Lite Salt™

Combine all ingredients in a blender or food processor and process until well mixed but still slightly chunky.

Serve as a topping for grilled fish or chicken or as a dip.

Yield: about 1 1/2 cups

Per serving:	Serving size	Calories	Fat (g)	Cholesterol (mg)	Fiber (g)	Sodium (mg)
	2 Tbsp	13	0	1	0	29

Citrus Dijon Sauce

This tangy, slightly hot sauce is wonderful on grilled tuna, salmon or halibut

1 1/2 cups fresh grapefruit juice
1/2 cup Dijon mustard
  (*or* use a sweet hot mustard)
2 tsp. fresh lemon juice

1 tsp. lemon zest
4 Tbsp. olive oil
1/2 tsp. dried tarragon

In a small saucepan, boil grapefruit juice until reduced to about 1/2 cup. Pour into a small bowl and cool. Mix in mustard, lemon juice and zest. Gradually whisk in oil and tarragon. Serve with grilled fish or chicken.

Yield: about 1 cup

Per serving:	Serving size	Calories	Fat (g)	Cholesterol (mg)	Fiber (g)	Sodium (mg)
	2 Tbsp	97	7	0	0	11

Dijon Mustard Sauce

1 cup plain non-fat yogurt
1 to 2 Tbsp. Dijon mustard
1/2 tsp. dried basil, tarragon,
  ***or* dill**

Combine all ingredients in a small bowl. Chill before serving.

Use as a topping for baked potatoes, grilled fish or chicken, as a salad dressing or as a dip for fresh vegetables.

Variation: Add 3 Tbsp. low-calorie Dijon vinaigrette salad dressing and 1 Tbsp. light, cholesterol-free mayonnaise. Great with artichokes.

Yield: 1 1/4 cups

Per serving:	Serving size	Calories	Fat (g)	Cholesterol (mg)	Fiber (g)	Sodium (mg)
	2 Tbsp	16	0	1	0	55

Fresh Tomato Sauce

Vine ripened tomatoes give this simple sauce its fresh from the garden flavor

1 tsp. olive oil
1 onion, chopped
3 lb. ripe tomatoes, cored and chopped
1 to 2 cloves garlic, minced
1 Tbsp. fresh lemon juice
1/4 cup chopped parsley

1 Tbsp. chopped fresh basil *or*
 1 tsp. dried
2 tsp. chopped fresh thyme *or*
 1/2 tsp. dried
1/2 tsp. Lite Salt™
Freshly ground black pepper

Heat oil in a non-stick skillet. Saute onion until soft, about 3 minutes. Add tomatoes and simmer 10 minutes or until sauce begins to thicken. Add remaining ingredients and simmer an additional 2 to 3 minutes. Serve over hot pasta.

Yield: about 3 cups

Per serving:	Serving size	Calories	Fat (g)	Cholesterol (mg)	Fiber (g)	Sodium (mg)
	1/2 Cup	63	1	0	2	92

Grilled Red Pepper Salsa

Serve this brightly colored salsa over grilled fish or chicken

3 grilled red peppers (page 226)
1/4 cup black olives, rinsed,
  drained and chopped
2 Tbsp. Parmesan cheese (optional)
1 Tbsp. olive oil

1 Tbsp. balsamic *or* red wine vinegar
2 Tbsp. chopped fresh basil
2 Tbsp. chopped fresh parsley
1/4 tsp. dried oregano
Dash cayenne pepper

Chop grilled peppers finely and combine with remaining ingredients. Cover and let stand 30 to 60 minutes at room temperature before serving.

Yield: about 1 1/2 cups

Per serving:	Serving size	Calories	Fat (g)	Cholesterol (mg)	Fiber (g)	Sodium (mg)
	1/4 Cup	50	4	2	1	73

Green Sauce

This creamy green sauce offers a color and flavor contrast to
mild whitefish such as sole, flounder and orange roughy

1 anchovy fillet
1 cup plain non-fat yogurt
1/4 cup low-fat sour cream
2 cups fresh spinach leaves
1/4 cup chopped parsley

2 green onions, chopped
1 clove garlic
1 Tbsp. chopped fresh dill
1 Tbsp chopped fresh mint

Soak anchovy in warm water for 10 minutes; rinse well, drain and pat dry. Combine with remaining ingredients in food processor or blender. Puree until just smooth. Transfer to a covered container and refrigerate for 1 to 2 hours before serving.

Yield: about 2 cups

Per serving:	Serving size	Calories	Fat (g)	Cholesterol (mg)	Fiber (g)	Sodium (mg)
	2 Tbsp	17	1	1	40	22

Mignonette Sauce

Colorful bits of vegetables add flavor and flair to this tart, tangy sauce

$^1/_2$ **cup dry white wine**
$^1/_2$ **cup white wine vinegar**
1 carrot, peeled and grated
$^1/_4$ **cup each diced red and green pepper**
3 Tbsp. chopped shallots

1 tsp. minced fresh ginger
1 tsp. freshly ground black pepper
1 tsp. chopped fresh thyme *or*
  $^1/_4$ **tsp. dried**

In a small bowl, whisk all ingredients together. Serve drizzled over fresh oysters on the half shell; also good with grilled fish or chicken

Yield: about 1 cup

Per serving:	Serving size	Calories	Fat (g)	Cholesterol (mg)	Fiber (g)	Sodium (mg)
	2 Tbsp	22	0	0	0	7

Herbed Oil

1 cup olive oil
2 cloves garlic, crushed
1 Tbsp. minced shallots

$^1/_2$ **tsp. dried basil**
$^1/_4$ **tsp. *each:***
  dried rosemary, thyme, oregano, fennel seed

Heat oil and pour over garlic, shallots and herbs. Let stand 2 to 3 hours for flavors to blend. Strain then place oil in a tightly covered container.

Brush on fish or chicken before cooking or mix with vinegar to use as a salad dressing.

Yield: 1 cup

Per serving:	Serving size	Calories	Fat (g)	Cholesterol (mg)	Fiber (g)	Sodium (mg)
	1/5 Tbsp	60	7	0	0	0

Orange-Curry Sauce

Goes well with grilled or baked fish

1 cup plain non-fat yogurt
2 Tbsp. low-sugar orange marmalade
1 Tbsp. fresh lime juice
1 tsp. lime zest

1 tsp. curry powder
1 green onion, thinly sliced
1/4 cup toasted almond slices

In a small bowl, combine all ingredients. Cover and chill before using.

Yield: 1 1/4 cups

Per serving:	Serving size	Calories	Fat (g)	Cholesterol (mg)	Fiber (g)	Sodium (mg)
	2 Tbsp	44	2	1	0	22

Pesto

This classic Italian sauce accompanies fish, chicken, omelettes and salads as well as pasta

1/4 cup pine nuts
3 cloves garlic
2 cups packed fresh basil leaves

1/4 cup chopped parsley
2/3 cup olive oil
Freshly ground black pepper

Place nuts, garlic, basil and parsley in a food processor and process until finely ground. With motor running, gradually add oil until pesto is the consistency of mayonnaise. Add pepper to taste. Transfer to a small jar and pour a thin film of olive oil over the surface of the pesto. Cover tightly and store in refrigerator.

Yield: about 2 cups

Per serving:	Serving size	Calories	Fat (g)	Cholesterol (mg)	Fiber (g)	Sodium (mg)
	1 Tbsp	48	5	0	0	0

Pineapple Salsa

2 cups fresh pineapple, diced
1 red bell pepper, cored,
  seeded and diced
1/2 cup chopped red onion
1 jalapeño chili, seeded and diced

1 Tbsp. grated fresh ginger
1 Tbsp. fresh lime juice
1 tsp. lime zest
1/2 cup chopped fresh cilantro

Combine pineapple, red pepper, onion, chili and ginger in a food processor and pulse until coarsely chopped. Stir in lime juice, zest and cilantro. Pour into a small bowl; cover and let stand for 1 to 2 hours at room temperature.

Serve with grilled fish or chicken.

Variation: Add 1 to 2 Tbsp. Pommery (grainy) mustard.

Yield: about 3 cups

Per serving:	Serving size	Calories	Fat (g)	Cholesterol (mg)	Fiber (g)	Sodium (mg)
	1/4 Cup	19	0	0	1	14

Quick Tomato Sauce

1 28-oz can. crushed plum tomatoes,
  undrained
1 8-oz can. salt-free tomato sauce
1/2 cup salt-free tomato paste
1 Tbsp. Parmesan cheese (optional)
1/2 cup chopped parsley

1 bay leaf
2 Tbsp. chopped fresh basil *or*
  1/2 tsp. dried
1/2 tsp. dried oregano
1/4 tsp. dried thyme

Combine all ingredients in a medium saucepan. Bring to a boil, stirring occasionally. Reduce heat and simmer until thickened, about 20 minutes. Stir occasionally. Serve hot. Freezes well.

Serve over pasta or use as a pizza sauce. Best when made a day ahead.

Yield: about 4 cups

Per serving:	Serving size	Calories	Fat (g)	Cholesterol (mg)	Fiber (g)	Sodium (mg)
	1/2 Cup	37	0	1	3	142

Slim Gravy

1/4 cup unbleached flour
2 cups salt-free chicken *or* beef broth, defatted
1/4 cup defatted meat *or* poultry juices (optional)

In a covered jar, shake together flour and 1/2 cup broth to form a smooth paste. In a small saucepan, heat broth and meat juices to boiling. Gradually stir in flour mixture. Simmer 5 to 10 minutes, stirring frequently until thickened.

Variations:

• Add 1/2 cup dry white wine to broth; increase flour by 2 Tbsp.

• Substitute 1 cup non-fat milk for 1 cup of the broth.

Yield: 2 cups

Per serving:	Serving size	Calories	Fat (g)	Cholesterol (mg)	Fiber (g)	Sodium (mg)
	2 Tbsp	9	0	0	0	1

Sweet and Sour Mustard Sauce

3 Tbsp. grainy mustard (Pommery)
3 Tbsp. white wine vinegar
1/4 cup brown sugar
1 Tbsp. dry mustard

1/4 tsp. Lite Salt™
1/4 tsp. pepper
1/8 tsp. cardamom
1/3 cup olive oil

In a small bowl, whisk together mustard, vinegar, brown sugar, dry mustard, salt, pepper and cardamom. Gradually whisk in oil until sauce is thick.

Serve with grilled fish or chicken or use as a sandwich spread.

Yield: about 1 cup

Per serving:	Serving size	Calories	Fat (g)	Cholesterol (mg)	Fiber (g)	Sodium (mg)
	1 Tbsp	57	5	0	0	53

*Deli*tefully HealthMark

ORDER FORM

Send to: HealthMark Centers, Inc., 5889 Greenwood Plaza Blvd., Suite 200
Englewood, CO 80111; (303) 694-5060

NAME_____ TELEPHONE_____ (day) _____(eve)

STREET ADDRESS_____

CITY/STATE/ZIP_____

	Quantity	Price	Tax*	Total
*Deli*tefully HealthMark	_____	$16.95	$ 1.13 per book	_____
Cooking for a Healthier Ever After	_____	$16.95	$ 1.13 per book	_____
The HealthMark Program for Life	_____	$16.95	$ 1.13 per book	_____

Plus $3.00 shipping and handling per book _____

TOTAL ENCLOSED _____

Please make checks payable to: Healthmark Centers, Inc. Please do not send cash. Sorry, no COD's.

* Colorado Residents only

ORDER FORM

Send to: HealthMark Centers, Inc., 5889 Greenwood Plaza Blvd., Suite 200
Englewood, CO 80111; (303) 694-5060

NAME_____ TELEPHONE_____ (day) _____(eve)

STREET ADDRESS_____

CITY/STATE/ZIP_____

	Quantity	Price	Tax*	Total
*Deli*tefully HealthMark	_____	$16.95	$ 1.13 per book	_____
Cooking for a Healthier Ever After	_____	$16.95	$ 1.13 per book	_____
The HealthMark Program for Life	_____	$16.95	$ 1.13 per book	_____

Plus $3.00 shipping and handling per book _____

TOTAL ENCLOSED _____

Please make checks payable to: Healthmark Centers, Inc. Please do not send cash. Sorry, no COD's.

* Colorado Residents only

Index

A

Acapulco Salad 53
All Day Chile Verde 209
Almond Macaroons................................273
Aloha Muffins 79
Amaretto Fruit Loaf 267
Ann's Bread...76

Appetizers
  Avocado Cilantro Dip 7
  Avocado Sesame Dip 7
  Bagel Chips 11
  Ceviche...13
  Chicken Pate...19
  Chicken Rumaki....................................18
  Chutney Cheese Spread 8
  Citrus Marinated Seafood 19
  Confetti Spread 3
  Creamy Garlic Dip..................................3
  Crisp Garbanzo Nuts.............................21
  English Tavern Dip 9
  Green Chile-Cilantro Dip 8
  Green Onion Dip.....................................6
  Golden Chicken Nuggets 18
  Herbed Cheese Spread.............................4
  Herbed Tomato Bread 14
  Hot and Sour Nuts 21
  Mandarin Chicken Bites 17
  Marinated Flank Strips...........................20
  Mary's Guacamole..................................6
  Mexican Pizza 12
  Mexican Salsa 10
  Oriental Dip...9
  Oriental Meatballs 16
  Pesto Cheese Spread 4
  Pita Chips...11
  Pizza Potato Skins.................................14
  Red Pepper Dip......................................5
  Roquefort Dip 5
  Salsa Dip...7
  Salsa Verde 10
  Salsafied Seafood 15
  Spicy Cucumber Bites 15
  Tangy Onion Spread................................4
  Tortilla Crisps 12
  Turkey Montmorency 16

Apple
  Baked Butterfish 180
  Brandied Baked Apples 239
  CranApple Oatmeal 98
  Oatmeal Muffins 79
  Pie 257
  Pumpkin Apple Bundt Cake 262
  Rocky Mountain Apple Bread 71
  Sweet Potato and Apple Casserole 231

Applesauce
  Cake 258
  Date Bars 273
  Filled Acorn Squash 231
  Raisin Bran Muffins 80
  Summer Fresh Applesauce 249

Apricot
  Squares 274
  Sweet and Sour Sauce 162
  Orange Souffle 250
Arroz con Pollo.....................................147

Asparagus
  Soup 29
  Chilled Asparagus
    in Dijon Mustard Sauce...................217
  Gingered Beef and Asparagus Stir-Fry....211
  Oriental Asparagus Salad 114
  Stir-Fried Asparagus with Cashews 217

Avocado
  Bisque...25

Cilantro Dip...7
Sesame Dip...7
Brown Rice and Avocado Salad..............63
California Avocado Sandwich..................43
Citrus Avocado Salad................................54
Mary's Guacamole......................................6
Salsafied Seafood.....................................15
Seafood Avocado Salad in Pita..............46
Turbot with Avocado Cream.................196

B

Bagel Chips..11
Baked Pears with Apricot Glaze............243
Balsamic Vinaigrette...............................279

Banana

Date Bread...72
Honey Cream......................................105
Oatmeal Pancakes.............................102
Smoothie...96
Grilled Banana and Papaya................239
Peanut Butter Banana Muffins.............87
Sherry Baked Bananas.........................240
Barbequed Seafood with Plum Sauce......196
Basic Omelette..109

Beans

'n' Greens Soup.....................................29
Bistro Three Bean Salad.......................136
Black and White Salad.........................135
Black Bean Salad.................................134
Black Beans and Brown Rice...............141
Blackeye Pea Soup.................................31
Broccoli and Bean Salad.....................135
Calico Bean Soup...................................30
Crisp Garbanzo Nuts.............................21
Cuban Beans..140
Denver Baked Beans............................139
Enchiladas..144

Fiesta Salad...205
Hummus in Pita Bread.............................45
Indian Spiced Garbanzos......................142
Kidney Beans with Rice.........................139
Lentil Confetti Salad..............................134
Lentil Curry..143
Lentils in Pita Pockets.............................43
Lentils with Spinach..............................143
Lima Bean Salad....................................133
Marinated Lentil Salad..........................136
Mediterranean Salad...............................66
Mexicali Pasta.......................................122
Mexican Pasta Salad.............................117
Microwave Lentils.................................142
Pasta E Fagioli.......................................141
Pickled Blackeye Peas..........................137
Pinto Bean Soup......................................31
Quick Baked Beans...............................138
Quick Chili...137
Southwestern Stir-Fry...........................213
Spinach and Black Bean Soup................32
White Bean Salad..................................133
White Chili...138

Beef

All Day Chile Verde...............................209
Carne Asada Jalisco..............................210
Cool Beef and Veggie Salad.................208
Curried Orange Beef Kabobs................212
Fiesta Salad...205
Gingered Beef and Asparagus Stir-Fry....211
Mustard Marinated Beef........................209
Oriental Beef Salad...............................206
Southwest Grilled Beef..........................207
Southwestern Stir-Fry...........................213
Tabbouleh with Beef.............................207
Thai Sesame Beef..................................210
Marinated Flank Strips............................20

Index

Beets
Chilled Beet Soup 25
Beer Boiled Shrimp 202
Berries 'n' Cream 240
Bistro Three Bean Salad 136
Bittersweet Chocolate Sauce 272
Black and White Salad 135
Black Bean Salad 134
Black Beans and Brown Rice 141
Blackeye Pea Soup 31
Blueberry
Ginger Muffins 81
Mint Sorbet 247
Oatmeal Muffins 82
Instant Sorbet 248
Bombay Lime Sauce 289
Bran
Maple Bran Muffins 86
Old Fashioned Bran Muffins 83
Pumpkin Bran Muffins 89
Brandied Baked Apples 239
Brandied Pumpkin Pudding 256
Breads
Ann's 76
Banana Date 72
Heart-y Date Loaf 73
Judy's Whole Grain 77
Herbed Tomato 14
Pumpkin Oatmeal 75
Rocky Mountain Apple 71
Whole Wheat Raisin 74
Breakfast Split 97
Broccoli
and Bean Salad 135
Soup 29
Creamy Cheesy Broccoli Soup 33
Curried Broccoli Soup 34

Spicy Orange Broccoli 218
Stir-Fried Broccoli 219
Brown Rice and Avocado Salad 63
Brussels Sprouts with Chestnuts 218
Bulgur
and Spinach Salad 64
Mediterranean Salad 66
Swiss Breakfast Combo 100
Tabbouleh with Beef 207
Burrito
Chicken 148
Buttermilk Herb Chicken 149
Buttermilk Oatmeal Pancakes 102
Butterscotch Pudding 255
Buttery Baked Fish 182

C

Cabbage
Firecracker Cole Slaw 60
Orange Slaw 60
Pineapple Cole Slaw 61
Shredded Cabbage Soup 35
Sweet and Sour Red Cabbage 221
Three Cabbage Stir-Fry 220
Caesar Salad 51
Cakes
Amaretto Fruit Loaf 267
Applesauce 258
Chocolate Pound 260
Date Nut Torte 267
Fudge Nut 259
Mocha Pound 260
Orange Pound 260
Pineapple Oatmeal 261
Poppy Seed 262
Pumpkin Apple Bundt 262
Pumpkin Fruit 266

Spiced (Bean) 263
Sunshine Breakfast 108
Sherried Fruit 265
Triple Ginger 264
Calico Bean Soup.....................................30
California Avocado Sandwich 43
Carne Asada Jalisco...............................210

Carrot
Gingered Carrot Soup 33
Oatmeal Muffins 84
Mustard Glazed Carrots 219
Raspberry Carrots..................................220

Catfish
Creole Catfish 181
Southern Baked Catfish 180

Cauliflower
Chunky Salad..52
Celery Seed Dressing 279

Cereal
CranApple Oatmeal 98
Grape Nutty Oatmeal..............................99
Mom's Best Oats 99
Spiced Oatmeal with Dates....................98
Swiss Breakfast Combo 100
Yogurt Parfait...96
Ceviche...13
Cheese Omelette....................................109
Cheese Sauce..288

Cheesecake
Coffee 268
Chocolate Amaretto 268
Mocha Cheesecake.................................268
Piña Colada 268
Pittsfield 268
Pumpkin Cheesecake 268

Chicken
Arroz con Pollo......................................147

Burritos 148
Buttermilk Herb 149
Cinnamon Scented 150
Club Sandwich..45
Cranberry Glazed...................................147
Curried Orange 152
Easy Orange Glazed...............................155
Fajita Sandwich..44
Fajitas 153
Five Spice 154
Golden Chicken Nuggets 18
Grand Marnier 154
Grilled with Mango Salsa 156
Herbed Chicken Grill..............................151
Herbed Chicken in Wine........................157
Lemony Chicken 151
Mandarin Chicken Bites 17
Mexican...160
in Orange Sauce 159
Pate..19
Pesto Primavera 158
Pineapple...159
Posole 150
Quick Chick...169
Rumaki 18
Salad Pesto..69
Sesame Cashew 161
Sesame Honey 158
Shanghai Chicken Salad............................67
Skinny Chicken Salad................................47
Spice Islands 162
Spring Roll Ups 163
Stir-Fried with Cashews 164
Stuffed Chicken Marinara.......................157
Tandoori..187
Tossed Chicken Salad................................68
with Fresh Tomatoes...............................156

Chile

All Day Chile Verde 209

Relleno Brunch Casserole.....................110

Quick Chili 137

Red, White and Green Chili 171

White Chili 138

Chilled Asparagus

in Dijon Mustard Sauce.................217

Chilled Beet Soup 25

Chinese Steamed Trout.........................195

Chocolate

Almond Macaroons..............................273

Amaretto Cheesecake...........................268

Bittersweet Chocolate Sauce 272

Frozen Yogurt......................................246

Mint Parfait 254

Pound Cake 260

Pudding 255

Chunky Salad...52

Chunky Vegetable Marinara Sauce..........128

Chutney Cheese Spread 8

Cinnamon

French Toast..104

Rolls..78

Scented Chicken 150

Sticks 229

Citrus

Avocado Salad 54

Dijon Sauce 289

Marinated Seafood 19

Melon Soup 26

Rice 128

Coffee Cheesecake...............................268

Cold Spinach Soup..................................27

Cole Slaw

Firecracker Cole Slaw 60

Orange Slaw 60

Pineapple Cole Slaw 61

Confetti Spread 3

Cookies

Almond Macaroons..............................273

Applesauce Date Bars 273

Apricot Squares....................................274

Carrot Raisin Cookies...........................275

Chocolate Almond Macaroons..............273

Oatmeal Cookie Squares......................274

Peanut Butter Crunchers......................276

Peanut Butter Oatmeal Cookies............275

Raspberry Squares................................276

Cool Beef and Veggie Salad 208

Cool Mango Soup 26

Corn

and Barley Salad 63

Chowder 36

Jalapeño Corn Casserole 221

Jalapeño Corn Muffins............................85

Mexican Pasta Salad.............................117

Muffins..85

Cottage Cheese

Berries 'n' Cream 240

Cheesecake

Coffee 268

Chocolate 268

Mocha 268

Piña Colada 268

Pittsfield...268

Pumpkin 268

Chocolate Mint Parfait 254

Chutney Cheese Spread 8

Confetti Spread 3

Cottage Cakes 103

Creamy Garlic Dip....................................3

Creamy Caramel Dip 269

Creamy Herbed Dressing 281

Confetti 3
English Tavern Dip 9
Fudge Nut Cake 259
Green Chile Cilantro Dip 8
HealthMark Sour Cream....................287
Herbed Cheese Spread.........................4
Mocha Cheesecake Parfait 254
Orange Honey Creamed Cheese 107
Pesto Cheese Spread 4
Red Pepper Dip..................................5
Roquefort Dip 5
Salsa Dip..7
Couscous
Primavera.....................................130
Salad with Dill Vinaigrette.................65
CranApple Oatmeal 98
Cranberry
CranApple Oatmeal 98
Cran-Raspberry Sorbet 247
Crunch...241
Glazed Chicken 147
Orange Muffins 82
Ruby Fruit Soup 27
Tart Cranberry Relish.......................236
Walnut Sauce.................................236
Cream Soup Mix 29
Creamed Spinach..............................229
Creamy
Caramel Dip 269
Cheesy Broccoli Soup 33
Cucumber Salad................................54
Garlic Dip...3
Herbed Dressing 281
Orange Dressing 280
Orange Topping 105
Seafood Pasta.................................125
Creole Catfish 181

Creole Syrup 106
Crisp Garbanzo Nuts.........................21
Crispy Breaded Eggplant 222
Crispy Coating 179
Crunchy Green Pea Salad 59
Cuban Beans..................................140
Cucumber
Creamy Cucumber Salad......................54
Dressing.......................................281
Gazpacho Salad................................56
Greek Cucumber Salad 54
Spicy Cucumber Bites 15
Oriental Cucumbers...........................55
Curried
Broccoli Soup 34
Orange Beef Kabobs 212
Orange Chicken...............................152
Orange Roughy 188
Curry Sauce 288

D

Date
Amaretto Fruit Loaf 267
Applesauce Date Bars 273
Banana Date Bread 72
Heart-y Date Loaf.............................73
Nut Torte......................................267
Orange Date Muffins...........................88
Spiced Oatmeal with Dates...................98
Walnut Muffins 86
Denver Baked Beans...........................139
Desserts (see individual names)
Dijon Mustard Sauce..........................290
Dijon Sea Bass 179
Dill Pasta Salad with Shrimp 116
Dips
Avocado Cilantro Dip 7

Index

Avocado Sesame Dip 7
Creamy Garlic Dip.........................3
English Tavern Dip 9
Green Chile Cilantro Dip 8
Green Onion Dip.........................6
Oriental Dip.........................9
Red Pepper Dip.........................5
Roquefort Dip 5
Dressings
Balsamic Vinaigrette.........................279
Celery Seed.........................279
Creamy Herbed.........................281
Creamy Orange.........................280
Cucumber.........................281
Dill Vinaigrette.........................65
Fabulous French.........................282
HealthMark Ranch 282
Herbed Dijon Vinaigrette 283
Lemony Mustard 283
Mustard Vinaigrette.........................284
Orange Vinaigrette.........................284
Poppy Seed 280
Sesame Cilantro 285
Sesame Orange Vinaigrette 285
Thousand Island.........................286
Tomato Vinaigrette 286

E
Easy Orange Glazed Chicken.........................155
Eggplant
Crepes.........................223
Crispy Breaded.........................222
Grilled Eggplant Sandwich 44
Herbed Eggplant 222
Parmesan 224
Enchiladas
Bean 144

Turkey.........................166
English Tavern Dip 9
Ensalada Escabeche 55
Evaporated Skim Milk
Creamy Orange Topping 105
Creole Syrup 106
Frozen Raspberry Mousse 252
Garden Linguine 123
Strawberry Margarita Mousse 252

F
Fabulous French Dressing 282
Fajitas
Chicken 153
Chicken Fajita Sandwich.........................44
Fettuccine with Fresh Herbs 127
Fiesta Salad 205
Fillets with Basil Sauce.........................183
Firecracker Cole Slaw 60
Fish and Seafood (see individual names)
Fish in Foil 182
Five Spice Chicken.........................154
Flank Steak
Carne Asada Jalisco.........................210
Cool Beef And Veggie Salad.........................208
Marinated Flank Strips.........................20
Mustard Marinated Beef.........................209
Oriental Beef Salad 206
Southwest Grilled Beef.........................207
Florentine Omelette 109
Flummery.........................242
Four Onion Soup 37
Fresh Tomato Sauce 290
Frozen Raspberry Mousse 252
Frozen Yogurt.........................246
Fruit (see individual types)
'n' Yogurt Pops.........................245

Ruby Fruit Soup 27
Fudge Nut Cake 259

G

Gala Grapefruit 241
Garden Linguine 123
Garden Pasta Salad 116
Garlic Croutons 51
Gazpacho Salad 56
Gingered Beef and Asparagus Stir-Fry 211
Gingered Carrot Soup 33
Glazed Vegetables 234
Golden
  Chicken Nuggets 18
  Fruit Compote 97
  Mashed Potatoes 227
  Pasta Salad 113
  Pepper Soup 34
Grape Nutty Oatmeal 99
Greek Cucumber Salad 54
Greek Pasta Salad 115
Green
  and Gold Soup 35
  Beans Italian 223
  Beans Nicoise 57
  Chile-Cilantro Dip 8
  Chile Omelette 110
  Onion Dip 6
  Sauce 291
Grilled
  Banana and Papaya 239
  Chicken with Mango Salsa 156
  Eggplant Sandwich 44
  Onion Salad 57
  Peppers 226
  Red Pepper Salsa 291

Ground Beef
  Fiesta Salad 205
Ground Turkey
  Fiesta Salad 205
  Italian Turkey Burgers 165
  Oriental Meatballs 16
  Turkey Enchiladas 166

H

Halibut
  with Chile-Cilantro Salsa 185
  Orange Pecan Halibut 186
  Sesame Halibut 186
  Tandoori Halibut 187
HealthMark
  Mayonnaise 287
  Ranch Dressing 282
  Sour Cream 287
Heart-y Date Loaf 73
Herb Omelette 109
Herbed
  Cheese Spread 4
  Chicken Grill 151
  Chicken in Wine 157
  Dijon Vinaigrette 283
  Eggplant 222
  Oil 292
  Summer Vegetables 235
  Tomato Bread 14
Holiday Stuffing 91
Honey
  Mustard Swordfish 194
  Spiced Honey 107
Horseradish Mustard 20
Hot and Sour Nuts 21
Hot Pasta Salad with Tuna 121
Hummus in Pita Bread 45

I

Indian Spiced Garbanzos 142
Instant Sorbet 248
Italian
  Eggplant Crepes 223
  Eggplant Parmesan 224
  Green Beans Italian...............................223
  Herbed Eggplant 222
  Omelette...109
  Parmesan Tomatoes..............................232
  Pesto Cheese Spread 4
  Pizza Potato Skins 14
  Quick Pizzas...49
  Stuffed Chicken Marinara.....................157
  Tomatoes with Pesto.............................232
  Turkey Burgers 165
  Turkey Parmesan 170
  Turkey Scallopini...................................173
  Turkey Marinara Sauce.........................175

J

Jalapeño Corn Casserole 221
Jalapeño Corn Muffins..............................85
Judy's Whole Grain Bread 77

K

Kidney Beans with Rice............................139

L

Lasagne
  Mexican Lasagne...................................118
Lemon Zucchini Salad 58
Lemony
  Barley Pilaf..130
  Chicken 151
  Mustard Dressing 283

Lentil
  Confetti Salad.......................................134
  Curry...143
  in Pita Pockets..43
  Marinated Lentil Salad 136
  Microwave Lentils................................142
  with Spinach 143
Lima Bean Salad 133
Lime Marinated Swordfish.......................194

M

Mahi Mahi Hawaiian 188
Mandarin Chicken Bites 17
Maple Bran Muffins...................................86
Marinades
  Barbecued Seafood with Plum Sauce 196
  Carne Asada Jalisco..............................210
  Ceviche..13
  Chicken Fajitas.....................................153
  Chicken Fajita Sandwich........................44
  Chicken Rumaki.....................................18
  Cinnamon Scented Chicken 150
  Golden Chicken Nuggets 18
  Lime Marinated Swordfish....................194
  Mahi Mahi Hawaiian 188
  Marinated Flank Strips...........................20
  Marinated Lentil Salad 136
  Marinated Spaghetti Salad 62
  Mustard Marinated Beef.......................209
  Oriental Beef Salad 206
  Peppery Shrimp and Scallops 198
  Sesame Cashew Chicken.......................161
  Sesame Honey Chicken 158
  Sesame Scallops...................................199
  Southwest Grilled Beef.........................207
  Spice Islands Chicken 162
  Stir-Fried Chicken with Cashews 164

Tandoori Halibut.....................................187
Teriyaki Grilled Fish 185
Thai Sesame Beef.................................210
Trout with Orange Vinaigrette 195
Turkey Steaks 167

Marinated
Flank Strips 20
Lentil Salad 136
Spaghetti Salad.....................................162
Marmalade Sauce 250
Mary's Guacamole................................6
Mediterranean Salad 66
Meringue Shells 269
Mexicali Pasta 122

Mexican
Acapulco Salad 53
Arroz Con Pollo 147
Carne Asada Jalisco..............................210
Ceviche...13
Chicken Burritos 148
Chicken Fajita Sandwich.......................44
Chicken Fajitas.....................................153
Chicken Posole 150
Chile Relleno Brunch Casserole 110
Ensalada Escabeche 55
Fiesta Salad 205
Gazpacho Salad....................................56
Green Chile Omelette 110
Jalapeño Corn Casserole 221
Jalapeño Corn Muffins..........................85
Lasagne 118
Mary's Guacamole 6
Mexicali Pasta......................................122
Mexican Brown Rice.............................129
Mexican Chicken..................................160
Mexican Pasta Salad.............................117
Mexican Pizza 12

Mexican Salsa.......................................10
Red, White and Green Chili 171
Salsa Verde 10
Salsafied Seafood 15
Southwest Grilled Beef..........................207
Southwestern Stir-Fry............................213
Spanish Rice Soup.................................37
Tortilla Crisps 12
Microwave Lentils.................................142
Mignonette Sauce 292
Minted Tomato Salad 58
Mocha Cheesecake...............................268
Mocha Cheesecake Parfait 254
Mocha Pound Cake...............................260
Mom's Best Oats 99
Monkfish with Creamy Tomato Sauce 189
Moroccan Salad 59

Muffins
Aloha Muffins 79
Apple-Oatmeal Muffins.........................79
Applesauce Raisin Bran Muffins 80
Blueberry Ginger Muffins 81
Blueberry Oatmeal Muffins 82
Carrot Oatmeal Muffins.........................84
Corn Muffins 85
Cranberry Orange Muffins.....................82
Date Walnut Muffins 86
Jalapeño Corn Muffins...........................85
Maple Bran Muffins...............................86
Oatmeal Raisin Muffins.........................87
Old Fashioned Bran Muffins...................83
Orange Date Muffins.............................88
Peanut Butter Banana Muffins 87
Pumpkin Bran Muffins...........................89
Raspberry Poppy Seed Muffins 89
Spiced Pumpkin Marmalade Muffins.......90

Mushroom

Omelette.................................109
Sherried Cream of Mushroom Soup.........38
Soup 29
Sherry Glazed Fish 184
Provencal.................................225

Mustard

Chilled Asparagus
   in Dijon Mustard Sauce...................217
Citrus Dijon Sauce 289
Dijon Mustard Sauce........................290
Dijon Sea Bass 179
Glazed Carrots 219
Herbed Dijon Vinaigrette 283
Horseradish Mustard 20
Lemony Mustard Dressing.....................283
Oriental Dip.................................9
Sweet and Sour Mustard Sauce 295
Vinaigrette...............................284

N

New Eggs 108

O

Oat

Apple-Oatmeal Muffins.......................79
Applesauce Raisin Bran Muffins 80
Banana Oatmeal Pancakes....................102
Blueberry Oatmeal Muffins 82
Buttermilk Oatmeal Pancakes 102
Carrot Oatmeal Muffins......................84
Cornmeal Waffles...........................103
CranApple Oatmeal 98
Crust 256
Grape Nutty Oatmeal........................99
Mom's Best Oats 99
Oatmeal Cookie Squares.....................274

Oatmeal Raisin Muffins.......................87
Pumpkin Oatmeal Bread 75
Spiced Oatmeal with Dates....................98
Swiss Breakfast Combo 100
OJ Shake.................................95
Old Fashioned Bran Muffins...................83
Olive Salsa...............................228

Orange

Apricot Orange Souffle......................250
Chicken in Orange Sauce....................159
Creamy Orange Dressing 280
Curried Orange Chicken 152
Curry Sauce 288
Date Muffins 88
Easy Orange Glazed Chicken...............155
Glazed Sweet Potatoes 228
Glazed Turkey............................169
Honey Creamed Cheese....................107
Pecan Halibut 186
Pound Cake 260
Raspberry Orange Sauce....................272
Sesame Orange Vinaigrette 285
Sherried Oranges 243
Slaw....................................60
Spicy Orange Broccoli 218
Trout with Orange Vinaigrette 195
Turkey with Zesty Currant Sauce 165
Vinaigrette................................284

Orange Roughy

Curried...................................188

Oriental

Asparagus Salad 114
Beef Salad 206
Cucumbers................................55
Dip 9
Meatballs.................................16
Melon Compote 242

Sesame Beans 224
Turkey Stir-Fry 172

P

Pancakes
Banana Oatmeal 102
Buttermilk Oatmeal...............................102
Cottage Cakes 103
Whole Wheat Buttermilk........................100
Whole Wheat Raisin 101
Parmesan Sauce....................................288
Parmesan Tomatoes...............................232

Pasta
Couscous Salad with Dill Vinaigrette.......65
Creamy Seafood Pasta...........................125
Dill Pasta Salad with Shrimp 116
E Fagioli 141
Fettuccine with Fresh Herbs..................127
Fresca with Basil 127
Garden Linguine...................................123
Garden Pasta Salad 116
Golden Pasta Salad 113
Greek Pasta Salad.................................115
Hot Pasta Salad with Tuna.....................121
Marinated Spaghetti Salad......................66
Mexicali Pasta......................................122
Mexican Pasta Salad.............................117
Neptune...125
Oriental Asparagus Salad 114
Primavera in Cheese Sauce 124
Provencal...126
Sesame Noodles...................................119
Tomato Fettucine
     with Piñon Vinaigrette.....................126
Tri Color Pasta Salad 62
with Scallops and Peppers.....................198
Year of the Snake Noodles 120

Pate
Chicken 19
Pavlova 270
Peach Mousse 251
Peachy Frappe 95
Peachy Syrup 106
Peanut Butter
Banana Muffins 87
Crunchers 276
Oatmeal Cookies 275
Pears
Baked with Apricot Glaze 243
Poached with
     Raspberry Orange Sauce 244
Peppers
Chicken Pesto Primavera.......................158
Golden Pepper Soup 34
Grilled Peppers 226
Red Pepper Dip.......................................5
Roasted Pepper Salad.............................56
Stuffed Red Peppers 227
Vegetable Medley Saute 235
Pesto..293
Cheese Spread 4
Chicken Pesto Primavera.......................158
Potato Salad 69
Shark with Pesto...................................187
Tomatoes with Pesto.............................232
Pickled Blackeye Peas...........................137
Pie
Apple...257
Pie Crust 257
Pilaf
Lemony Barley......................................130
Piña Colada Cheesecake 268
Pineapple
Chicken 159

Index

Cole Slaw.................................61
Freeze....................................244
Oatmeal Cake......................261
Salsa.....................................294
Pinto Bean Soup......................31
Pita
   Chips...................................11
   Hummus in..........................45
   Salmon in.............................46
   Seafood Avocado Salad in.......46
   Lentils in..............................43
   Tuna...................................48
   Zucchini Pockets....................49
Pittsfield Cheesecake..............268
Pizza
   Omelette.............................109
   Potato Skins.........................14
Poached Pears
      with Raspberry Orange Sauce........144
Poppy Seed Dressing...............280
Poppy Seed Cake....................262
Potato
   Pesto Potato Salad..................67
   Pizza Potato Skins..................14
   Roasted Potato Packets..........225
Pound Cake
   Chocolate...........................260
   Mocha................................260
   Orange...............................260
Pudding
   Butterscotch........................255
   Chocolate...........................255
   Vanilla................................255
Pumpkin
   Apple Bundt Cake.................262
   Bran Muffins........................89
   Frozen Yogurt......................245

Fruit Cake.............................266
Maple Cheesecake..................268
Oatmeal Bread.......................75

Q

Quick Baked Beans.................138
Quick Chick...........................169
Quick Quick Chili...................137
Quick Quick Pizzas.................49
Quick Quick Tomato Barley Soup.............38
Quick Quick Tomato Sauce....................294

R

Raisin
   Whole Wheat Raisin Bread......74
   Whole Wheat Raisin Pancakes............101
Raspberry
   Carrots...............................220
   Mousse..............................253
   Orange Sauce.......................272
   Poppy Seed Muffins...............89
   Squares..............................276
Red Pepper Dip.......................5
Red, White and Green Chili....................171
Rhubarb-Raspberry Sherbet....................249
Rice
   Citrus................................128
   Florentine...........................129
   Mexican Brown Rice..............129
   Spanish Rice Soup.................37
Roasted Pepper Salad..............56
Roasted Potato Packets............225
Rocky Mountain Apple Bread....................71
Rolls
   Cinnamon...........................78
Roquefort Dip.........................5
Round Steak
   All Day Chile Verde...............209

Carne Asada Jalisco.................................210
Southwestern Stir-Fry.............................213
Tabbouleh with Beef 207
Thai Sesame Beef....................................210
Ruby Fruit Soup 27

S

Salads

Acapulco 53
Brown Rice and Avocado........................63
Bulgur and Spinach.................................64
Caesar...51
Chicken Salad Pesto................................69
Chunky 52
Citrus Avocado..54
Corn and Barley......................................63
Couscous with Dill Vinaigrette...............65
Creamy Cucumber..................................54
Crunchy Green Pea.................................59
Ensalada Escabeche 55
Firecracker Cole Slaw 60
Gazpacho Salad......................................56
Greek Cucumber.....................................54
Green Beans Nicoise................................57
Grilled Onion 57
Lemon Zucchini......................................58
Marinated Spaghetti 62
Mediterranean...66
Minted Tomato..58
Moroccan 59
Orange Slaw 60
Oriental Cucumbers................................55
Pesto Potato 67
Pineapple Cole Slaw 61
Roasted Pepper 56
Seafood Avocado 46
Sesame Spinach 52

Shanghai Chicken 67
Skinny Chicken 47
Sweet Potato 61
Sweet and Sour Spinach..........................53
Tossed Chicken 68
Tri Color Pasta...62

Salad Dressing (see Dressings)
Salad Sandwich.......................................43
Salmon in Pita Bread...............................46

Salsa
Dip 7
Chile-Cilantro 185
Grilled Red Pepper..................................291
Mango 156
Mexican..10
Olive...228
Papaya 190
Pineapple..294
Baked Fish 183
Verde 10
Salsafied Seafood 15
San Francisco Cioppino 197

Sandwiches
California Avocado 43
Chicken Club..45
Chicken Fajita...44
Grilled Eggplant......................................44
Hummus in Pita Bread 45
Lentils in Pita Pockets.............................43
Salad...43
Salmon in Pita Bread...............................46
Seafood Avocado Salad in Pita 46
Tuna Pita 48
Zucchini Pockets.....................................49

Sauces
Apricot Sweet and Sour...........................162
Basil Sauce..183

Index

Bechamel..................................288
Bombay Lime...........................289
Cheese......................................288
Chunky Vegetable Marinara.................128
Citrus Dijon..............................289
Creamy Tomato.........................189
Curry...288
Dijon Mustard...........................290
Fresh Tomato.............................290
Green...291
HealthMark Mayonnaise.................287
HealthMark Sour Cream.................287
Herbed Oil................................292
Horseradish Mustard.........................20
Mignonette................................292
Orange......................................159
Orange Curry.............................293
Parmesan..................................288
Pesto...293
Plum..196
Quick Tomato............................294
Raspberry Orange.....................272
Sherry Mushroom......................288
Slim Gravy.................................295
Sweet and Sour Mustard................295
Turkey Marinara........................175
Veloute......................................288
White (Bechamel).....................288

Scallops
Barbecued Seafood with Plum Sauce....196
Ceviche..13
Greek Pasta Salad......................115
Peppery Shrimp and Scallops...............198
Salsafied Seafood..........................15
San Francisco Cioppino..............197
Seafood Curry............................201
Seafood Oriental........................200

Seafood Pesto Saute.................199
Seafood Saute with Mushrooms...........201
Sesame......................................199
Stir-Fried..................................200

Seafood
Avocado Salad in Pita...................46
Curry...201
Omelette....................................109
Oriental.....................................200
Pesto Saute...............................199
Salsafied......................................15
Saute with Mushrooms..............201

Sesame
Cashew Chicken........................161
Cilantro Dressing.......................285
Crisped Fillets...........................182
Halibut.......................................186
Honey Chicken..........................158
Noodles....................................119
Orange Vinaigrette....................285
Scallops....................................199
Spinach Salad..............................52
Shanghai Chicken Salad..................67
Shark with Pesto........................187
Sherried Cream of Mushroom Soup........38
Sherried Fruit Cake....................265
Sherried Oranges.......................243
Sherry Baked Bananas...............240
Sherry Mushroom Sauce.............288

Shrimp
Barbequed Seafood with Plum Sauce....196
Beer Boiled...............................202
Creamy Seafood Pasta...............125
Dill Pasta Salad with Shrimp.............116
Greek Pasta Salad......................115
Peppery Shrimp and Scallops.............198
Salsafied Seafood.........................15

San Francisco Cioppino 197
Seafood Curry 201
Seafood Oriental 200
Seafood Pesto Saute 199
Seafood Saute with Mushrooms 201
Year of the Snake Noodles 120

Sirloin Steak
Curried Orange Beef Kabobs.................212
Gingered Beef and Asparagus Stir-Fry....211
Mustard Marinated Beef........................209
Southwest Grilled Beef..........................207
Thai Sesame Beef..................................210
Skinny Chicken Salad.............................47
Slim Gravy 295
Smoked Salmon Omelette......................109

Snapper
Cozumel 191
Veracruz 189
with Papaya Salsa 190

Snow Peas
Stir-Fried 230

Sole
Florentine...193
Roulades Poached in Wine 191
Veronique 192
with Almonds..190
with Tomatoes and Mushrooms.............193

Soups
Asparagus 29
Avocado Bisque 25
Bean 'n' Greens 21
Black Bean 140
Blackeye Pea...31
Broccoli 29
Calico Bean 30
Chilled Beet 25
Citrus Melon 26

Cold Spinach 27
Cool Mango...26
Corn Chowder 36
Cream Soup Mix....................................29
Creamy Cheesy Broccoli 33
Curried Broccoli....................................34
Four Onion 37
Gingered Carrot 33
Golden Pepper.......................................34
Green and Gold 35
Mushroom 29
Quick Tomato Barley 38
Pinto Bean 31
Ruby Fruit 27
Sherried Cream of Mushroom 38
Shredded Cabbage 35
Spanish Rice 37
Spinach and Black Bean.........................32
Summer Tomato 28
Sweet Potato Vichyssoise 28
Turkey 39
Zucchini Pesto 40
Southern Baked Catfish 180
Southwest Grilled Beef..........................207
Southwestern Stir-Fry.............................213

Spaghetti
Creamy Seafood Pasta...........................125
Fettuccine with Fresh Herbs 127
Garden Linguine 123
Marinated Spaghetti Salad......................62
Mexicali Pasta......................................122
Mexican Pasta Salad..............................117
Pasta Neptune.......................................125
Pasta Primavera in Cheese Sauce 124
Sesame Noodles....................................119
Year of the Snake Noodles 120
Spanish Rice Soup.................................37

Spice Islands Chicken 162
Spiced
  (Bean) Cake...263
  Honey...107
  Oatmeal with Dates 98
  Pumpkin Marmalade Muffins 90
  Waffles..104
Spicy
  Cucumber Bites...................................15
  Orange Broccoli..................................218
Spinach
  and Black Bean Soup 32
  Bean 'n' Greens Soup...........................29
  Bulgur and Spinach Salad 64
  Cold Spinach Soup...............................27
  Creamed 229
  Omelette...109
  Sole Florentine 193
  Szechwan 230
Spreads
  Confetti 3
  Chutney Cheese 8
  Herbed Cheese 4
  Orange Honey Creamed Cheese...........107
  Pesto Cheese..4
  Tangy Onion 4
Spring Roll Ups 163
Squash (see Zucchini)
Stir-Fry
  Asparagus 217
  Broccoli 219
  Chicken with Cashews..........................164
  Scallops 200
  Snow Peas...230
Strawberry Margarita Mousse 252
Stuffed Chicken Marinara.......................157
Stuffed Onions 226

Stuffed Red Peppers 227
Stuffing
  Holiday...91
Summer Fresh Applesauce 249
Summer Tomato Soup 28
Sunshine Breakfast Cake 108
Sweet and Sour
  Mustard Sauce 295
  Red Cabbage.......................................221
  Spinach Salad 53
  Zucchini 233
Sweet Potato
  and Apple Casserole 231
  Cinnamon Sticks 229
  Golden Mashed Potatoes 227
  Orange Glazed 228
  Salad 61
  Vichyssoise 28
Swordfish
  Honey Mustard 194
  Lime Marinated 194
Swiss Breakfast Combo 100
Syrup
  Banana Honey Cream...........................105
  Creamy Orange Topping 105
  Creole 106
  Peachy 106
Szechwan Spinach 230

T

Tabbouleh with Beef 207
Tandoori Chicken...................................187
Tandoori Halibut....................................187
Tangy Onion Spread.....................................4
Tart Cranberry Relish..............................236
Teriyaki Grilled Fish 187
Thai Sesame Beef...................................210

Thousand Island Dressing 286
Three Cabbage Stir-Fry 220
Tomato
   and Basil Omelette................................109
   Fettucini with Piñon Vinaigrette 126
   Herb Bread 14
   Minted Tomato Salad 58
   Monkfish with Creamy Tomato Sauce ...189
   Parmesan Tomatoes................................232
   Provencal..233
   Quick Tomato Barley Soup......................38
   Sole with Tomatoes and Mushrooms 193
   Summer Tomato Soup 28
   Vinaigrette...286
   with Pesto 232
Tortilla Crisps 12
Tossed Chicken Salad...............................68
Tri Color Pasta Salad 62
Triple Ginger Cake 264
Tropical Shake...96
Trout
   Chinese Steamed...................................195
   with Orange Vinaigrette 195
Tuna Pita 48
Turbot with Avocado Cream....................196
Turkey
   Cutlets Dijon...166
   Enchiladas...166
   Hawaiian 167
   Indienne..168
   Italian Turkey Burgers............................165
   Marinara Sauce 175
   Marsala 169
   Montmorency 16
   Orange Glazed 169
   Oriental Meatballs 16
   Oriental Turkey Stir-Fry 172

Parmesan 170
Red, White and Green Chili 171
Sausage Patties......................................176
Scallopini 173
Soup 39
Steaks..167
Van Gogh Turkey-Lentil Salad 174
with Zesty Currant Sauce 165

V
Van Gogh Turkey-Lentil Salad 174
Vanilla Pudding......................................255
Vegetables (see also individual names)
   Glazed 234
   Herbed Summer.....................................235
   Medley Saute 235
Veggie Omelette 109
Veloute Sauce 288

W
Waffles
   Oat Cornmeal 103
   Spiced 104
Whipped Topping One.............................271
Whipped Topping Two 271
White
   (Bechamel) Sauce..................................288
   Bean Salad 133
   Chili..138
Whole Wheat
   Buttermilk Pancakes..............................100
   Raisin Bread...74
   Raisin Pancakes 101

Y
Year of the Snake Noodles 120

Yogurt

Avocado Cilantro Dip 7

Avocado Sesame Dip 7

Banana Smoothie 96

Bombay Lime Sauce............................289

Chocolate Frozen 246

Creamy Herbed Dressing 281

Creamy Orange Dressing 280

Curry Dip..17

Fruit 'n' Yogurt Pops............................245

Green Sauce 291

HealthMark Mayonnaise......................287

OJ Shake 95

Oriental Dip...9

Peachy Frappe 95

Parfait 96

Pumpkin Frozen..................................245

Swiss Breakfast Combo 100

Tropical Shake......................................96

Z

Zucchini

Green and Gold Soup 35

Lemon Zucchini Salad 58

Pesto Soup 40

Pizza..234

Pockets 49

*De**lite**fully HealthMark*

ORDER FORM

Send to: HealthMark Centers, Inc., 5889 Greenwood Plaza Blvd., Suite 200
Englewood, CO 80111; (303) 694-5060

NAME_____ TELEPHONE_____ (day) _____(eve)

STREET ADDRESS_____

CITY/STATE/ZIP _____

	Quantity	Price	Tax*	Total
*De**lite**fully HealthMark*	_____	*$16.95*	*$ 1.13 per book*	_____
Cooking for a Healthier Ever After	_____	*$16.95*	*$ 1.13 per book*	_____
The HealthMark Program for Life	_____	*$16.95*	*$ 1.13 per book*	_____

Plus $3.00 shipping and handling per book _____

TOTAL ENCLOSED _____

I am interested in receiving information about the HealthMark programs. _____

Please make checks payable to: Healthmark Centers, Inc. Please do not send cash. Sorry, no COD's.

* Colorado Residents only

ORDER FORM

Send to: HealthMark Centers, Inc., 5889 Greenwood Plaza Blvd., Suite 200
Englewood, CO 80111; (303) 694-5060

NAME_____ TELEPHONE_____ (day) _____(eve)

STREET ADDRESS_____

CITY/STATE/ZIP _____

	Quantity	Price	Tax*	Total
*De**lite**fully HealthMark*	_____	*$16.95*	*$ 1.13 per book*	_____
Cooking for a Healthier Ever After	_____	*$16.95*	*$ 1.13 per book*	_____
The HealthMark Program for Life	_____	*$16.95*	*$ 1.13 per book*	_____

Plus $3.00 shipping and handling per book _____

TOTAL ENCLOSED _____

I am interested in receiving information about the HealthMark programs. _____

Please make checks payable to: Healthmark Centers, Inc. Please do not send cash. Sorry, no COD's.

* Colorado Residents only

The HealthMark Philosophy

The HealthMark cookbooks, *Cooking for a Healthier Ever After* and *Delitefully HealthMark,* were created by Susan Stevens, M.A., R.D., Director of Nutrition at HealthMark to help graduates of the HealthMark preventive medicine programs maintain their healthy lifestyle. Recipes were developed according to HealthMark dietary guidelines to be low in fat, cholesterol, sodium and calories.

Current medical research clearly shows the relationship between diet, lifestyle and disease. Eight of the leading causes of death in the United States are related to poor dietary habits, lack of exercise, smoking and stress: heart disease, stroke, high blood pressure, adult onset diabetes, lung, colon, breast and prostate cancer

A healthy diet, regular exercise and stress reduction can significantly delay — or often prevent — the onset of these diseases.

HealthMark Centers, Inc. is a preventive medicine clinic founded in 1985 in Denver, Colorado by Dr. Robert A. Gleser in response to the need for education about lifestyle changes to lower risk for life-threatening disease. To date, over 5,000 people have completed one of HealthMark's preventive medicine/education programs and are leading healthier lives as a result. The programs focus on what you CAN eat and still reduce your intake of fat, cholesterol, sodium and calories. We offer positive programs for a lifetime of good health.

Supermarket shelf-labeling programs and a successful restaurant program help graduates — as well as the community — make healthier food choices. The ease and convenience of these programs motivate and help many people maintain their newly developed eating and exercise habits.

If you would like to know more about the exciting programs offered at HealthMark, please send us the card below.

☐ Please send more information about the HealthMark Programs

☐ Please have a HealthMark representative call me

Name _____

Street Address _____

City/State/Zip _____

Telephone: Day_____ Evening_____

HealthMark Centers, Inc. • Associated with Saint Joseph Hospital
5889 Greenwood Plaza Blvd., Suite 200 • Englewood, Colorado 80111 • (303) 694-5060

Return Address Information

_____
_____
_____

HealthMark Centers, Inc,
5889 Greenwood Plaza Blvd., Suite 200
Englewood, CO 80111